74

The Bare Essentials

Form A

Third Edition

The Bare Essentials

Form A

Third Edition

Sarah Norton
Brian Green

English Writing Skills

Holt, Rinehart and Winston of Canada, Limited
Toronto

Canadian Cataloguing in Publication Data

Norton, Sarah, date
The bare essentials: form A

3rd ed.
ISBN 0-03-922674-3

1. English language – Rhetoric. 2. English language – Grammar – 1950– . I. Green, Brian. II. Title.

PE1408.N674 1989 808′.042 C89-095164-0

PUBLISHER: *David Dimmell*
ACQUISITIONS EDITOR: *Heather McWhinney*
DEVELOPMENTAL EDITOR: *Graeme Whitley*
PUBLISHING SERVICES MANAGER: *Karen Eakin*
EDITORIAL CO-ORDINATOR: *Jill Parkinson*
EDITORIAL ASSISTANT: *Tess Fragoulis*
COPY EDITOR: *Cy Strom*
TYPESETTING AND ASSEMBLY: *Q Composition Inc.*
PRINTING AND BINDING: *Webcom Ltd.*

Printed in Canada

2 3 4 5 94 93 92 91

preface

Most of the changes in this revision of *The Bare Essentials, Form A* are responses to suggestions from our colleagues across Canada who are using *The Bare Essentials* in their classrooms. We are grateful for their ideas, comments, and support.

In addition to many new and updated exercises, we have added a chapter on sentence combining to test and reinforce the beginning writer's mastery of sentence structure. We have simplified the explanation of the apostrophe in possessive constructions, and we have moved that chapter to the unit on punctuation. Those who are familiar with the original Forms A and B should note that the chapters in this revision have been renumbered in consequence of these changes. We have also rewritten the chapter "Revising the Paper," emphasizing the importance of audience and structure as well as technical correctness. Two of the readings are new; one is an essay written in class by a first-term student. And finally, in response to continuing requests from the grammatically faithful, we have included a glossary. Students wishing to know the definitions of grammatical terms used in the text – as always, we have kept these to a minimum – can find both definitions and examples in the List of Grammatical Terms at the back of the book.

Like its predecessors, *The Bare Essentials, Form A Third Edition* is designed for Canadian college students taking a first-semester or first-year writing course. The concise explanations, numerous exercises, and answers, however, make it as suitable for individualized, self-paced learning programs as it is for conventional composition classes.

As the title suggests, *The Bare Essentials* covers only those points of grammar, usage, and mechanics that are indispensable to clear expository writing: organization of ideas, sentence structure, grammar, spelling, diction, and punctuation. This book teaches the basic skills, leaving the teacher free to supplement the text according to the special needs of the class or the specific objectives of the course.

Each "essential" is presented in a discrete unit. A glance at the table of contents will show that we have arranged the units in what might be called the "order of visibility" of composition errors – starting with spelling and ending with organization and diction – but the instructor may introduce the units in any order. The chapters within a unit should, however, be covered in the order in which they appear.

We believe that students can learn to write clear, error-free prose if they understand the principles involved, master the principles through practice with given sentences, and then apply the principles in their own writing. And they have to want to learn. Thus, we begin most chapters with a few words about the practical significance of the material. A short, nontechnical explanation of the writing principle appears next, followed by examples. Where the material is complex, we've broken it down into several easy-to-follow steps. Most of each chapter is devoted to practice exercises of gradually increasing difficulty, and the student is directed to do as many as necessary to master the rule. Taken sometimes from student work, sometimes from professional writing, the exercises are all designed to appeal to the interests of Canadian college students. In fact we have given the entire book an informal tone, to engage and motivate the student.

Several features of the book make it especially helpful and easy to use. First, the student can do most of the exercises right in the book. Second, the answers are printed on detachable pages at the back of the book, so students can easily correct their own work, getting immediate feedback about their errors. Finally, on the inside of the back cover is a Revision Guide, which can be used both as a checklist for revision and rewriting and as a subject index to the book. Teachers may wish to duplicate the Revision Guide, attach it to a student's paper, and use it to guide and explain grading.

We wish to express our appreciation to all those who offered suggestions for improvement to this third edition of the book. Special thanks are due to Tom Hartley of Centennial College, who assisted both with the manuscript and with the Instructor's Manual, and to students Janet Read and Marty J. Chan, who contributed two of the essays we've included in the Readings.

Sarah Norton
Centennial College
Scarborough, Ontario

Brian Green
Niagara College
Welland, Ontario.

introduction

Why You Need This Book

Who needs to write well, anyway? If I get a factory or general labour job, I won't ever need to write, and if I'm in management, a secretary will fix all my mistakes.

college student

We can train a person on the job to do the specific tasks we require in about two weeks . . . maximum. What we need you people at the colleges to do is teach them to communicate – with other workers, with their supervisors – orally and in memos, reports, and letters.

president of a steel-fabricating firm speaking to the technical faculty at an Ontario community college

You look at the guys who move up in this industry. They're the ones who can write intelligently and who can read and understand other people's writing. Hard work helps, and so does being the owner's nephew . . . but you've got to be able to read and write reasonably well to move past manual labour – and the guys who can't do it know that better than anyone. Ask them.

former employee in the Canadian mining industry

To an employer, any employee is more valuable if he or she is able to write correctly and clearly. No one can advance very far in a career without the ability to construct understandable sentences. It's that simple. Fairly or unfairly, employers and others will judge your intelligence and ability on the basis of your use of English. If you want to communicate effectively and earn respect, both on and off the job, you need to be able to write clearly.

That's the bad news. The good news is that *anyone who wants to* can achieve the standards of written English that are acceptable anywhere. All that is needed from you, really, is *caring*. If you care enough – about what others think of you, about advancement in a career – then you'll put out the effort necessary, whether that means looking up spelling, rereading what you've written, or doing all the exercises in this book twice!

How To Use This Book

In each chapter, we do three things: explain a point, illustrate it with examples, and give exercises to help you master it. The exercises are arranged in **sets** that get more difficult as you go along. By the end of the last set in a chapter, you should have a good grasp of the skill.

Here's how to proceed:

1. Read the explanation. Do this even if you think you understand the point being discussed.
2. Study the examples carefully.
3. Now turn to the exercises. If you've found an explanation easy and feel you have no problems with the skill, try a set near the end of the group of exercises following the explanation. If you get all the sentences right, do one more set. If you get that one all right too, skip the rest and go on to the next point. Skip ahead only if you're really confident, though.

   If you don't feel confident, don't skip anything. Start with the first set and work through all the exercises until you're sure you understand the point.
4. ALWAYS CHECK YOUR ANSWERS TO ONE SET OF EXERCISES BEFORE GOING ON TO THE NEXT. If you ignore this instruction, we can't help you. Only if you check after every set can you avoid repeating your mistakes and possibly reinforcing your error.
5. When you discover a mistake, go back to the explanation and examples and study them again. Make up some examples of your own to illustrate the rule. When you're sure you understand, continue with the exercises.

Finally, on the inside of the back cover you'll find the Revision Guide. Use it to check over your papers before handing them in. This book is meant to be a practical tool, not a theoretical reference. Apply the lessons in the writing assignments we've included and in all the writing you do. Explanations can identify writing problems and show you how to solve them, exercises can give you practice in eliminating errors, but only writing and revising can bring real and lasting improvement.

Publisher's Note to Instructors and Students

This text book is a key component of your course. If you are the instructor of this course, you undoubtedly considered a number of texts carefully before choosing this as the one that will work best for your students and you. The authors and publishers of this book spent considerable time and money to ensure its high quality, and we appreciate your recognition of this effort and accomplishment.

If you are a student, we are confident that this text will help you to meet the objectives of your course. You will also find it helpful after the course is finished, as a valuable addition to your personal library. So hold on to it.

As well, please don't forget that photocopying copyright work means the authors lose royalties that are rightfully theirs. This loss will discourage them from writing another edition of this text or other books, because doing so will simply not be worth their time and effort. If this happens, we all lose – students, instructors, authors, and publishers.

And since we want to hear what you think about this book, please be sure to send us the stamped reply card at the end of the text. This will help us to continue publishing high-quality books for your courses.

contents

spelling

Three Suggestions for Quick Improvement

We will deal with spelling first because, of all the errors you might make in writing, spelling is the one that is noticed by everyone, not just English teachers. No piece of writing that is full of misspellings can be classified as good. Misspellings can cause misunderstanding, as when the English teacher promised his students a course with "a strong *vacational* emphasis." (Those students who weren't misled wondered what he was doing teaching English.)

Sometimes misspellings cause confusion. Take this sentence, for example:

> Mouse is a desert with a base of wiped cream.

It takes a few seconds to "translate" the sentence into a definition of *mousse*, a dessert made with whipped cream.

Most often, though, misspellings are misleading, in that they spoil the image you want to present. You want, naturally, to be seen as intelligent, careful, and conscientious. But, if your writing is riddled with spelling errors, your reader will think you careless, uneducated, or even stupid. It is not true, by the way, that intelligence and the ability to spell go hand in hand. It *is* true, though, that people generally think they do. So, to prevent both confusion and embarrassment, it is essential that you spell correctly.

There are three things you can do to improve your spelling almost instantly:

1. Buy and use a good dictionary.

A good dictionary is the one indispensable tool of the writer. You will need it *every time* you write. Most of your doubts about spelling can be answered if you take the time to check in your dictionary. The time you spend looking up words will not be wasted; your rewards will be the increased accuracy of your writing and the increased respect of your reader. Useful dictionaries are Holt, Rinehart and Winston's *Compact Dictionary of Canadian English* (a light, easy-to-carry dictionary, convenient for school), *The Gage Canadian Dictionary* (a Canadian reference, ideal for use at home or in the office), and the *Merriam-Webster Unabridged Dictionary*.

If you wonder how it's possible to look up a word that you can't spell, look at the dictionaries we've recommended. At the front of each is a "Guide to the Dictionary," and in the Guide is a chart showing the common spellings for all the sounds in the English language. If you know only how to pronounce a word, the chart will help you find its spelling. Another way to find a word you can't spell is to look up a *synonym* — a word that means the same thing. In the dictionary entry for the synonym, you'll probably find the word you're looking for.

> 2. Ask a good speller.

Most good spellers are secretly proud of their talent and pleased to demonstrate it. Don't be afraid to ask. Remember, they probably aren't as good as you are at something else; you may have a talent they could use in exchange.

> 3. Learn three basic spelling rules.

English spelling is frustratingly irregular, and no rule holds true in *all* cases. But there are three simple rules that do hold for most words, and mastering these rules will help you avoid many common errors.

Before learning the three rules, you need to know the difference between **vowels** and **consonants**. The vowels are **a, e, i, o,** and **u** (and sometimes **y**). All the other letters are consonants.

Rule 1: Dropping the Final *e*

The first rule tells you when to drop the final, silent *e* when adding an ending to a word.

> *Drop* the final, silent *e* when adding an ending beginning with a vowel.
> *Keep* the final, silent *e* when adding an ending beginning with a consonant.

Keeping the rule in mind, look at these examples:

Endings Beginning with a Vowel	Endings Beginning with a Consonant
-ing: amuse + ing = amusing	*-ment:* amuse + ment = amusement
-ed: live + ed = lived	*-ly:* live + ly = lively
-able: like + able = likable	*-ness:* like + ness = likeness
-ible: force + ible = forcible	*-ful:* force + ful = forceful
-er: use + er = user	*-less:* use + less = useless

Exercises

Combine each word with the ending to form a new word. When you have finished, check your answers in the back of the book. (Answers begin on p. 265. You can tear them out if you want to.) If you miss even one answer, go over the rule and the examples again to find out why. If you get all the answers to exercises 1 and 2 correct, skip ahead to exercise 4.

1

1. sure + ly =
2. like + ing =
3. believe + able =
4. arrange + ment =
5. move + ing =
6. bare + ly =
7. radiate + or =
8. experience + ing =
9. absolute + ly =
10. use + ing =

2

1. safe + ly =
2. argue + ing =
3. size + able =
4. accelerate + ing =
5. extreme + ly =
6. improve + ment =
7. reduce + ing =
8. use + able =
9. immediate + ly =
10. require + ing =

3

1. sincere + ly =
2. cohere + ence =
3. value + able =
4. guide + ance =
5. discourage + ing =
6. ice + y =
7. complete + ly =
8. purchase + ing =
9. collapse + ible =
10. encourage + ment =

4

Add *e* in the blank space wherever it's needed to complete the spelling of these words. If no *e* is needed, leave the space blank.

1. bor_____ing
2. mov_____ment
3. scarc_____ly
4. unus_____able

5. car_____ful
6. advertis_____ment
7. excus_____able
8. provid_____ing
9. sens_____ible
10. improv_____ment

5

Add *e* in the blank space wherever it's needed.

1. saf_____ty
2. rang_____ing
3. reduc_____ible
4. balanc_____ing
5. entir_____ly
6. insur_____ance
7. definit_____ly
8. car_____less
9. respons_____ible
10. distanc_____ing

6

Make up sentences, using all of the words you got wrong in exercises 1 through 5.

Exceptions to Rule 1

Three common words do not follow the rule. Here they are:

argue + ment = argument
nine + th = ninth
true + ly = truly

There is one more exception to rule 1: after soft *c* (as in *notice*) and soft *g* (as in *change*), keep the final, silent *e* when adding an ending beginning with *a* or *o*. Here are two examples:

notice + able = noticeable
outrage + ous = outrageous

Rule 2: Doubling the Final Consonant

The second rule tells you when to double the final consonant when adding an ending to a word.

> When adding an ending beginning with a vowel (such as *-able*, *-ing*, *-ed*, or *-er*), double the final consonant of the root word if the word
> 1. ends with a *single* consonant preceded by a *single* vowel
>   AND
> 2. is stressed on the last syllable.

Notice that a word must have *both* characteristics for the rule to apply. Let's look at a few examples:

begin + er	ends with a single consonant (*n*) preceded by a single vowel (*i*) and is stressed on the last syllable (*begín*), so the rule applies, and we double the final consonant:	**beginner**
control + ed	ends with a single consonant (*l*) preceded by a single vowel (*o*) and is stressed on the last syllable (*contról*), so the rule applies:	**controlled**
drop + ing	ends with a single consonant (*p*) preceded by a single vowel (*o*) and is stressed on the last syllable (there is only one: *dróp*), so the rule applies:	**dropping**
appear + ing	ends with a single consonant (*r*) preceded by *two* vowels (*ea*), so the rule does not apply, and we do not double the final consonant:	**appearing**
turn + ed	ends with *two* consonants (*rn*), so the rule does not apply:	**turned**
open + er	ends with a single consonant (*n*) preceded by a single vowel (*e*) but is *not* stressed on the last syllable (*ópen*), so the rule does not apply:	**opener**

(In words such as *equip*, *quit*, and *quiz*, the *u* should be considered part of the *q* and not a vowel. These words then follow the rule: *equipping*, *quitter*, and *quizzed*.)

Exercises

Combine each word with the ending to form a new word. Check your answers to each set of ten before going on. If you make no mistakes in exercises 7 and 8, skip ahead to exercise 11. If you make even one mistake, do exercises 9 and 10.

7

1. plan + ing =
2. stop + ing =
3. admit + ed =
4. nail + ing =

5. stir + ed =
6. commission + er =
7. put + ing =
8. write + ing =
9. map + ing =
10. interrupt + ed =

8

1. ship + er =
2. begin + ing =
3. drop + ed =
4. train + ing =
5. forget + ing =
6. appear + ance =
7. plan + ed =
8. happen + ing =
9. stop + er =
10. insist + ed =

9

1. suffer + ing =
2. quiz + ed =
3. permit + ing =
4. strip + ed =
5. meet + ing =
6. compel + ing =
7. crop + ed =
8. tip + ing =
9. allot + ing =
10. quarter + ed =

10

1. prefer + ing =
2. omit + ed =
3. transfer + ing =
4. develop + ing =
5. control + er =
6. occur + ed =
7. equip + ing =
8. forgot + en =
9. bite + ing =
10. prefer + ed =

11

1. bid + ing =
2. comfort + ing =
3. forget + ful =
4. admit + ing =
5. avail + able =
6. regret + ing =
7. regret + able =
8. control + able =
9. disappear + ance =
10. defer + ed =

12

1. overlap + ed =
2. expel + ing =
3. quiz + ed =
4. acquit + ed =
5. focus + ing =
6. excel + ing =
7. develop + ed =
8. transfer + ed =
9. parallel + ed =
10. rebel + ing =

13

1. occur + ence =
2. exist + ence =
3. cohere + ence =
4. concur + ing =
5. interfere + ence =
6. subsist + ence =
7. differ + ence =
8. depend + ence =
9. recur + ence =
10. insist + ence =

When it comes to adding *-ence*, three words are especially troublesome. *Prefer, refer*, and *confer* all appear to require a doubled final consonant. But they don't, because, when you add *-ence*, the stress shifts to the *first* syllable of the word. So you write:

prefér	preférring	preférred	but	*préference*
refér	reférring	reférred	but	*réference*
confér	conférring	conférred	but	*cónference*

Exercise

14

Make up sentences in which you use the words you got wrong in exercises 7 through 13.

Rule 3: Words Containing *ie* or *ei*

There are almost a thousand common English words containing *ie* or *ei*, so remembering the rule that governs them is worthwhile. It helps to keep in mind that *ie* occurs roughly twice as often as *ei*.

The old rhyme tells you most of what you need to know to spell these words:

> Write *i* before *e*, except after *c*
> Or when sounded like *ā*, as in *neighbour* and *weigh*.

If you remember this rhyme, you'll have no difficulty in spelling words like *belief*, *piece*, *ceiling*, *receive*, and *freight*.

Unfortunately, the rhyme covers only two of the cases in which we write *e* before *i*: after *c*, and when the syllable is pronounced with a long *ā* sound. So an addition to the rule is necessary:

> If short *ĕ* or long ī is the sound that is right,
> Write *e* before *i*, as in *their* or in *height*.

This rule covers words such as *Fahrenheit*, *seismic*, *heir*, and *leisure* (pronounce it to rhyme with *pleasure*). *Either* and *neither* can be pronounced "eye-ther" and "nye-ther," so they too require *ei*.

There are, of course, exceptions. This silly sentence contains the most common ones:

The *friend* of a *weird species* of *sheik seized caffeine, codeine,* and *protein.*

Exercises

Fill in the blanks with *ie* or *ei*. After you finish each set, check your answers.

15

1. br____f
2. cash____r
3. rec____ve
4. p____rce
5. rel____f
6. retr____ve
7. c____ling
8. bel____ve

9. dec_____tful
10. hyg_____ne

16

1. th_____f
2. p_____ce
3. gr_____f
4. conc_____ve
5. pr_____st
6. front_____r
7. ach_____ve
8. conc_____t
9. b_____ge
10. Fahrenh_____t

17

1. Each w_____ner w_____ghed 85 g.
2. The fr_____ght yard was under police surv_____llance.
3. She gave me a rec_____pt for_____ght dollars.
4 There is no rel_____f from his conc_____t.
5. Elizabeth II now r_____gns; Prince Charles is her h_____r.

18

1. I ordered chow m_____n and a st_____n of beer.
2. N_____ther of us knows how to use a G_____ger counter.
3. Our n_____ghbour has offered to hire our n_____ce.
4. I dropped the horse's r_____ns and fell out of the sl_____gh.
5. It is conc_____vable that_____ther one could do the job.

19

1. I gr_____ved when Dracula struck a v_____n.
2. It is th_____r bel_____f that too much prot_____n is unhealthy.

3. That spec____s of ape grows to a h____ght of 2 m.

4. The police s____zed the rec____vers of for____gn gold.

There are three or four more spelling rules we could explain here, but we won't — for two reasons. First, there are many exceptions to the remaining "rules" for English spelling. And, second, you don't need to memorize more rules *if you use your dictionary*. Now is the time to read the "Guide to the Dictionary" in the front of your dictionary. Reading it won't be very entertaining, but it will be well worth your while. The Guide outlines the kinds of information given for each word in the dictionary and explains the abbreviations and symbols that are used. You will discover, for example, that you don't need to memorize long lists of irregular plurals: your dictionary provides the irregular plurals of the nouns you look up. It also gives the irregular forms of verbs, adjectives, and adverbs. (If you've forgotten how *regular* plurals, verb forms, adjectives, and adverbs are formed, the Guide will remind you.) Your dictionary will also tell you how to add various endings to root words and even where you can divide a word when you need to hyphenate it at the end of a line. Take half an hour to read the Guide in your dictionary; then do the following exercises.

Exercises

Use your dictionary to do these exercises. Check your answers to each set of ten before going on to the next.

20

Write the plural form of each word.

1. hero
2. history
3. criterion
4. ghetto
5. personnel
6. crisis
7. data
8. phenomenon
9. nucleus
10. appendix

21

Combine each root word with the ending given.

1. lonely + ness =
2. copy + ed =
3. crazy + ness =
4. easy + er =

5. pretty + est =
6. reply + s =
7. reply + ing =
8. thirty + eth =
9. unnecessary + ly =
10. traffic + ing =

22

Using hyphens, show where each word could be divided at the end of a line. (Some words can be divided in two or more places — for example, *ice-break-er*.)

1. employer
2. consists
3. success
4. management
5. process
6. shipping
7. accounting
8. through
9. distribution
10. business

chapter 2

Sound-Alikes, Look-Alikes, and Spoilers

Using a dictionary, asking a good speller for help, and applying the three spelling rules will make an immediate improvement in your spelling. By following two additional suggestions you will further increase your spelling accuracy, but the skills involved will take longer to master. First, learn to tell apart words that are often confused because they sound or look alike. Second, learn to spell the words that most people find difficult — words we have called Spelling Spoilers. Don't try to master all of these words at once. Instead, memorize a few each week, and review them frequently. In two or three months, you could be one of the people poor spellers turn to for help!

Sound-Alikes and Look-Alikes

Some of your spelling troubles are probably caused by your using words that either sound or look like the words you really want. Careful pronunciation sometimes helps to correct this problem. For example, if you pronounce the words *accept* and *except* differently, you'll be less likely to confuse them in your writing. It is also useful to make up memory aids to help yourself remember the difference between words that sound alike but have very different meanings.

accept
except

Accept means "t**a**ke." It is always a verb. *Except* means "**ex**cluding."

Everyone *except* Brian *accepted* my explanation.

advice
advise

The difference in pronunciation makes the difference in meaning clear. *Advise* (rhymes with *wise*) is a verb. *Advice* (rhymes with *nice*) is a noun.

I *advise* you not to listen to free *advice*.

affect
effect

Affect is a verb meaning "influence." *Effect* is a noun meaning "result." If you can substitute *result*, then *effect* is the word you need. (Occasionally *effect* can be a verb — meaning "bring about" — but you probably won't need to use it that way.)

Learning about the *effects* of caffeine *affected* my coffee-drinking habits.

a lot
allot

A lot (often misspelled *alot*) should be avoided. Use *many* or *much* instead. *Allot* means "distribute" or "assign."

He still has ~~a lot of~~ *many* problems, but he's coping ~~a lot~~ *much* better.
The teacher will *allot* the marks according to the difficulty of the questions.

are
our

Are is a verb. *Our* shows ownership.

Pierre Berton and Margaret Atwood *are* two of Canada's best-known writers.
Canada is *our* home and native land.

choose
chose

Pronunciation gives the clue here. *Choose* rhymes with *booze* and means "select." *Chose* rhymes with *rose* and means "selected."

Please *choose* a topic.
I *chose* film making.

coarse
course

Coarse means "rough, unrefined." (Remember: the word ***arse*** is co**arse**.) For all other meanings, use *course*.

That sandpaper is too *coarse*.
You'll enjoy the photography *course*.
Of *course* you'll do well.

complement
compliment

A *complement* compl**e**tes something. A *compl**i**ment* is a gift of praise.

A glass of wine would be the perfect *complement* to the meal.
Some people are embarrassed by *compliments*.

conscience
conscious

Your *conscience* is your sense of right and wrong. *Conscious* means "aware" or "awake" — able to feel and think.

After Katy cheated on the test, her *conscience* bothered her.
Katy was *conscious* of having done wrong.
The injured man was *unconscious* for an hour.

consul
council
counsel

A *consul* is a government official stationed in another country. A *council* is an assembly or official group. Members of a council are *councillors*. *Counsel* can be used to mean both "advice" and "to advise."

The Canadian *consul* in Mexico was very helpful.
The Women's Advisory *Council* meets next month.
Maria gave me good *counsel*.
She *counselled* me to hire a lawyer.

desert
dessert

A *désert* is a dry, barren place. As a verb, *desért* means "leave behind." *Dessért* is "double good," the kind of food you'd like two servings of, so give it two *s's*.

The tundra is Canada's only *desert* region.
My neighbour *deserted* her husband and children.
Dessert is my favourite part of the meal.

dining
dinning

You'll spell *dining* correctly if you remember the phrase "wining and dining." You'll probably never use *dinning*. It means "making a loud noise."

The children are in the *dining* room.

We are *dining* out tonight.
The sounds from the disco next door were *dinning* in my ears.

does
dose

Pronunciation provides the clue. *Does* rhymes with *buzz* and is a verb. *Dose* rhymes with *gross* and refers to a quantity of medicine.

John *does* drive fast, *doesn't* he?
My grandmother gave me a *dose* of cod liver oil.

forth
fourth

Forth means "forward" or "onward." ***Four**th* contains the number **four**, which gives it its meaning.

Please stop pacing back and *forth*.
The B.C. Lions lost their *fourth* game in a row.

hear
here

*H**ear*** is what you do with your **ear**s. *Here* is used for all other meanings.

Now *hear* this!
Ray isn't *here*.
Here is your assignment.

it's
its

It's is a shortened form of *it is*. The apostrophe takes the place of the *i* in *is*. If you can substitute *it is*, then *it's* is the form you need. If you can't substitute *it is*, then *its* is the correct word.

It's really not difficult. (*It is* really not difficult.)
The book has lost *its* cover. ("The book has lost *it is* cover" makes no sense, so you need *its*.)

It's is also commonly used as the shortened form of *it has*. In this case, the apostrophe takes the place of the *h* and the *a*.

It's been a bad month for mussels.

later
latter

Late**r* refers to time and has the word ***late in it. *Latter* means "the second of two" and has two *t's*. It is the opposite of *former*.

It is *later* than you think.
You take the former, and I'll take the *latter*.

loose
lose

Pronunciation is the key to these words. *Loose* rhymes with *goose* and means "not tight." *Lose* rhymes with *ooze* and means "misplace" or "be defeated."

A *loose* electrical connection is dangerous.
Some are born to win, some to *lose*.

miner
minor

A ***miner*** works in a **mine**. *Minor* means "lesser" or "not important." For example, a *minor* is a person of less than legal age.

Liquor can be served to *miners*, but not if they are *minors*.
For me, spelling is a *minor* problem.

moral
morale

Again, pronunciation provides the clue you need. *Móral* refers to the understanding of what is right and wrong. *Moràle* refers to the spirit or mental condition of a person or group.

People often have to make *moral* decisions.
The low *morale* of the workers prompted the strike.

peace
piece

Peace is what we want on **ea**rth. *Piece* means "a part or portion of something," as in "a **pie**ce of **pie**."

Everyone hopes for *peace* in the Middle East.
A *piece* of the puzzle is missing.

personal
personnel

Personal means "private." *Personnel* refers to the group of people working for a particular employer or to the office responsible for maintaining employees' records.

The letter was marked "*Personal* and Confidential."
We are fortunate in having hired highly qualified *personnel*.
Nellie works in the *Personnel* Office.

principal
principle

Principal means "main." A *principle* is a rule.

A *principal* is the main administrator of a school.
Oil is Alberta's *principal* industry.
The *principal* and the interest totalled more than I could pay. (In this case, the principal is the main amount of money.)
One of the teacher's *principles* is to refuse to accept late assignments.

quiet
quite

If you pronounce these words carefully, you won't confuse them. *Quiet* has two syllables; *quite* has only one.

The librarian asked us to be *quiet*.
We had not *quite* finished our homework.

stationary
stationery

Stationary means "fixed in place." *Stationery* is writing paper.

Did you want a portable or a *stationary* computer?
Please order a new supply of *stationery*.

than
then

Than is used in comparisons. Pronounce it to rhyme with *can*. *Then* refers to time and rhymes with *when*.

Peter is a better speller *than* I.
He made his decision *then*.
Ted withdrew from the competition; *then* he realized the consequences.

their
there
they're

Their indicates ownership. *There* points out something or indicates place. It includes the word ***here***, which also indicates place. *They're* is a shortened form of *they are*. (The apostrophe replaces the *a* in *are*.)

It was *their* fault.
There are two weeks left in the term.
You should look over *there*.
They're late, as usual.

too
two
to

The *too* with an extra *o* in it means "more than enough" or "also." *Two* is the number after one. For all other meanings, use *to*.

He thinks he's been working *too* hard. She thinks so, *too*.
There are *two* sides *to* every argument.
The *two* women knew *too* much about each other *to* be friends.

were
where
we're

If you pronounce these three carefully, you won't confuse them. *Were* rhymes with *fur* and is a verb. ***Where*** is pronounced "hwear," includes the word ***here***, and indicates place. *We're* is a shortened form of *we are* and is pronounced "weer."

You *were* joking, *weren't* you?
Where did you want to meet?
We're on our way.

who's
whose

Who's is a shortened form of *who is* or *who has*. If you can substitute *who is* or *who has* for the *who's* in your sentence, then you are using the right spelling. Otherwise, use *whose*.

Who's coming to dinner? (*Who is* coming to dinner?)
Who's been sleeping in my bed? (*Who has* been sleeping?)
Whose calculator is this? ("*Who is* calculator" makes no sense, so you need *whose*.)

woman
women

Confusing these two is guaranteed to irritate your women readers. *Wo***man** is the singular form; compare **man**. *Wo***men** is the plural form; compare **men**.

A *woman's* place is wherever she chooses to be.
The *women's* movement promotes equality between *women* and men.

you're
your

You're is a shortened form of *you are*. If you can substitute *you are* for the *you're* in your sentence, then you're using the correct form. If you can't substitute *you are*, use *your*.

You're welcome. (*You are* welcome.)
Unfortunately, *your* hamburger got burned. ("*You are* hamburger" makes no sense, so *your* is the word you want.)

Exercises

Choose the correct word in each pair. If you don't know an answer, go back and reread the explanation. Check your answers after each set of ten questions (answers begin on p. 268). When you get five sets entirely correct, you may skip ahead to exercise 11.

1

1. Unemployment is having an (affect effect) on the kinds of (coarses courses) college students choose.
2. (Are Our) offer was not (accepted excepted).
3. Fresh fruit is a better (desert dessert)(than then) cake.
4. When (your you're) travelling abroad, (losing loosing) your ticket is a nightmare.
5. It was so (quite quiet) that you could (hear here) a pin drop.
6. He is the one (who's whose)(conscience conscious) ought to be troubled.
7. Alex, the (forth fourth) child, was nine years younger (then than) his sister.

8. Don't buy expensive luggage; (its it's) bound to get scratched during (its it's) travels.
9. The SPCA will (advice advise) you on what kind of dog to (chose choose).
10. (Does Dose) the (dining dinning) room serve fish and chips?

2

1. If a (principal principle) is always a rule, is a (principal principle) always a pal?
2. Finally, on the (forth fourth) try, I (choose chose) the right key.
3. We all enjoyed the dinner, (accept except) for the (desert dessert).
4. (Your You're) acting as if you had a guilty (conscience conscious).
5. If you aren't (quiet quite), I won't be able to (here hear) him.
6. In all my courses (except accept) English, I'm having only (miner minor) problems.
7. If they (loose lose) this game (to two too), the (moral morale) of the team will suffer.
8. Let your (conscience conscious) be (your you're) guide.
9. A (stationary stationery) engine is one that is fixed in (its it's) place.
10. (Does dose) the average (woman women) really worry about getting her laundry "whiter than white"?

3

1. Did you (hear here) that Margaret Atwood is expected to speak (hear here) next week?
2. When the (stationary stationery) was delivered, we found (to too two) printing errors in the letterhead.
3. It's not whether you win or (loose lose); (its it's) how you play the game.
4. In (your you're) opinion, (miners minors) shouldn't be allowed to drive, let alone drink.
5. Your (conscious conscience) will guide you in (chosing choosing) the right (coarse course) of action.
6. The scientist was pleased to (accept except) a National Research (Counsel Council) grant.
7. The (coarse course) fabric spoiled the (affect effect).
8. All I want for Christmas is (peace piece) and (quite quiet).
9. (Whose Who's) afraid of (woman's women's) liberation?
10. A long (peace piece) of rope swung back and (forth fourth) in the breeze.

4

1. Drawings of what look like extraterrestrials can be found in (a lot, allot, many) of the world's great (desserts deserts).

2. (Were We're Where) can I find a (quite quiet) place to study?
3. Of the (to too two) proposals, the (later latter) seems preferable.
4. We found the (consul council counsel) to be a man of (principal principle).
5. (A lot of, Allot of, Many) people take up jogging to try to (loose lose) weight.
6. (Your You're) supposed to swallow four teaspoons as (your you're) daily (does dose).
7. I thought I had mastered the "*i* before *e*" (principal principle), but (than then) they told me about the exceptions.
8. (Its It's)(later latter) than you think.
9. The thieves came back (later latter) and took everything (accept except) the radio.
10. It's no longer (quiet quite) so unusual for a (woman women) to be elected to public office.

5

1. They plan to (a lot, allot) $1,500 for the redecoration of their (dining dinning) room.
2. Let there be (peace piece) in (are our) time.
3. Edmund Burke believed manners were more important (than then)(morales morals).
4. (Were We're Where) do you think (were we're where) going to get the money?
5. I found it impossible to remain (stationary stationery), so I walked rapidly back and (forth fourth).
6. I (hear here)(your you're) sorry you (choose chose) this (coarse course).
7. Do you think Canadians (are our)(conscience conscious) of (there their they're) national identity?
8. Your ability to learn is (affected effected) by your (personal personnel) well-being.
9. He is a person (whose who's)(advice advise) I value.
10. Inflation and unemployment are the (principal principle) concerns of Canadians; world (peace piece) is considered almost a (miner minor) problem in comparison.

6

1. Prolonged unemployment (affects effects) one's (moral morale).
2. A (complement compliment) is sometimes more welcome (than then) a kiss.
3. Following your (advise advice), I applied to the bank for a (personal personnel) loan.

4. As a coal (miner minor), he (does dose) run an increased risk of developing lung disease.
5. I suggest that (there their they're) behaviour can hardly be described as (moral morale).
6. If I (hear here) one more complaint, (your you're) going to stay home.
7. (Whose Who's) been using my (personal personnel)(stationary stationery)?
8. If I had to (chose choose) between the two, I'd follow the (later latter)(coarse course) of action.
9. Two helpings of (desert dessert) should be (quiet quite) sufficient.
10. (To Too Two) many people don't look (were we're where) they're going.

7

1. I made the turn and (than then) saw the sign: "No left turn; busses (accepted excepted)."
2. If you let the dog run (loose lose), you must (accept except) the consequences.
3. Surely (its it's) a question of (principal principle).
4. The student asked the guidance counsellor to (advice advise) her on a (personal personnel) matter.
5. The young musician gratefully (accepted excepted) our (complements compliments).
6. Some (miners minors) have little difficulty in convincing a bartender that (their there they're) of age.
7. She (choose chose) to work in the (dining dinning) room of the Banff Springs Hotel.
8. Judging by the pinging sounds I (hear here), I'd say (your you're) car needs a tune-up.
9. I'd rather write an essay (than then) do an oral report in front of (are our) whole class.
10. The salt was (to too two)(coarse course)(to too two) pass through the holes of the shaker.

8

1. Moments after (its it's) take-off, the plane banked (to too two) sharply (to too two) the right.
2. I do not intend to (choose chose) the one (who's whose) application was late.
3. Check with the (Personal Personnel) Department first; (than then) hire legal (consul council counsel).

4. Until I reached home, I was not (conscience conscious) of the drug's (affect effect).
5. If he (does dose) that again, it will (affect effect) his chances for promotion.
6. The Canada (Council Counsel) will announce (its it's) awards (later latter) this month.
7. My (personal personnel) opinion is that (woman women) are safe drivers.
8. Whenever I receive a (complement compliment), I feel a little self- (conscience conscious).
9. (A lot, Many, Much) Post Office (personal personnel) suffer from low (moral morale).
10. (Whose Who's) turn is it to find the (complement compliment) of the angle?

9

1. The camel's (coarse course) hair protects it from the (desert dessert) sun.
2. If you could remember the three rules, (than then) (your you're) spelling troubles would be over.
3. Thinking Barry's (advice advise) would be sound (cunsul council counsel), I (accepted excepted) it.
4. (Their There They're) are many children who believe the tooth fairy will come if they (loose lose) a tooth.
5. The (woman women) and her daughter own a (stationary stationery) store.
6. The (miner minor) skirmish before the game had the (affect effect) of making us determined to win.
7. It's (to too two) bad, but we're (to too two) tired (to too two) go.
8. The impressionist painters were particularly (conscience conscious) of the (affects effects) of light on the landscape.
9. Each province establishes (its it's) own minimum wage, (dose does) it not?
10. Ontario colleges are governed by a (consul council counsel) (who's whose) function is to (advice advise) the Minister of Education.

10

Correct all the spelling errors you find in the following paragraphs.

There once was a sailor who, loosing his job to a steam engine, set out to become a successful business man. His first venture was as encyclopedia salesman, but he found that he didn't have the necessary personnel touch to win exceptance from his customers. Indeed, he was fortunate to escape one encounter with his life, after calling his prospective customer "Matey" throughout they're negotiations.

He next sought the relative piece and quite of the skilled trades, turning his hand to carpentry. The affect of that decision was even more unhappy, for he no sooner set fourth on the venture then he lost too fingers while attempting to cut a board with a dull saw. Latter, after he regained conscienceness, he swore (rather coursely) that he would never again try a job that required him to handle sharp implements.

The sailor then became a minor, but concluded that his fellow minors were to unfriendly, and so he desserted. He tried his hand (or what remained of it) at selling stationary, working in a tire repair shop, and bartending. It was on this last job that he recieved the advise that would lead to his success. A women who relieved him at 8:00 every night recommended that he forget his principals and turn to politics. Her advice was sound.

From local counsel to provincial politics, and on to Parliament, our sailor leapt from success to success. He found that his previous jobs had prepared him well for his new career. His moral soared. In campaign speeches he was able to say, "As you're MP, I shall guide the ship of state, while nailing down new reforms and toiling beneath the surface to draft legislation. I shall go door to door to ask for you're support and when I get it, I shall serve you tirelessly!" He was irresistible. Election after election, his constituency choose him as their representative.

11

Your own writing is the best test of your spelling accuracy. Write ten sentences using sound-alikes and look-alikes. Try to use those that cause you the most difficulty.

12

Write a short paragraph on any topic you choose. In your paragraph, use at least five of the sound-alikes and look-alikes you have had trouble with. Refer to the explanations, if necessary, and don't forget to use your dictionary!

Spelling Spoilers

Here is a list of words that are frequently misspelled. Have someone dictate the list to you. Circle the ones you misspell and memorize them, a few at a time. Try to learn ten each week. Review your list often, until you have mastered every word. Making up memory aids for especially troublesome words will help you conquer them. Here are some examples to get you started:

accommodate:	It means "make room for," and the word itself makes room for two *c*'s and two *m*'s.
business:	Bu**sin**ess is no **sin**.
environment:	The word *env**iron**ment*, like the earth, has ***iron*** in it.
friend:	He is a fri**end** to the **end**.
grammar:	Poor gram**mar** will **mar** your writing.

absence
accommodate
achievement
acknowledge
across

adolescence
among
answer
argument
beginning

business
careful
category
clothes
committee

conscious
criticism
definitely
dependent
desperate

development
disappear
disappoint
discipline
dissatisfied

doesn't
eighth
embarrassed
environment
exercise

existence
explanation
extremely
familiar
February

finally
forty
friend
gauge
government

grammar
guarantee
guidance
height
hoping

hypocrisy
immediately
independent
laboratory
license (*or* licence)

likely
loneliness
lonely
maintenance
marriage

mentally
necessary
ninety
ninth
occasionally

omission
opinion
opportunity
paid
parallel

perform
planned
possess
prejudice
privilege

procedure
proceed
professor
psychology
recommend

relevant
repetition
restaurant
rhythm
ridiculous

safety
schedule
separate
shining
similar

somewhat
speech
studying
succeed
superintendent

surprise
technique
thorough
tragedy
truly

unnecessary
until
unusual
usually
vacuum

Wednesday
writing
written

Exercise 13

Make up sentences containing the words you misspelled when the list of Spelling Spoilers was dictated. Underline the Spelling Spoiler(s) in each sentence. (If you do this exercise once a week, you will master the list very quickly.)

One final suggestion. You may find that, despite all your efforts, there are a few words you just cannot spell correctly. The solution? Either write them out on the inside cover of your dictionary or, even simpler, don't use them. Look in your dictionary or a thesaurus to find synonyms (different words with the same or similar meanings), and use those instead. Two thesauruses are available in inexpensive paperback editions: *Roget's Thesaurus* and Soule's *Dictionary of English Synonyms*.

unit 2

sentence structure

chapter 3

Cracking the Sentence Code

There is nothing really mysterious or difficult about the sentence itself; you've been speaking sentences successfully since you were two. The difficulty arises when you go to write — not sentences, oddly enough, but paragraphs. Almost all college students, if asked to write ten sentences on ten different topics, could do so without an error. But, if those same students were to write paragraphs, sentence fragments and run-on sentences would creep in — errors that confuse or annoy readers.

The solution to fragment and run-on problems has two parts:

> Be sure every sentence you write
> 1. sounds right
> and 2. has a subject and a verb.

Your ear is the best instrument with which to test your sentences. If you read your sentences aloud, you'll probably be able to tell by the sound whether they are complete, clear, and satisfactory. A complete sentence is one that makes sense by itself.

Read these sentences aloud:

> Windsurfing is one of the world's newest sports.
> Although windsurfing is still a young sport.

The second "sentence" doesn't sound right, does it? It does not make sense on its own and is in fact a sentence fragment.

Testing your sentences by reading them aloud won't work if you read your paragraphs straight through from beginning to end. The trick is to read from end to beginning. That is, read your last sentence aloud, and *listen* to it. If it sounds all right, then read aloud the next-to-last sentence, and so on, until you have worked your way back to the first sentence you wrote.

Now, what do you do with the ones that "sound funny"? Before you can fix them, you need to be able to "decode" each sentence to find out whether it has a subject and a verb. The subject and the verb are the bare essentials of the sentence; every sentence you write must have both. (The only exception is the *command*, in which the subject is understood rather than expressed. Consider this command: "Put your signature here." The subject *you* is understood.)

Finding Subjects and Verbs

A sentence is about *someone* or *something*. That someone or something is the **subject**. The word (or words) that tells what the subject *is* or *does* is the **verb**. The verb will express some sort of action, or condition, or occurrence.

Find the verb first. One way is by finding the word or group of words whose form can be changed to indicate a change in time. In the sentence

> The prime minister has called an election.

has called (in the past) can be changed to *is calling* (present) or *will call* (future), so *has called* is the verb.

Once you have found the verb, find the subject by asking *who* or *what* the verb refers to.

Look at these examples. We have underlined the subjects once and the verbs twice.

> Jean helped me.
> (Helped expresses an action and is the verb.
> Who or what helped? Jean helped, so Jean is the subject.)

> Finding verbs is relatively easy.
> (Is expresses a condition and is the verb.
> Who or what is [easy]? Finding, which is the subject.)

> How you do it remains a mystery to me.
> (Remains expresses a condition and is the verb.
> Who or what remains [a mystery]? How you do it, which is the subject.
> Notice that the subject can be more than one word.)

> Canada was described as "the land God gave to Cain."
> (Was described expresses an occurrence and is the verb.
> Who or what was described? Canada.)

> Their rehabilitation program seems successful.
> (Seems expresses a condition and is the verb.
> Who or what seems [successful]? The program.)

Exercise

I

Find the subject and the verb in each of the following sentences. Underline the subject with one line and the verb with two. When you have finished, check your answers on p. 270. If you make even one mistake, carefully reread "Finding Subjects and Verbs." Be sure you understand this material thoroughly before you go on.

1. Algy met a bear.
2. A bear met Algy.
3. The bear was bulgy.

4. Sad to say, the bulge was Algy.
5. Grizzlies are famous for their unpredictability.
6. Meeting bears unexpectedly is clearly risky.
7. According to an old myth, bears never run downhill.
8. Believe me. They do.
9. Females with cubs are known to be especially vicious.
10. How to defend oneself presents a real problem.

Usually the subject comes before the verb in a sentence, but not always. Occasionally we find it after the verb:

> Back to the refreshment stand for the fourth time stumbled the weary father.
> (Who or what stumbled? The father.)

> At the bottom of the page, in red ink, was my grade.
> (Who or what was? My grade.)

In sentences beginning with *There* + some form of the verb *to be*, or with *Here* + some form of the verb *to be*, the subject is generally found after the verb.

> There are three good reasons for learning to write well.
> (Who or what are? Reasons.)

> There will be a test next week.
> (Who or what will be? A test.)

> Here are the solutions to last week's problem set.
> (Who or what are? Solutions.)

In questions, the subject often follows the verb:

> Are you sure about this?
> (Who or what are? You.)

> Is he late again?
> (Who or what is? He.)

But notice that, in questions beginning with *who*, *whose*, *what*, or *which*, the subject and verb are in "normal" order:

> Who met the bear?
> Whose belly was bulgy?

> What happened to Algy?
> Which grizzly ate Algy?

Exercises

Find the subject and the verb in each of the following sentences. Underline the subject with one line, the verb with two. Check your answers to each set of ten sentences before you go on.

2

1. Canada is a country with two official languages.
2. The word "Ai!" means "hello" in Inuktitut.
3. Newfoundland is a piece of rock entirely surrounded by fog.
4. Are you from B.C.?
5. In Norway, drinking drivers are jailed for three weeks.
6. No exceptions are made.
7. There is the CN Tower, the world's tallest freestanding structure.
8. Crime is the product of a diseased society.
9. To the traditional baseball fan, playing in the SkyDome is a crime.
10. Just out of reach behind the dresser lay my car keys.

3

1. Money, like manure, does no good until it is spread.
2. Here are the steps to follow.
3. Flin Flon is named after the hero of a ten-cent novel published in 1905.
4. Whose idea was this, anyway?
5. Drive carefully.
6. Study makes the eyes weak and the brain strong.
7. Turn it down!
8. Historically, Canada's most disliked city is Toronto.
9. Love comes after marriage. (Inuit proverb)
10. Only in North America and Europe is the concept of leisure time widely understood.

4

1. Doing grammar exercises is boring.
2. A man's best friend is his dog — better even than his wife. (Inuit proverb)
3. Were they happy with their choice?
4. In the playground were thirty-four screaming children.
5. Are you still angry with me?
6. In July each year, in Calgary, Alberta, the famous Stampede is held.
7. Replacing ceramic tiles is messy, but not difficult.
8. Please stop at the next corner.
9. Santa Claus' address is c/o The North Pole, Canada, HOH OHO.
10. Peace, order, and good government are guaranteed in the Constitution Act.

More about Verbs

The verb in a sentence may be a single word, as in most of the exercises you've just done, or it may be a group of words. **Helping verbs** are often added to main verbs, so that an idea can be expressed precisely. The words *shall*, *should*, *may*, *might*, *can*, *could*, *must*, *ought*, *will*, *would*, *have*, *do*, and *be* are helping verbs.

> The complete verb in a sentence consists of the main verb + any helping verbs.

Here are a few of the forms of the verb *write*. Notice that in questions the subject may come between the helping verb and the main verb.

You may write now.
He certainly can write!
We should write home more often.
I shall write tomorrow.
He could have written yesterday.
She is writing her memoirs.
Did he write to you?
He had written his apology.
You ought to write to him.
We will have written by then.
I will write to the editor.
The proposal has been written.
Orders should have been written.
Could you have written it in French?

One verb form, in particular, always takes a helping verb. Here is the rule:

> A verb ending in *-ing* MUST have a helping verb (or verbs) before it.

Here are a few of the forms an *-ing* verb can take:

I am writing the report.
You will be writing a report.
He should have been writing it.
Is she writing the paper for him?
She must have been writing all night.
You are writing illegibly.
I was writing neatly.
Have you been writing on the wall?

Beware of certain words that are often confused with helping verbs:

> Words such as *not*, *only*, *always*, *sometimes*, *never*, *ever*, and *just* are NOT part of the verb.

These words sometimes appear in the middle of a complete verb, but they are modifiers, not verbs. Do not underline them:

I have just won the lottery!
He is almost always chosen first.
Most people do not welcome unasked-for advice.

Exercises

Underline the subject once and the complete verb twice. Correct each set of ten sentences before you go on to the next.

5

1. He is sleeping again, unfortunately.
2. You should have been paying attention.
3. Should we write the report now?
4. In Canada fall comes one month before winter.
5. What mark did you get?
6. We do not want to hear about your date.
7. Where and when are we meeting?
8. Old men will always think young men fools.
9. Their coach has just begun to suffer.
10. Back and forth, lazily but without stopping, swam the shark.

6

1. The whole country is covered with hip-deep snow for several months.
2. Why would anyone want to go over the falls in a barrel?
3. Canadians are becoming more concerned about the national debt.
4. Never again will I agree to ride with you!
5. A person may forgive an injury, but not an insult.
6. There have been better, but not more determined, players.
7. You can become addicted to coffee.
8. How long did you stay in Prince Rupert?
9. Have you ever been to the Yukon?
10. Only recently has our track coach become interested in chemistry.

7

1. By the year 2000, gasoline made from coal will be commercially available.
2. At the end of this year, a fibre-optic network will have been completed, linking all campuses into a single system.
3. Why are the official records of Canada's Parliament known as Hansard?
4. The wise man will take everything seriously except himself.
5. Canada's provinces were literally railroaded into Confederation.
6. I am always studying for some test or another, only to forget everything the next day.
7. Could any government have managed the economy worse than the last one?
8. Have you ever been caught cheating on a test?
9. Very little is known about the War of 1812, except that we won.
10. Aren't you glad to be finished?

More about Subjects

Very often, groups of words called **prepositional phrases** come before the subject in a sentence, or between the subject and the verb. When you're looking for the subject in a sentence, prepositional phrases can trip you up unless you know this rule:

> The subject of a sentence is never in a prepositional phrase.

You have to be able to identify prepositional phrases, so that you will know where *not* to look for the subject. A prepositional phrase is a group of words that begins with a preposition and ends with the name of something or someone (a noun or a pronoun). Often a prepositional phrase will indicate the direction or location of something. Here are some prepositional phrases:

about the book
above the book
according to the book
after the meeting
against the wall

behind the desk
below the window
beside the book
between the desks
by the book

from the office
in the book
inside the office
into the elevator
in front of the door

along the hall
among the books
among them
around the office
before lunch

concerning the memo
despite the book
down the hall
except the staff
for the manager

like the book
near the wall
on the desk
onto the floor
of the typist

over a door
to the staff
through the window

under the book
until the meeting
up the hall

with a book
without the book
without them

When you're looking for the subject in a sentence, you can make the task easier by crossing out any prepositional phrases. For example,

The keyboard ~~of your computer~~ should be cleaned occasionally.
What should be cleaned? The keys (not the typewriter).

~~In case of an emergency~~, one ~~of the group~~ should go ~~to the nearest ranger station for help~~.
Who should go? One (not the group).

Exercises

First cross out the prepositional phrase(s) in each sentence. Then underline the subject once and the verb twice. Check your answers to each set of ten sentences before going on. When you get three sets entirely correct, skip ahead to exercise 13.

8

1. A bird in the hand is worth two in the bush.
2. Only a few of us have done our homework.
3. Some of your answers are entertaining but wrong.
4. More than a dozen brands of video recorder are now on the market.
5. Meet me at six at the corner of Bathurst and Dupont.
6. A couple of hamburgers should be enough for each of us.
7. Do you know anything about the latest rumours of scandal in the government?
8. There is a show about laser technology on television tonight.
9. After eight hours of classes, the thought of collapsing in front of the TV set is very appealing.
10. One episode of *All My Children* was more than enough.

9

1. The verb in this sentence is "is."
2. For many students, lack of money is probably the most serious problem.
3. In the middle of May, after the end of term, the Intercollegiate Arm-Wrestling Championships will be held.
4. One strand of fibre optics can carry both telephone and television signals.
5. During the second week of term, the class will be taken on a tour of the resource centre.
6. Contrary to your expectations, and despite the rumours, your instructor does not bite.
7. On Callisto, one of Jupiter's thirteen moons, snow may "fall" up, not down.
8. On the shore of Vancouver Island, you can find both oysters and clams.
9. One of the most entertaining comedies of the 1980s was *A Fish Called Wanda*.
10. In similar circumstances, most of us would probably have taken his money.

10

1. By this time, you must be tired of the pointless game shows on TV.
2. The happiness of every country depends upon the character of its people.
3. Above my desk hangs someone else's diploma.
4. During the course of the discussion, several of us lost our tempers.
5. In the evenings and on weekends, he works on his 1958 Chevy.
6. The "short side" of a goalie is the side closer to the post.
7. New steps should be taken to encourage the flow of capital into small businesses.
8. After waiting for more than an hour, we finally left without you.

9. So far only two of your answers to the questions have been incorrect.
10. One of the country's most distinguished reporters will speak on the responsibilities of the press.

11

1. The average height of Canadian women, excluding those in Quebec, is 165 cm.
2. By waiting on tables, babysitting, and doing other jobs, I manage to make ends meet.
3. The pile of books and papers on your desk is about as neat as a tossed salad.
4. Only a few of the news reporters on television are responsible for researching and writing in addition to reading the news.
5. Except for me, everyone understands prepositions.
6. No book of Canadian humour would be complete without a couple of "Newfie" jokes.
7. Our teacher's uncertainty about the date of the War of 1812 made us less than confident about his knowledge of Canadian history.
8. A daily intake of more than 600 mg of caffeine can result in headaches, insomnia, and heart palpitations.
9. Six to ten cups of coffee will contain 600 mg of caffeine.
10. Despite its strong taste, espresso contains no more caffeine than regular coffee.

12

1. The current trend in electronics is to put telephones in our pockets and televisions in our telephones.
2. Along with many other Canadian expressions, the term *bluenose*, meaning a Nova Scotian, is of uncertain origin.
3. Within a week, please give me your report on the pyrazine anion project.
4. In the spring, parked in front of his TV set, Barry trains for the Stanley Cup playoffs.
5. Government programs to encourage training in basic skills have been cut back steadily over the past few years.
6. In the Arctic wastes of Ungava, there is a mysterious stone structure in the shape of a giant hammer standing on end.
7. There is no obvious explanation for its presence in this isolated place.
8. According to archeologist Thomas E. Lee, it may be a monument left by Vikings in their travels west from Greenland.
9. Here, on an island called Pamiok, are the ruins of what may have been a Viking longhouse.

10. If so, then centuries before Columbus' "discovery" of America, the Vikings were in what is now northern Quebec.

13

Write ten sentences of your own. Cross out all the prepositional phrases, and underline the subject once and the complete verb twice.

Multiple Subjects and Verbs

So far you have been working with sentences containing only one complete subject and one complete verb. Sentences can, however, have more than one subject and verb. Here is a sentence with a multiple subject:

> Southlands and West Point Grey are suburbs of Vancouver.

This sentence has a multiple verb:

> He elbowed and wriggled his way along the aisle of the bus.

And this sentence has a multiple subject and a multiple verb:

> The psychiatrist and the intern leaped from their chairs and seized the woman.

The elements of a multiple subject or verb are usually joined by *and* or *or*. Multiple subjects and verbs may contain more than two elements, as in the following sentences:

> Clarity, brevity, and simplicity are the basic qualities of good writing.
> I finished my paper, put the cat outside, took the phone off the hook, and crawled into bed.

Exercises

Find and underline the subjects once and the verbs twice. Be sure to underline all the elements in a multiple subject or verb. Check your answers after completing each set of ten sentences.

14

1. Jack and Jill went up the hill.
2. Georgie Porgie kissed the girls and made them cry.
3. Jack and Jill went up the hill and fetched a pail of water.
4. Maple sugar and wild rice are native Canadian products.
5. I tried and tried but didn't succeed.
6. Jim or Brian will go next.
7. The two canoeists and their dog were missing for four days.
8. Timothy Findley now farms, writes, and lectures — in that order.

9. Wait ten minutes and then phone again.
10. Shooting often and scoring occasionally are not marketable talents.

15

1. Misspellings can create misunderstanding and cause embarrassment.
2. About fifteen years ago, the *Durham County Review* printed an article about a British military leader.
3. In the article, the old soldier was highly praised but unfortunately was described as "battle-scared."
4. Furious, the soldier called the paper and demanded an apology.
5. The writer and the editor soothed the old man and promised to publish a retraction.
6. In the retraction, the paper apologized for the error and explained, "What we really meant, of course, was 'bottle-scarred.' "
7. "Drive slowly and see our city; drive fast and see our jail."
8. Good drivers obey all traffic regulations and never lose their heads.
9. Drink if you want, but don't drive if you do.
10. Come-by-Chance, Blow-me-Down, Run-by-Guess, and Jerry's Nose are places in Newfoundland.

16

1. "Take only pictures. Leave only footprints." (Sign posted in Banff National Park)
2. Jan and I studied for more than a week but failed the exam anyway.
3. In the pond were two goldfish, an old green tennis ball, and a couple of broken bottles.
4. He worked and saved all his life and died miserable and alone.
5. Everybody but me went to camp or spent a few weeks at a cottage.
6. Among the many kinds of cheese made in Canada are Camembert, Fontina, and Quark.
7. Shoe companies, book publishers, and equipment manufacturers are all profiting from the fitness craze.
8. We took a train from Clarenville to Bonavista and then went by bus to St. John's.
9. The politicians of our time attempt in vain to change the world but seldom try to change themselves.
10. According to its election literature, the government will provide every Canadian with a job, eliminate the national debt, find a cure for cancer, land a Canadian on Pluto, and win the World Series, all in the first year of office.

17

This exercise is a review. Find and underline the subjects once and the verbs twice. Be sure to underline all the elements in a multiple subject or verb. No answers are given for this exercise.

To an American visiting our country for the first time, Canadian customs and values may seem quite strange, even exotic. True, shopping centres, corn chips, *thirtysomething*, fitness programs, video games, ecological movements, and interest rates dominate the culture on both sides of the border. Nevertheless, in contrast to their American counterparts, Canadians live rather placid and orderly lives. In Canada's major cities, there are no slums, little graffiti, and not much litter. Vancouver's murder toll in 1982 was 41; Toronto's was 44; Montreal's was 84. Compare these figures with those for Chicago (668), Los Angeles (853), and New York (1,668). Things haven't changed much since then; Canadians walk and jog on city streets and in public parks both day and night, without fear of being molested. Some restaurants and even a few stores in the heart of Canada's major cities stay open 24 hours a day. In most places, drivers can safely leave their cars unlocked. In fact, in Canada we are more likely to have our bicycles stolen than our cars!

chapter 4

Still More about Verbs (For Those Who Need It)

Every verb has four forms:

1. the **base form:** used by itself or with *can, may, might, shall, will, could, would, should, must*;
2. the **past tense** form: used by itself;
3. the **-ing form:** used with *am, is, are, was, were*;

and 4. the **past participle** form: used with *have, has, had* or with *am, is, are, was, were.*

These forms are the **principal parts** of a verb. Here are some examples:

Base	Past Tense	-ing Form	Past Participle
walk	walked	walking	walked
learn	learned	learning	learned
seem	seemed	seeming	seemed
enjoy	enjoyed	enjoying	enjoyed

To use verbs correctly, you must know their principal parts. Knowing two facts will help you. First, your dictionary will give you the principal parts of certain verbs (irregular ones). Just look up the base form, and you'll find the past tense and the past participle beside it, usually in parentheses. If the past tense and past participle are *not* given, the verb is **regular**. So, the second thing you need to know is how to form the past tense and the past participle of regular verbs: by adding *-ed* to the base form. The examples listed above — *walk, learn, seem,* and *enjoy* — are regular verbs.

Many of the most common verbs are **irregular**. Their past tense and past participle are formed in a variety of ways. Following is a list of the principal parts of some of the most common irregular verbs. (We have not included the *-ing* form, because it never causes any difficulty. It is always made up of the *base form + ing.*)

The Principal Parts of Irregular Verbs

Base (Use with *can*, *may*, *might*, *shall*, *will*, *could*, *would*, *should*, *must*.)	**Past Tense**	**Past Participle** (Use with *have*, *has*, *had* or with *am*, *is*, *are*, *was*, *were*.)
be (am, is, are)	was, were	been
bear	bore	borne
become	became	become
begin	began	begun
bid (offer to pay)	bid/bade	bid/bidden
bite	bit	bitten
blow	blew	blown
break	broke	broken
bring	brought	brought
build	built	built
burst	burst	burst
buy	bought	bought
catch	caught	caught
choose	chose	chosen
come	came	come
cost	cost	cost
deal	dealt	dealt
dive	dived/dove	dived
do	did	done
draw	drew	drawn
drink	drank	drunk
drive	drove	driven
eat	ate	eaten
fall	fell	fallen
feel	felt	felt
fight	fought	fought
find	found	found
fling	flung	flung
fly	flew	flown
forget	forgot	forgotten/forgot
forgive	forgave	forgiven
freeze	froze	frozen
get	got	got/gotten
give	gave	given
go	went	gone (*not* went)
grow	grew	grown
hang (suspend)	hung	hung
hang (put to death)	hanged	hanged
have	had	had
hear	heard	heard

Base	Past Tense	Past Participle
hide	hid	hidden
hit	hit	hit
hold	held	held
hurt	hurt	hurt
keep	kept	kept
know	knew	known
lay	laid	laid
lead	led	led
leave	left	left
lend	lent	lent
lie	lay	lain
lose	lost	lost
make	made	made
mean	meant	meant
meet	met	met
pay	paid	paid
put	put	put
ride	rode	ridden
ring	rang	rung
rise	rose	risen
run	ran	run
say	said	said
see	saw (*not* seen)	seen
sell	sold	sold
set	set	set
shake	shook	shaken
shine	shone	shone
sing	sang	sung
sit	sat	sat
sleep	slept	slept
slide	slid	slid
speak	spoke	spoken
speed	sped	sped
spend	spent	spent
stand	stood	stood
steal	stole	stolen
strike	struck	struck
swear	swore	sworn
swim	swam	swum
swing	swung	swung
take	took	taken
teach	taught	taught
tear	tore	torn

Base	Past Tense	Past Participle
tell	told	told
think	thought	thought
throw	threw	thrown
wear	wore	worn
win	won	won
wind	wound	wound
write	wrote	written

Exercises

In the blank, write the correct form (either the past tense or the past participle) of the verb shown to the left of the sentence. Do not add or remove helping verbs. Answers begin on p. 273.

I

1. become After much practice, the team__________better at scoring.
2. bring The subject should have been__________up at last week's meeting.
3. have If only we could have__________your advice last month!
4. sing I__________my heart out, but the audience didn't seem to appreciate my efforts.
5. fling Ignoring the "Fragile" sticker, the clerk__________the parcel into the chute.
6. freeze A blast of icy air__________them in their tracks.
7. get We have__________out of shape during the winter.
8. lend To help the young couple get started, we__________them our tools.
9. swing Stiffly, he__________from the saddle.

10. lay — After spending an hour reading, she __________ the book down and went to bed.

2

1. lead — She __________ them through several back alleys and down a narrow street they had never seen before.
2. lose — Before long they were aware that they had __________ their way.
3. say — Neither of them __________ anything, afraid of making her angry.
4. sleep — After several hours of travelling, they stopped and __________.
5. swim — Back on the trail again, she brought them to a river that both of them had __________ when they were small.
6. tell — After they crossed, she __________ them that the journey was half over.
7. throw — By this time, they were so tired that her next suggestion ______ them into a panic.
8. steal — She wanted them to smuggle across the border a car she had __________.
9. ride — Despite their fear, they __________ with her as far as the customs building.
10. write — After their adventure, they decided to publish the journal they had __________.

The sentences in exercises 3 through 10 require both the past tense and the past participle of the verb shown at the left. Write the required form in each blank. Do not add or remove helping verbs.

3

1. wear — We__________ the same thing we had__________ last year on Halloween.
2. build — The house was__________ in a matter of days by the same men who__________ my uncle's house so quickly five years ago.
3. slide — As children, we had for many years__________ down the river bank where as adults we__________ our canoe into the water.
4. blow — The wind__________ so hard this time that it ripped apart a shed that had already been__________ down.
5. bear — Politely we__________ his complaining, until we could not have__________ it another minute.
6. hit — After making four errors in left field, George came to bat and __________ the ball harder than he'd ever__________ it before.
7. ride — Having__________ a cow once, I wouldn't mind if I never __________ one again.
8. spend — I__________ more on his present than I have__________ on my mother over the whole year.
9. win — When I__________ the contest, I was delighted, for I had never__________ anything before.

10. tell Sandie____________her dog to lie down; she should have ____________it to play dead.

4

1. wind Mary____________the clock, not knowing that Peter had ____________it the night before.
2. tear Alberto____________the sheet into strips; when the sheet was all____________, he tied the strips together and escaped through the window.
3. lie The cat____________defiantly right where the dog had______ all morning.
4. bite He____________his nails whenever he was nervous; as a result, his fingernails were____________to the quick.
5. grow The vine____________until it had____________over the window and onto the roof.
6. have I____________a funny feeling that I had been____________.
7. burst The little boy____________into tears when he saw that his balloon had____________.
8. run With Mr. McGregor chasing him, Peter____________faster than he'd ever____________before.
9. make The kite you____________flies better than mine, which was ____________in China.
10. bring Visitors from Chile____________us a copper tray, not knowing that we had____________one back ourselves.

5

1. bid	Lewis__________$200 for the ceramic bear with a clock in its stomach; luckily, someone else had already__________$225.
2. ring	The bell is supposed to be__________every half hour, but the last time it__________was at nine o'clock.
3. see	I would not believe that you__________a Sasquatch if I hadn't__________it too.
4. break	The talks were__________off yesterday, just after Canada __________diplomatic ties with South Africa.
5. fight	At our last meeting, we__________over the same issues that we have__________over for years.
6. keep	The snow__________falling, which meant that the children had to be__________indoors.
7. put	He__________his paper in the pile in which the other students had__________theirs.
8. write	I finally __________to my parents, who complained that I should have__________weeks ago.
9. throw	Adam__________the ball that Emily had__________over the fence.
10. take	Before anyone else could have__________it, I__________ the last piece of cake.

6

1. think	I__________she would have__________to ask you to dinner while your roommate was away.

2. begin — We had just __________ to unpack the lunch when the rain __________.

3. feel — When I had my tonsils out, I __________ worse than I had ever __________ before.

4. buy — We __________ twenty lottery tickets, which was more than we'd __________ the year before.

5. do — We ought not to have __________ it, but we __________ it anyway.

6. give — For my birthday, Uncle Herbert __________ me the tie I had __________ him for Christmas.

7. pay — We __________ what they asked for the car, but it was more than I thought we should have __________.

8. lend — I __________ her the money, even though I had __________ her ten dollars a week earlier.

9. go — After everyone else had __________, I __________ home.

10. hurt — It __________ me to learn that you had been __________ by my careless remark.

7

1. come — When Anna __________ to the door, we could see we had __________ earlier than she had expected.

2. rise — I __________ from my bed to see if the sun had __________.

3. leave — We __________ at midnight; otherwise we would have been the only ones __________ to clean up.

4. speed — Having __________ home from school, Jimmy __________ off to the park on his bike.

5. teach — I have __________ you all I know, but you __________ me very little in return.

6. fall — The old man slipped and __________ on the sidewalk, right where I had __________ the day before.

7. choose — Despite the fact that we __________ carefully, I'm afraid that we have __________ the wrong man for the job.

8. hear — I __________ a slightly different story from the one you had __________.

9. fly — The plane we __________ in looked old enough to have been __________ by the Wright brothers.

10. strike — A visit to the island __________ us as a good idea, but when we got there we found the same idea had __________ about two thousand other people as well.

8

1. hold — Knowing that I could not have __________ on much longer, Gerry __________ me as tightly as he could.

2. steal — Chuck __________ a motorcycle that had been __________ from Keith the month before.

3. swing — Her hair __________ out behind her as she was __________ round by her partner.

4. hide Biggs__________his money in the rented garage where Roy had__________the van.

5. say She__________she would do it, but she's__________so before, hasn't she?

6. draw As the master of ceremonies__________the winning tickets, I prayed that my number would be__________.

7. meet I'm sure I__________Ruth for the first time yesterday, but she insists we have__________before.

8. swear She__________she would never tell anyone, and I have __________to give her a black eye if she does.

9. forgive Lucie__________Ralph, but he has not yet__________her.

10. lay Jim__________his passport on the official's desk, where all the others had been__________.

9

1. drive Laura had already__________to the airport twice that day, but she cheerfully__________us anyway.

2. mean I__________what I said, but no insult was__________by the remark.

3. hang The butcher__________the beef for three weeks before he cut it, but, judging by its toughness, it should have been______ for at least five weeks.

4. deal In that game, I__________the cards face up, and play began when five cards had been__________to each player.

5. find — Today I __________ only three balls, although at times I have __________ a dozen or more.

6. lead — Since Terry had __________ his campers to the beach, I __________ mine to the mountain.

7. know — I had not __________ that you __________ of this place.

8. forget — My wife __________ our anniversary again; this is the third year in a row she's __________ it.

9. sell — We __________ most of the stuff at the garage sale. The TV set was the first thing to be __________.

10. speak — I __________ to Barb about her having __________ so thoughtlessly to you.

10

1. hang — The judge sentenced the man to be __________ by the neck until dead, and they __________ him the next morning.

2. stand — We __________ in line for two hours; we couldn't have __________ any longer.

3. lose — You __________ control of the ball, and we have __________ the game as a result.

4. get — Brian __________ one of the best grade-point averages any student has ever __________ at his college.

5. sleep — Julie __________ for ten hours and would have __________ longer if we had let her.

6. freeze — I__________the meat, as you asked me to, but I'm sure it's been__________before.

7. shake — After I had__________the money out of the envelope, I__________the envelope once more to be sure I had got it all.

8. set — Greg__________the jack in place, but it was not__________ straight.

9. swim, dive — After not having__________or__________for years, we __________and__________all afternoon in the Jacksons' pool.

10. eat, drink — They__________and__________until they could have __________and__________no more.

---

chapter 5

Solving Sentence-Fragment Problems

Any group of words that is punctuated as a sentence but that does not have a subject or a complete verb is a **sentence fragment**. Fragments are perfectly appropriate in conversation and in some kinds of writing, but normally they are unacceptable in college, technical, and business writing. You've already learned how to spot a sentence fragment: read the words aloud, and check to see whether the subject or the verb (or both) is missing. Let's look at a few examples:

> Now, as always, is greatly influenced by her wilful neighbour.
> (Who or what is influenced? The sentence doesn't tell you. The subject is missing.)

> Historians attempting to analyze Canada's role in World War II.
> (Part of the verb is missing. Remember that a verb ending in *-ing* must have a helping verb in front of it.)

> For motorcycle riders in every province but Manitoba.
> (Subject and verb are both missing.)

> Regarding the student we discussed last week.
> (Subject and verb are both missing.)

Now, what do you do with the fragments you've found?

> To change a sentence fragment into a complete sentence, add whatever is missing: a subject, a verb, or both.

You may need to add a subject:

> Now, as always, Canada is greatly influenced by her wilful neighbour.

You may need to add part of a verb:

> Historians are attempting to analyze Canada's role in World War II.

Sometimes it's better to change the form of the verb:

> Historians attempt to analyze Canada's role in World War II.

You may need to add both a subject and a verb:

Helmets are required for motorcycle riders in every province but Manitoba.

And sometimes you need to add more than just a subject and a verb:

I have written the Registrar regarding the student we discussed last week.

Don't let the length of a fragment fool you. Students often think that if a string of words is long it must be a sentence. Not so. No matter how long the string of words is, if it doesn't have both a subject and a verb, it is not a sentence. Here is an example, taken from "The Men of Moosomin," by Sara Jeannette Duncan:

> Here and there a ruddy little pond, like a pocket looking glass dropped on the prairie, with a score or so of wild ducks swimming in it, or a slight round hollow where a pond used to be, with the wild ducks flying high.

Do you know what's missing? Can you change the fragment into a sentence?

Exercises

Read each "sentence" aloud. Put S before each complete sentence and F before each sentence fragment. Make each fragment into a complete sentence by adding whatever is missing: a subject, a verb, or both. After you complete each set of ten sentences, check your answers. If you get three sets of ten entirely correct, you may skip the rest. Answers begin on p. 275.

I

1. _____About sentence fragments.
2. _____To go to the wall.
3. _____Glad to do it for you.
4. _____Falling asleep in class, after working all night.
5. _____The pinochle players meeting in the upper lounge.
6. _____Look at the helicopter.
7. _____Watching television a cheap form of entertainment.
8. _____Hoping to hear from you soon.

9. ____Having saved for just such an emergency.

10. ____Thinking the class was over, I left.

2

1. ____To whom it may concern.

2. ____Turtles being both cheap and easy to train.

3. ____Never cared for them, frankly.

4. ____Learning how to write a computer program.

5. ____The establishment of the colleges in 1966.

6. ____Kim Basinger, of *Batman* fame.

7. ____Are you sure about that?

8. ____Many of whom have seen the film dozens of times.

9. ____Burst without any warning.

10. ____Never put off until tomorrow what you can put off until next week.

3

1. ____As you can see, procrastination is my downfall.

2. ____Can the Blue Jays ever win the Pennant?

3. ____The reason being he loves hockey.

4. ____When you feel you have no friends.

5. ____Unable to locate your account number.

6. ____The look he gave us when we came in late.

7. ____Hope that you are feeling better.

8. ____The ability to learn from mistakes.

9. _____This, along with his addiction to video games.

10. _____Makes him an unlikely candidate for a job.

4

1. _____To suffer for his carelessness and his neglect of his family.

2. _____Playing Trivial Pursuit with you is a real challenge.

3. _____Making the team being the most important achievement of his life.

4. _____Unless you know what is more than enough.

5. _____A singer called Tracy Chapman who never wears a dress?

6. _____The child developing a habit that is most irritating.

7. _____Skip it.

8. _____Not letting me finish, he turned away.

9. _____Another boring Saturday night, watching television and eating popcorn.

10. _____The twentieth century belongs to Canada.

5

1. _____Unless you have a better suggestion.

2. _____A new you: trim, firm, and full of energy.

3. _____Halley's Comet appears every seventy-six years.

4. _____Knowing how to confound one's enemies.

5. _____For you don't need even a high school diploma.

6. _____The word *pot pourri*, a French translation of Spanish words meaning "rotten pot."

7. _____Not having to punch a clock every morning at 08:15 and every afternoon at 16:00.

8. _____To qualify a verb with an adjective?

9. _____Teenagers often being forced to accept unreasonable parental demands.

10. _____As Canada's biggest trading partner expects and gets raw materials for less than world-market prices.

Independent and Dependent Clauses

A group of words containing a subject and a verb is a clause. There are two kinds of clauses. An **independent clause** is one that makes complete sense on its own. It can stand alone, as a sentence. A **dependent clause**, as its name suggests, cannot stand alone as a sentence; it *depends* on another clause to make complete sense.

Dependent clauses are easy to recognize, because they begin with words such as these:

Dependent Clause Cues

after	so that
although	that
as, as if	though
as soon as	unless
as long as	until
because	what, whatever
before	when, whenever
even if, even though	where, wherever
if	whether
in order that	which, whichever
provided that	while
since	who, whom, whose

Whenever a clause begins with one of these words or phrases, it is dependent.

> A dependent clause must be attached to an independent clause. If it stands alone, it is a sentence fragment.

Here is an independent clause:

I am a poor speller.

If we put one of the dependent clause cues in front of it, it can no longer stand alone:

Because I am a poor speller

We can correct this kind of fragment by attaching it to an independent clause:

Because I am a poor speller, I have chained my dictionary to my wrist.

Exercises

Put an S before each clause that is independent and therefore a sentence. Put an F before each clause that is dependent and therefore a sentence fragment. Underline the dependent clause cue in each sentence fragment.

6

1. _____Although I tried hard.
2. _____Before you buy one.
3. _____Since he quit school.
4. _____Whose decision this is.
5. _____Until the matter is settled.
6. _____As I told you last week.
7. _____If you meet me at noon.
8. _____Provided that you pay, I'll go.
9. _____Before the school day begins.
10. _____I worked quickly so that I could leave early.

7

1. _____After the game was over.
2. _____Whatever Lola wants.
3. _____Even if I did agree to go with you.
4. _____As long as we understand each other.
5. _____When the revolution comes.

6. _____Unless you can pass a simple spelling test.
7. _____The people who finish before the time is up.
8. _____I went since no one else was interested.
9. _____When you move to a new apartment.
10. _____Repulsive, although it seems to belong here.

8

1. _____In order that you can learn the whole operation.
2. _____Though the decision was not easy.
3. _____Since I believe she's doing the best she can.
4. _____If you miss the next class, too.
5. _____Provided that the company is pleased with your work.
6. _____Even if that toad turns into a prince.
7. _____Before the college accepted me, I worked as a babysitter.
8. _____Whenever we meet like this.
9. _____Luckily, the horse that we bet on won.
10. _____Occasionally, so that you don't get lonely.

9

1. _____All those who are late coming back from lunch.
2. _____The party that was in power being full of scoundrels.
3. _____Although we're poor, we're happy.
4. _____What he thinks doesn't matter.
5. _____Where you left them yesterday, I guess.

6. _____Frequently, when he's away on business.

7. _____Whether she believes him or not.

8. _____In a situation like this, whichever decision you make.

9. _____Despite our efforts to help him, until he decides he wants to learn.

10. _____In view of the fact that you lied about your age, education, and work experience.

10

1. _____She frowns because it gives people the impression she's thinking.

2. _____Though most of us don't even know who the candidates are.

3. _____A job that demands intelligence, physical fitness, and a genuine liking for people.

4. _____Wherever you go, I'll follow.

5. _____Whether or not you want me is irrelevant.

6. _____Unless you conceal yourself, I'll be there.

7. _____If I wrote his letters for him and typed his résumé.

8. _____Because the network has decided that all of the *General Hospital* characters need shaking up.

9. _____Until death do us part, or as long as we love each other, whichever comes first.

10. _____When George approached the table where the five of us sat indulging in quantities of food — food prepared by the students themselves.

Most sentence fragments are dependent clauses punctuated as sentences. Fortunately, this is the easiest kind of fragment to recognize and fix. All you need to do is join the dependent clause either to the sentence that comes before it or to the one that comes after it — whichever linkage makes better sense. Keep one final point in mind: if you join your clause fragment to the independent clause that follows it, you must separate the two clauses with a comma (see chapter 18, p. 174).

Read the following example to yourself; then read it aloud (remember, last sentence first).

> Montreal is a sequence of ghettos. Although I was born and brought up there. My experience of French was a pathetically limited and distorted one.

The second "sentence" sounds incomplete, and the dependent-clause cue at the beginning of it is the clue you need to identify it as a sentence fragment. You could join the fragment to the sentence before it, but then you would get "Montreal is a sequence of ghettos, although I was born and brought up there," which doesn't make sense. Clearly the fragment should be linked to the sentence that follows it, like this:

> Montreal is a sequence of ghettos. Although I was born and brought up there, my experience of French was a pathetically limited and distorted one. (Mordecai Richler, "Quebec Oui, Ottawa Non!")

Exercise

11

Correct the sentence fragments in exercises 6 through 10. Make each fragment into a complete sentence by adding an independent clause either before or after the dependent clause. Remember to punctuate correctly: if a dependent clause comes at the beginning of your sentence, put a comma after it. When you have completed this exercise, exchange with another student and check each other's work.

Find the sentence fragments in the paragraphs below. Underline the dependent clause cue in each one.

12

Although spring is my favourite season and I look forward eagerly to its arrival after the long winter. There are some things about the season. That I could do without. When the warm weather begins. I am always tempted to buy new, fashionable shoes. Which are ruined in the wet muck. That is everywhere. Unless I act quickly. My dog also becomes a problem in the spring. She delights in tracking mud from the back yard into the house. After she creates a mess that Mr. Clean would need steroids to tackle. She will go back outside and find something sticky and smelly to roll in. Until the warm weather dries up the mud and my dog loses the annual urge to coat herself with disgusting substances. My joy at the arrival of spring is always a little restrained.

13

Fads in popular music come and go with astonishing speed. After the movie *Urban Cowboy*. Country and western music became popular. Among people who had never dreamed of wearing pointed boots with high heels. Though the C and W fad was short-lived. It did produce a host of new fans. Most of these quickly moved on to other musical trends. While those of us who had always loved C and W settled down to being cultural outcasts again. After our brief time in the limelight. As soon as John Travolta gave up his Stetson for dancing shoes. The western theme bars and restaurants threw out the barn board and cactuses and began redecorating. Most recently, however, since people like k.d. lang have brought a mainstream following back to country music. Sophisticated urban listeners are once again buying Conway Twitty and Ian Tyson. Even though musical tastes change quickly. There are die-hard C and W fans who can always be identified by their collection of Tommy Hunter records.

14

As you've already noticed, one effective way to correct sentence fragments is to join the fragment to a complete sentence that precedes or follows it. Use this technique to correct exercises 12 and 13 above and the following passage.

Since my marks at the end of high school were anything but impressive. I thought the chances of my acceptance at college or university were not very good. Secretly, however, I wasn't at all sure that college or university was where I wanted to go. I had also applied to the Armed Forces program that pays for your education. If you agree to serve for four years after graduation. Provided that you meet certain conditions. On the same day that the official transcript of my dismal marks appeared in the mail. Two schools I had applied to sent their rejections. As did the Armed Forces, calling me "an academic risk." Until the next day. When a fourth letter arrived. I hid the marks and the rejection letters from my parents and suffered. As I have never suffered before or since. Fortunately, since the fourth letter was an acceptance from an unusually enlightened (or desperate) school. I was able to enjoy the summer. Eventually I graduated with a respectable average. And became a writer. Last year I got my revenge on the Armed Forces for their lack of faith in my academic potential. When they bought three thousand copies of my text book–in order to teach their recruits how to write.

15

As a final test of your skill in correcting sentence fragments, try this exercise. Put S before each complete sentence and F before each sentence fragment. Make each fragment into a complete sentence. (No answers are given for this exercise.)

_____ 1. Because we often repeat the patterns of parenting that our own parents used on us.

_____ 2. George Orwell's memorable dictum from *Animal Farm*: "All animals are equal but some animals are more equal than others."

_____ 3. All things considered, her chances of being chosen Ms Teenage Tonawanda run from slim to nil.

_____ 4. In today's society, women choosing to work in non-traditional jobs such as plumbing, auto mechanics, and construction.

_____ 5. One of my favourite Canadian bluegrass groups, all the way from Dewfrost, Manitoba: Humphrey and the Dump Trucks!

_____ 6. Lake Ontario, the water supply for about 8 million people, American and Canadian, being seriously imperiled by dangerous practices of Niagara River region chemical companies like the one that contaminated the Love Canal.

_____ 7. I couldn't believe it when my son asked for a computer game called *Skate or Die*.

_____ 8. Elmo's continued insistence that his hero, Elvis Presley, is alive and well and working as a truck driver in the Ozarks.

_____ 9. After staying out until dawn and getting only two hours of sleep to be awakened by a scowling roommate.

_____10. The problem being that a tree surgeon can't avoid making woods calls.

Solving Run-On Problems

Just as a sentence can lack certain elements and thus be a fragment, so can it contain too many elements. A sentence with too much in it is a **run-on**. Run-ons most often occur when you write in a hurry or when you're disorganized and not thinking clearly. If you think about what you want to say, and proceed slowly and carefully, you shouldn't have any problems with them.

There are two varieties of run-on sentence: the comma splice and the true run-on.

The Comma Splice

As the name suggests, the **comma splice** occurs when two complete sentences (independent clauses) are joined together, with only a comma between them. Here's an example:

That dog's obedient, it's been well trained.

> The easiest way to fix a comma splice is to replace the comma with a semicolon.

That dog's obedient; it's been well trained.

To be sure you understand how to use semicolons correctly, read chapter 19, p. 182.

> Another way to fix a comma splice is to add an appropriate linking word between the two clauses.

Two types of linking words will work.

1. You can insert one of these words: *and*, *but*, *or*, *nor*, *for*, *so*, *yet*. These should be preceded by a comma.

   That dog's obedient, for it's been well trained.

2. You can insert one of the dependent clause cues listed on p. 55.

   That dog's obedient because it's been well trained.

The third way to fix a comma splice is to make the run-on sentence into two short sentences.

That dog's obedient. It's been well trained.

All three solutions to the comma splice problem require that you replace the comma with a word or punctuation mark strong enough to come between two independent clauses.

Exercises

Correct the following sentences where necessary. Then check your answers. (Answers begin on p. 277.) Since there are several ways to correct comma splices, your answers may differ slightly from ours. If you find that you're confused about when to use a semicolon and when to use a period, be sure to read p. 182 before going on.

1

1. Kevin is lazy, Allan is no better.
2. Stop me if you've heard this one, there was this bus driver on his first day at work.
3. I'd like to help, but I have my own problems to worry about.
4. Ronnie says he likes hiking, but he never goes very far, maybe that's why he's still overweight.
5. Just because the train was two hours late, you shouldn't have lost your temper like that.
6. It bothers me to see her playing cards all the time, she could easily fail her semester.
7. Dennis was transformed, overnight he had turned from a plain-looking student into a fashion plate.
8. Fall is my favourite time of year, the colours are beautiful.
9. A fine mess this is, I'll never forgive you for getting me into this situation.
10. Carefully backing the car onto the road, she fought her nervousness and concentrated on driving.

2

1. I want to play the banjo, the only thing stopping me is a complete lack of musical talent.
2. If I were rich, my garage would contain a Ferrari.
3. There are many good films made in Hollywood, I wish I could tell which they were before paying my admission to the cinema.
4. The Irish Wolfhound is the largest dog in the world, if my memory is correct.

5. This is an excellent book, the authors must be very intelligent.
6. In the early days in Canada, the Americans were seen as a constant threat, even Ottawa was not considered safe.
7. Let him come on his knees and beg for it, that's the only way he'll ever get the money from me!
8. Chocolate is Annie's favourite indulgence, unless she has changed a great deal since we last saw her.
9. More people are heating their homes with woodstoves these days, the result is "ecologists' smog."
10. The fog is closing in, we'll be lucky to get home before dawn unless the weather changes.

3

1. Give careful thought to your answer, a great deal depends on what you decide.
2. Cooking is my favourite pastime, though I don't enjoy it much when I have to do it, only when I want to.
3. Although David enjoys fishing and hiking, he clearly prefers to live in the city, a preference that puzzles his close friends.
4. My chiropractor has given me several exercises he says will make my back stronger, in time I'm sure he will be proven right.
5. Karen was given the choice of joining her father's firm as a general labourer or continuing at school, she's sure to take the job if I know Karen!
6. Despite his overpowering shyness, Terry wants to get into politics, where, he hopes, his sincerity will shine through his fears of public exposure.
7. When our hockey team travels to Moncton, we always stay at the same motel, it's not expensive but is close to the arena and appears to be well maintained.
8. Go to the door and see who's there, I'm too busy with my homework right now.
9. There is a great deal to be said for woodcutting as a career, much of it bad.
10. You'll find that the biggest drawbacks to owning tropical fish are that you get soaked whenever you pet them, and they take a long time to grow big enough to eat.

4

Correct each of these sentences where necessary. Remember the three methods of changing comma splices into correct sentences; this might be a good time to review those methods.

1. I don't know whose those shoes are, they were left here after our last party, probably they belong to one of your friends.

2. With her huge, brown, adoring eyes and obedient disposition, my dog runs my life, I know I'll never find a woman who can compare.
3. Cats are the most wonderful of creatures, they are often more human than humans, as any true cat lover can tell you.
4. In comparing cars, there are many factors to consider, the most important of these is probably price.
5. Let's go the other way, to get there as quickly as possible is our most important task at the moment.
6. I completely understand his feelings of rejection after hearing that his family moved to another city while he was out getting a pizza for supper.
7. Fast food is generally less nutritious than home-cooked meals, though I know of some home cooking that rates below cardboard in nutritional value, I still prefer it as a rule.
8. Appraising his progress is difficult, when you realize that he has completed none of the assignments, written none of the tests, and attended only three of the classes, you can see why I despair.
9. This day has held quite enough excitement, I'm going to bed, so I get a good rest, please try to keep the noise to a minimum and don't turn on the light.
10. There's something very comforting about a fireplace, but a chimney fire is no joke, make sure your chimney is cleaned out twice a year.

5

Correct the comma splice errors in the following paragraph. Then turn to p. 279 to compare your revisions with ours.

Last term we had an exchange student from the south of France, her name was Sophie and she came to Canada to learn the language and experience something of our culture. She was amazed by our fondness for fast food, she found it inedible. Another cultural difference Sophie observed was the emphasis Canadian girls place on dress and cosmetics, they often applied fresh makeup between classes, they dressed as if they were going to a fashionable restaurant instead of school. Sophie loved to dress up, too, she delighted in the dramatic designs that the French are famous for, she wore them only on special occasions, however. The multicultural aspects of Canadian society, the newness of all the towns and cities, and the vast size of the country all impressed her during her visit, the huge expanses of untouched wilderness she found a little intimidating. Though she was homesick, especially at first, Sophie enjoyed her year in Canada, when she was packing to return to her home near Cannes, she was already planning her next visit — a canoeing holiday in Algonquin Park.

6

Here's a final test of your ability to spot and correct comma splices. Try to use all three ways of fixing comma splices as you correct the errors in this paragraph. (No answers have been given for this exercise.)

Videotaped instruction is now available for a wide variety of subjects and skills, even language instruction and personality improvement are only as far away as your VCR. I have learned an amazing amount thanks to the public library and my TV set, the art of fly fishing, which sites to visit in Paris, and how to fix my eavestroughs are among my recent excursions into the world of video-transmitted knowledge. With so little of value being broadcast on commercial television, I don't think I'd watch TV at all if it weren't for the availability of so many kinds of good videotapes, including the great classic films and the best of the new releases, there is so much good video, in fact, that I could easily become the dreaded "couch potato" if I didn't limit my viewing. Each week I permit myself two movies, two National Geographic specials, one National Film Board documentary, one hobby instruction tape, and one educational tape. The winter months go by very enjoyably under this strict "one tape per day" formula.

The Run-On Sentence

In the true **run-on sentence**, too many ideas are crowded into one sentence. In general, a sentence should convey no more than two ideas. There is no hard and fast rule about how many clauses you may have in a sentence, but more than two independent clauses can result in a sentence that's hard to read and even harder to understand.

> There were still twelve people at the party, but after Janice went home we decided it was time to leave, so we collected our coats and said good-bye to the others, and, after a careful drive home at 50 km/h, we drank coffee and stayed up until three a.m. discussing the evening's events.

It's obvious that the storyteller who created this monster got carried away with enthusiasm for the tale and just scribbled everything down without much thought. Take your time and keep your reader in mind, and you probably won't make this sort of error. If you do find run-on sentences in your writing, however, you can correct them by applying one of the three solutions to comma splices. Above all, remember this rule:

> Fix sentences that are too long by breaking them up into shorter sentences.

> There were still twelve people at the party, but after Janice went home we decided it was time to leave. So we collected our coats and said

good-bye to the others. After a careful drive home at 50 km/h, we drank coffee and stayed up until three a.m. discussing the evening's events.

Exercises

7

Using the four types of corrections you've learned in this chapter, make these sentences easier to read. There is more than one right way of fixing these; just be sure your resulting sentences are easy to read and make sense. The answers we've provided are only suggestions.

1. *Field of Dreams* is one of my favourite films because it seems so true to life, and I'm thinking of reading the short story, which is titled *Shoeless Joe Jackson Comes to Iowa*.
2. People tend to forget that a complete education involves the body as well as the mind, and in most high schools physical education isn't taken seriously, while at college there is almost no emphasis at all on athletics except for support of a few varsity teams, but all this would change if the Ministry of Education changed its policy, which doesn't seem likely.
3. When The Travelling Wilburys split up, my favourite group became Tom Petty and The Heartbreakers, and since rap has become popular I like Run DMC, but I don't listen to music much any more because my stereo's broken, and I lost my part-time job, so I can't afford to have it fixed.
4. Bruce hates alarm clocks and refuses to keep one in his apartment, he's the guy who used to go out with my sister, she dropped him because he was always late.
5. It's always best to tell the truth, because one lie leads to another, eventually you'll get caught.
6. They took up sailing last year, we haven't seen them since.
7. I'm tired, and I guess you must be, too, so let's just finish this last one and then turn in, and we can get an early start tomorrow and polish off the rest before noon so we can have the rest of the day to ourselves.
8. Foolish people are those who, through ignorance or stupidity, refuse to believe there's anything they don't know, but when a situation comes along that they aren't familiar with, and they don't know how to act, they just plough ahead without a care, and usually they end up making the situation worse and adding to their richly deserved reputation as fools.
9. I think there are many components of a sense of humour, one is the ability to see the absurd in normal situations, and another is the very rare gift of being able to see oneself as an object of fun or ridicule, almost no one has the latter ability to any degree.
10. Canadian politics are really very straightforward and simple, if you think about it, because we have several levels of government, each with its own

powers and jurisdictions and each responsible to its constituents, but difficulties arise when jurisdictions overlap or aren't clearly defined.

8

Correct the following paragraph by rewriting it to eliminate fragments, comma splices, and run-ons.

Having decided on a canoe trip to La Verendrye Park, north-east of Ottawa. Jean-Pierre and Bernard began to make plans, it did not take them long to discover that they really didn't know all that much about each other, and that, while Bernard was an experienced canoe tripper, Jean-Pierre had a great many fears and misconceptions. For example, he could not imagine what two people could eat for two whole weeks in the wilderness. Bernard, taking charge of the planning, and using his knowledge and experience to organize a list of supplies and equipment. The trip north to the park was their opportunity to become better acquainted, they found they had a great deal in common, including a love of music, Jean-Pierre could actually play an instrument, he was quite proficient with the banjo he had brought along. They rented a canoe near the park, registered with the park officials, and set about final preparations, however carefree they appeared on the surface, each had concerns about the trip, Jean-Pierre about what they would eat, and Bernard about his companion's canoeing ability.

Surviving the first day, despite a constant drizzle and a 500-metre portage that wound its way through swampy terrain, getting them soaked up to the knees, and dampening their spirits. The first camp was a huge success. Jean-Pierre proved to have a real talent for fishing, so they ate fresh-caught trout and the weather cleared and they sat around the fire and watched the moon come up, although eventually mosquitoes became a nuisance, forcing them into the protection of the tent. The two weeks flew by. Back home, when they reflected on the trip they agreed that their fears had been needless, for Jean-Pierre had put on three kilograms, and Bernard confessed that he had never canoed with a better bow-man, in fact, they had had such a good time they decided to make it an annual event.

9

Correct the following paragraphs where necessary. Your answers may differ somewhat from ours, which are on p. 281.

American gun laws continue to be a mystery to most Canadians. Who look at the annual death toll south of the border and compare it to our own more modest statistics. It seems obvious to us that our restrictive regulations are responsible for our relatively few gun incidents and we wonder at the blind prejudice of Americans that they cannot see as clearly as we do that open access to firearms leads to more gunshot deaths, in fact one statistic clearly proves our point of view, for every intruder killed by a privately owned handgun in the United States, two hundred innocent people are killed in domestic disputes or accidents.

In using such figures to question the wisdom of our southern neighbours, we overlook the reason for their insistence on free access to guns, that their country was born out of revolution against what they saw as a despotic king, the only thing that made the revolution possible (and ultimately successful) was that every household had at least one gun and at least one person who knew how to use it. In truth, armed civilians were responsible for the founding of America. A fact that led directly to the provision in their constitution that every citizen has the right to bear arms. (Though I know of more than one person who assumes this means that every American citizen has the constitutional right to wear short sleeves.) To argue against the right to bear arms is to be un-American in many minds and it is of little significance to such minds that the right to own a gun to protect America from her enemies is an outmoded concept in the age of Star Wars and missile-firing submarines.

10

Dire Straits is a band that transcends all the labels and loyalties associated with rock groups. There seems to be consensus that this is a group that defies categories. And yet picks up devoted fans from practically every branch of rock's broad range. At their most recent concert at a stadium that was within driving distance of our community, there was a great deal of excitement and enthusiasm, the amazing thing was that such a variety of people were determined to get tickets and arrange transportation. One friend of mine, a teacher in his mid-forties who snarls at little children and claims to like only kittens and puppies ... as long as they're well done. Behaved like a schoolboy in his eagerness to get good seats, and having got them, boasted openly about his success. Another friend, a serious rock musician who confesses to be an admirer of Dire Straits for their professionalism and for the fact that they are what he calls "a working band" rather than studio musicians, and he claims the lyrics of Mark Knopfler, the band's leader, are unsurpassed in contemporary music, while Knopfler's guitar playing is among the best in the business. At the other end of the scale, my neighbour's two teenage daughters squealed with delight and phoned practically every other fourteen-year-old in the county. When they were presented with tickets for a graduation gift. In short, everyone — young, old, and in-between — had a great time at the concert, Dire Straits proved their incomparable talent once again.

II

As a final test of your ability to identify and correct sentence errors, supply the appropriate sentence breaks to make this garble into a grammatically correct paragraph. (No answers have been provided.)

Computer Assisted Learning, or CAL, is an idea whose time has come and it's too bad that very few educational jurisdictions are taking advantage of its potential, especially at the post-secondary level, partly because it is so expensive to design and develop and partly because much of what has been produced up to now is either unsuitable or exorbitantly priced and also hardware in post-secondary institutions is not standardized, so programs cannot be shared or transported efficiently. Of all these problems, the cost of CAL is the major hurdle that must be overcome, but we should keep in mind that while it is undeniably expensive to produce, CAL is wonderfully efficient once it is installed because any number of students can take the same course at no cost to the school beyond the initial purchase price of the course program, which leads to another problem, the suspicion and mistrust of teachers who see their jobs threatened by a "teaching machine" that provides instruction at the level and pace of each individual student, providing remedial work or more challenging exercises as needed, *The Bare Essentials* is really a computer program written out in book form, every chapter asks you to read the explanation, try an exercise, then move backwards or forwards in the exercises depending on your success, and this, of course, is what a computer program could do with much more efficiency, choosing a route through the explanations, exercises, and tests that would match your individual ability and skill, rather than marching you through the instruction at the same pace as twenty or thirty other learners in a classroom or trusting you to recognize instinctively when you've mastered one concept and are ready to go on to another.

12

Write a letter to a friend who will soon be attending your school. Describe your experiences and provide any advice you think will be useful when your friend begins classes next year. Check your letter carefully to eliminate spelling errors and to make sure your sentences are correctly constructed. Watch especially for fragments and run-ons.

chapter 7

Solving Modifier Problems

The thieves were caught before much of the loot could be disposed of by the police.

Stamping her feet and switching her tail to brush away flies, Susan led the mare out of the barn.

At the age of five, the barber cut Jamie's hair, which curled to his shoulders nearly for the first time.

These sentences show what can happen to your writing if you aren't sure how to use modifiers. A **modifier** is a word or group of words that adds information about another word in a sentence. In the examples above, the underlined words are modifiers. Used correctly, modifiers describe or explain or limit another word, making its meaning more precise. Used carelessly, however, modifiers can cause confusion or, even worse, amusement. There's nothing more embarrassing than being laughed at when you didn't mean to be funny.

You need to be able to recognize and solve two kinds of modifier problems: misplaced modifiers and dangling modifiers.

Misplaced Modifiers

Modifiers must be as close as possible to the words they apply to. Usually a reader will assume that a modifier modifies whatever it's next to. It's important to remember this, because, as the following examples show, changing the position of a modifier can change the meaning of your sentence.

I told Mr. Jones only what I had done. (I didn't tell him anything else.)

I told only Mr. Jones what I had done. (I didn't tell anybody else.)

Only I told Mr. Jones what I had done. (Nobody else told Mr. Jones.)

I told Mr. Jones what only I had done. (No one else did it.)

> To make sure a modifier is in the right place, ask yourself, "What does it apply to?" and put it beside that word.

When a modifier is not close enough to the word it refers to, it is said to be misplaced. A **misplaced modifier** can be *a single word in the wrong place*:

The supervisor told me they needed someone who could type badly.

Is some company really hiring people to do poor work? Or does the company urgently need a typist? Obviously, the modifier *badly* belongs next to *needed*:

The supervisor told me they badly needed someone who could type.

> Be especially careful with these words: *almost*, *nearly*, *just*, *only*, *even*, *hardly*, *merely*, *scarcely*. Put them right before the words they modify.

Misplaced: I almost ate the whole thing.

Correctly placed: I ate almost the whole thing.

Misplaced: When he played short-stop for the Cardinals, Ozzie Smith nearly did back flips on the field before every game.

Correctly placed: When he played short-stop for the Cardinals, Ozzie Smith did back flips on the field before nearly every game.

A misplaced modifier can also be *a group of words in the wrong place*:

Scratching each other playfully, we watched the monkeys.

The modifier, *scratching each other playfully*, is too far away from the word it is supposed to modify, *monkeys*. In fact, it seems to modify *we*, making the sentence ridiculous. We need to rewrite the sentence:

We watched the monkeys scratching each other playfully.

Look at this one:

I worked for my father, who owns a sawmill during the summer.

During the summer applies to *worked* and should be closer to it:

During the summer, I worked for my father, who owns a sawmill.

Notice that a modifier need not always go right next to what it modifies; it should, however, be as close as possible to it.

Occasionally, as in the examples above, the modifier is obviously out of place. The writer's intention is clear, and the sentences are easy to correct. But sometimes modifiers are misplaced in such a way that the meaning is not clear, as in this example:

Lucy said on her way out she would give the memo to John.

Did Lucy *say* it on her way out? Or is she going to *deliver the memo* on her way out? To avoid confusion, we must move the modifier and, depending on which meaning we want, write either

On her way out, Lucy said she would give the memo to John.

or

Lucy said she would give the memo to John on her way out.

Exercises

Some of the sentences in these exercises contain misplaced modifiers. Rewrite the sentences as necessary, positioning the modifiers correctly. Check your answers to each set of ten before going on. (Answers begin on p. 282.) If you get the first two sets entirely correct, skip ahead to exercise 4.

1

1. Unless they're French or Italian, some people never go to movies.
2. Elmo bought a Dustbuster for his girlfriend that cost $29.95.
3. They nearly decided to pay me $350 a week.
4. I will ask you only one more time.
5. Wearing two left shoes and a funny little flowered hat, we laughed at the antics of the clown.
6. I hate parties where food is served to the guests on little paper plates.
7. Ferdinand has almost insulted everyone he's gone out with.
8. The angry hippo chased me towards the zookeeper in a rage.
9. My brother only could hope to win the jackpot.
10. The boss told me on Thursday I would be fired.

2

1. In Minoan Crete there are wall paintings of boys jumping over bulls with no clothes on.
2. Two suitable jobs only were advertised.
3. This course can be completed by anyone who has learned English grammar in six weeks.

4. The obituary column lists the names of people who have died recently for a small fee.
5. Alice discovered a mushroom walking through Wonderland.
6. She only ate one bite and found herself growing larger.
7. Every week they told me to come back and check the notice board.
8. Parents want to know what their children are doing in school for their own satisfaction.
9. The cause of the accident was a little guy in a small car with a big mouth.
10. Ferdinand spotted a dwarf hippo with his binoculars.

3

1. People who shoplift frequently get caught.
2. He almost watched television all night.
3. Tammy Faye tried to convince the members of her fan club to wear two or three sets of false eyelashes eagerly.
4. Stir the flour into the butter in the saucepan with the wooden spoon.
5. As someone who is concerned about fitness, you really should stop smoking.
6. No one is allowed to throw any pollutants into the river except petrochemical company executives.
7. He took a stand against a tree while waiting for the bear with only an old black-powder rifle.
8. I passed the security guard and two workmen walking to school.

9. I am pleased to meet student representatives of our twenty-two colleges here in Petawawa.
10. Perhaps you're on your own in Vancouver, with a sparkling city to explore and a couple of tickets to an event at the new covered stadium in your pocket. (B.C. travel flyer)

4

Make up three sentences containing misplaced modifiers; then correct them.

Dangling Modifiers

A **dangling modifier** occurs when there is *no appropriate word in the sentence* for the modifier to apply to. Or, a modifier is said to be "dangling" when the sentence does not contain a *specific word* or *idea* to which the modifier could sensibly refer. With no appropriate word to modify, the modifier *seems* to apply to whatever it's next to, often with ridiculous results:

After four semesters of hard work, my parents rewarded my good grades.

(This sentence seems to say that the parents are going to school.)

Jogging along the sidewalk, a truck swerved and nearly hit me.

(The *truck* was jogging along the sidewalk?)

Dangling modifiers are trickier to fix than misplaced ones; you can't simply move danglers to another spot in the sentence. There are, however, two ways in which you can fix them. One way requires that you remember this rule:

> When a modifier comes at the beginning of a sentence, it modifies the subject of the sentence.[1]

This means that you can avoid dangling modifiers by choosing the subjects of your sentences carefully. All you have to do is make sure the subject is an appropriate one for the modifier to apply to. Using this method, we can rewrite our two examples by changing the subjects:

[1] *Adverbial modifiers are exceptions to this rule, but they won't give you any trouble. Example: Quickly she did as she was told.*

After four semesters of hard work, I got my reward for my good grades.

Jogging along the sidewalk, I was nearly hit by a swerving truck.

Another way to correct a dangling modifier is by changing it into a dependent clause:

After I had completed four semesters of hard work, my parents rewarded me with a car.

As I was jogging along the sidewalk, a truck swerved and nearly hit me.

Sometimes a dangling modifier comes at the end of a sentence:

McDonald's would be a good place to go, not having much money.

Can you correct this sentence? Try it; then look at footnote[2], below.

Here is a summary of the steps to follow in solving modifier problems:

1. Ask "What does the modifier apply to?"
2. Be sure there is a word or group of words *in the sentence* for the modifier to apply to.
3. Put the modifier as close as possible to the word or word group it applies to.

Exercises

Most of the sentences in exercises 5 and 6 contain dangling modifiers. Make corrections by changing the subject of the sentence to one the modifier can appropriately apply to. There is no one "right" way to correct each sentence; our answers are only suggestions.

5

1. As a college English teacher, dangling modifiers are annoying.

2. Having rotted in storage, the farmers could not sell their grain for the profit they were counting on.

3. Before turning in for the night, your hairpiece should be placed on the plastic head.

[2] *Here are two suggestions: 1. Add a subject: Not having much money, I thought McDonald's would be a good place to go.*
2. Change the dangler to a dependent clause: McDonald's would be a good place to go since I don't have much money.

4. Driving through the Arizona desert, our mouths became drier and drier.
5. Turning to the appendix, the example I quoted is in the third paragraph.
6. The surface must be sanded smooth before applying the varnish.
7. Upon entering, the store was completely empty.
8. Attempting to hotwire an '88 Trans Am, the police were called and made an arrest.
9. Looking over his shoulder, the car slowly backed up.
10. In very cold weather, the engine should be thoroughly warmed up before attempting to drive.

6

1. After changing the tire, the jack should be released.
2. The next question is whether to order beer or wine, having decided on pizza.
3. After waiting for you for an hour, the evening was ruined.
4. Jogging through Stanley Park, a bronze horse came into view.
5. Most of the spare keys, after spending nine dollars on them, have been lost.
6. Having set the microwave on automatic, the turkey was quickly cooked to perfection.
7. Having completed the beginning, the ending is the next most important part of the essay.
8. Convicted of aggravated assault, the judge sentenced her to two years in Kingston.

9. After having been in prison for so long, the world seemed to be spinning at a hectic pace.
10. After shovelling the walks, the driveway, and the sidewalk, it snowed another 10 cm.

7

Correct the dangling modifiers in exercise 5 by changing them into dependent clauses.

8

Correct the dangling modifiers in exercise 6 by changing them into dependent clauses.

Correct the misplaced and dangling modifiers in exercises 9 through 11 in any way you choose. Our answers are only suggestions.

9

1. Being made of very thin crystal, the dishwasher breaks the glasses as fast as I can buy them.
2. Driving through Yellowstone, a buffalo blocked the road.
3. As a college student constantly faced with stress, the pressure is intolerable.
4. His socks were full of holes which were long and red.
5. Braised in wine, my guests loved the coq au vin.
6. After deciding whether the wine should be blended, sugar is added.
7. We were impressed as she rode by on a horse in a bikini.
8. The sign in the restaurant window read, "Our Establishment Serves Tea in a Bag Just Like Mother."
9. Peering out of my office window, the Goodyear Blimp sailed past.
10. Having broken its wings, they took the seagull to the SPCA.

10

1. Although he lives 50 km away, he nearly manages to come to every class.
2. The sign said students are only admitted to the pub.
3. The lion was recaptured before anyone was mauled or bitten by the trainer.
4. While asleep, the blankets were kicked off the bed.
5. I saw the Queen and her entourage arrive through a plate-glass window.
6. Having ruled out the other two Japanese imports, the Mazda is the one we'll choose.
7. Swimming isn't a good idea if cold or polluted.
8. The man wore a hat on his head which was hideous.
9. I learned about Joan's having a baby in last week's letter.
10. The counsellor who put his foot in his mouth recently has alienated the students.

11

1. After completing the study of staffing requirements, an assistant to the personnel manager will be hired.
2. Gnawing avidly on a bone, Joe found his dog.
3. He said on Tuesday we would have a test.
4. Left over from last week's party, our guests didn't find the meal very appetizing.
5. Employees who are late frequently are dismissed without notice.

6. Having forgotten to pick me up twice this week, I'm quitting Jim's car pool.
7. Green and mushy, Maria turned the avocados into great guacamole.
8. The thieves were caught before much of the loot could be disposed of by the police.
9. Though drunk daily, many people don't trust Lake Ontario water.
10. It is a tradition to pay one's respects to friends and relatives after they have died in a funeral parlour.

12

To test your mastery of modifiers, try this final exercise, for which no answers are provided.

1. While still in kindergarten, my parents moved me to Red Deer.
2. After finishing high school, college seemed like a good idea.
3. Having been overfertilized, my sister thinks the cactus will not survive.
4. A person who blacks out while drinking nine times out of ten is an alcoholic.
5. Hiking out into the wilderness, the weather grew ominous.
6. Elmo asked Dee Dee to marry him during the evening.
7. If caged, you can bring your Great Dane on the flight.
8. Being overinflated, Roderick thinks the inner tube will burst.
9. Weighing at least 80 kg, even Bettina couldn't move the baggage.
10. One morning I shot an elephant in my pajamas. How he got into my pajamas, I don't know. Then we tried to remove the tusks but they were

embedded so firmly that we couldn't budge them. Of course, in Alabama the Tuscaloosa. But that's entirely irrelephant. . . . (Groucho Marx)

chapter 8

The Parallelism Principle

When writing about items in a series, you must be sure all the items are **parallel**; that is, they must be written in the same grammatical form.

I like camping, fishing, and to hike.

The items in this list are not parallel. Two end in *ing*, but the third (*to hike*) is the infinitive form of the verb. To correct the sentence, you must make all the items in the list take the same grammatical form — either

I like to camp, to fish, and to hike.
or
I like camping, fishing, and hiking.

> Correct faulty parallelism by giving the items in a series the same grammatical form.

One way to tell whether all the items in a list are parallel is to picture (or actually write) the items in list form, one below the other. That way, you can make sure that all the elements are the same — that they are all words, or all phrases, or all clauses.

Not Parallel	**Parallel**
Sharon is kind, considerate, and likes to help.	Sharon is kind, considerate, and helpful.
I support myself by tending bar, piano, and shooting pool.	I support myself by tending bar, playing piano, and shooting pool.
Her upbringing made her neat, polite, and an obnoxious person.	Her upbringing made her neat, polite, and obnoxious.

Gordon tries to do what is right,
different things, and
make a profit.

Gordon tries to do what is right,
what is different,
and
what is profitable.

With his sharp mind,
by having the boss as his uncle, and
few enemies,
he'll go far.

With his sharp mind,
the boss as his uncle, and
few enemies,
he'll go far.

or

Having a sharp mind,
the boss as his uncle, and
few enemies,
he'll go far.

As you can see, achieving parallelism is partly a matter of developing an ear for the sound of a correct list. Practice, and the exercises in this chapter, will help. Once you have mastered parallelism in your sentences, you will be ready to develop ideas and arguments in parallel sequence and thus to write well-organized and clear paragraphs, letters, and essays. All this will be discussed in a later unit ("Organizing Your Writing"); we mention it now only to show you that parallelism, far from being a "frill," is a fundamental part of good writing.

Exercises

Correct the following sentences where necessary. As you work through these exercises, try to spot faulty parallelism and correct it from the sound of the sentences, before you examine them closely for mistakes. Check your answers to each set of ten before going on. Answers begin on p. 285.

I

1. The three main kinds of speech are demonstrative, informative, and the kind persuading someone of something.
2. The single mother faces many problems. Two of the most difficult are supporting her household and sole parent to her child.
3. He advised me to take two aspirins and that I call him in the morning.
4. Books provide us with information, education, and they're entertaining to read.

5. To make your court appearance as painless as possible, prepare your case thoroughly, and maintaining a pleasant, positive attitude.
6. The apostrophe is used for two purposes: contraction, and it shows possession.
7. Swiftly and with skill the woman gutted and scaled the fish.
8. I am overworked and not paid enough.
9. You need to develop skill and strategy and be agile to be a good tennis player.
10. The two main responsibilities of a corrections officer are security and controlling the inmates.

2

1. A part-time job can develop your decision-making skills, your sense of responsibility, and you feel more self-confident and independent.
2. The three keys to improving your marks are study, you must work hard, and bribing the teacher.
3. I couldn't decide whether I should become a chef or to study data processing.
4. The recent increase in teenage suicides can be attributed primarily to two causes: the widespread lack of strong religious beliefs and there are no strict moral codes either.
5. A course in logical reasoning will help us evaluate what we read and making sound decisions.
6. When you're buying a new car, you should look at more than just the size,

style, and how much it costs. The warranty, how much it costs to run, and trade-in value should also be taken into consideration.

7. Mrs. Hunter assigns two hours of homework every night, and we're expected to do an essay each week.
8. The two most important characteristics of a personal work space are how neat and well organized it looks, and the privacy.
9. Playing with small construction toys is beneficial to young children because it develops their fine motor skills, encourages concentration and patience, and their creative imagination is stimulated.
10. My supervisor told me that my performance was generally satisfactory but to improve my writing.

3

1. The role of the health instructor is to teach preventive medicine, care of the sick, and how to go about rehabilitating the injured.
2. The most common causes of snowmobile accidents are mechanical failure, the weather conditions might be poor, and the driver careless.
3. The portable classrooms are ill-equipped, poorly lighted, and there isn't any heat.
4. The advantages of a thesis statement are that it limits your topic, the contents of the paper are made very clear, and you show how your paper will be organized.
5. Unemployment deprives the individual of purchasing power, and the country's national output is reduced.

6. A good nurse is energetic, tolerant, sympathetic, and can be relied upon.
7. The money spent on space exploration should be used to provide aid to the underdeveloped countries, and medical research could be funded.
8. The best house cats are quiet, clean, affectionate, and should be somewhere else.
9. Springtime brings out some interesting emotions along with the flowers and leaves: a new appreciation for the beauty of nature, and members of the opposite sex are newly admired.
10. You can conclude a paper with a summary of main points, by posing a question, or you could end with a quotation.

4

1. Our winter has not been very pleasant with vicious ice storms, followed by heavy snowfalls, followed by freezing rain that is dangerous.
2. Baseball is a game that requires a high level of skill with natural talent in large measure.
3. Many foreigners see conservatism, a pride in our country, and an interest in being orderly as characteristic of Canadians.
4. Patience and dexterity will make you a good model builder, person who plays the piano, or cutter of meat.
5. Being a dutiful son, a loyal husband, and treating his children with affection made Jason so stressed that he took up boxing as an outlet for his aggression.

6. I shall prove to you that rock music is neither dangerous nor causes an addictive reaction.
7. Selena has three passions in her life: to dance with her boyfriend, listening to Ian Tyson's music, and fast cars.
8. After this year at school, I intend to go into nursing or I'll become a teacher.
9. After nine years of making up incorrect sentences for students to fix, Brian can no longer write properly or correctly express himself.
10. Both those in management positions and workers must make compromises if this committee is to succeed.

5

Make the following lists parallel. In each case there's more than one way to do it, because you can make your items parallel with any item in the list. Therefore, your answers may differ from ours. Here's an example:

wrong: stick handling	right: stick handling	right: handle the stick
score a goal	goal scoring	score a goal

1. wrong: mechanically	right:	right:
by using your hands		
2. wrong: nursing	right:	right:
being a pilot		
3. wrong: achieve her goals	right:	right:
finding true happiness		

	wrong:	right:	right:
4.	sense of humour wealthy intelligent		
5.	daily exercise wholesome food getting a checkup regularly		
6.	a good cigar drinking a glass of brandy conversation with friends		
7.	speed comfortable good cornering		
8.	look for bargains quality should be chosen value		
9.	security valuable safety		

10. wrong: tanned golden brown right: right:

    skimpy bathing suit

    big boyfriend

6

Create a sentence for each of the parallel lists you developed in exercise 5. Example: His stick handling was adequate, but his goal scoring was pitiful.

7

As a test for your ability to correct faulty parallelism, fix these sentences. (No answers are given.)

1. Down clothing is generally warmer, lasts longer, lighter, and costs more than the alternatives.
2. Jean has made her decision to be a wife and mother, and pursuing a career at the same time.
3. Sweetly and in silence, the tiny boy kissed his sleeping father.
4. My cat is noisy, smells, and not very well physically, but the whole family loves her.
5. It has all the ingredients of a very successful television series: sex, greedy people, and it's violent.
6. To ski in fresh powder and swimming in clear ocean water are two of my favourite vacation activities.
7. Both Canada and the United States are wealthy, have democratic forms of government, and can trace their roots back to Great Britain.
8. The computer is making my work faster, I find it easier, and it is much more accurate.

9. Phyllis wants to be either an actress, to practise medicine, or playing professional golf.
10. When canoeing, I value the silence most, but catching fish and bird watching and taking pictures are important to me, too.

8

Correct the faulty parallelism in this paragraph. (No answers are given for this exercise.)

There are many reasons why people buy the cars they do: safety, style, how fast they go, whether or not they're reliable, and reasons of economy. For some buyers, it seems the most important consideration is the impression the car will make on their relatives and those whom they like. Unfortunately, these would-be buyers often make an unfavourable impression on their loans officers or managers of their banks by choosing vehicles beyond their means. My friend Valerie has three criteria for choosing a car: it must be red, cost a great deal of money, and carry the name Ferrari on its hood. I'm sure you know people who have the same demanding standards; perhaps you're one of them. As I drive my rusty, elderly, lacking-in-comfort wreck along the road, I like to think that people who drive large, flashy sports cars with too much power are making up for other inadequacies.

9

Write a short paper on a topic you choose or on a topic assigned by your teacher. When you have completed your work, read it over carefully. Check your spelling. Check your sentence structure by reading your work aloud, from last sentence to first. Be sure to correct any unclear modifiers and errors in parallelism before handing in your paper.

You might like to try one of these topics:

1. Why a specific television commercial pleases (or irritates) you.

2. What makes your favourite restaurant the best in town.
3. How to be boring.
4. How the world would be different if everyone had a tail.
5. What you would wish for if you were granted one wish, and why.

Chapter 9

Refining By Combining

To reinforce what you've learned so far about sentence structure, try your voice and your hand (preferably with a pencil in it) at **sentence combining**. You've freed your writing of fragments; you've cast out demon comma splices; you're riding herd on run-ons. You may find, however, that your sentences — although technically correct — are choppy or repetitious. And you may be bored with conveying the same idea in the same old way. Sentence combining will not only test your mastery of sentence structure but also enable you to polish and refine your writing.

What is sentence combining? Sometimes called sentence generating, sentence building, sentence revising, or embedding, *sentence combining is a technique that enables you to avoid a choppy, monotonous style while at the same time producing correct sentences*. You can combine sentences in three ways:

1. Link two or more short sentences into a longer one using connecting words such as *and*, *or*, *but*.
2. Merge two or more short sentences into a longer one using dependent-clause cues (see p. 55).

or 3. Combine clusters of related sentences into paragraphs.

Let's look at an example.

Here are two short, technically correct sentences that could be combined:

> The paperboy collects on Fridays.
> The paperboy delivers the *Winnipeg Free Press* on Saturdays.

There are several ways of combining these two statements into a single smooth sentence:

> The paperboy delivers the *Winnipeg Free Press* on Saturdays and collects on Fridays.

> The paperboy, who delivers the *Winnipeg Free Press* on Saturdays, collects on Fridays.

> On Fridays, the paperboy collects for the *Winnipeg Free Press*, which he delivers on Saturdays.

The aim of sentence combining is to make good sentences, not long ones.

Don't forget that clarity is essential and that brevity has force. By rearranging words, changing their form, deleting repetitious or unnecessary words or phrases, and adding clear connectives, you are able to combine a number of short statements into several acceptable sentences.

Here's an example:

1. Correct but stilted sentences conveying an idea:

   Malcolm X was an influence.
   He influenced American culture.
   His influence was strong in the 1960s.

2. Correct and smooth sentences conveying the same idea:

   Malcolm X had a strong influence on American culture in the 1960s.

   Malcolm X strongly influenced American culture in the 1960s.

   In the 1960s, American culture was strongly influenced by Malcolm X.

The skills that you learn by combining sentences identify you as a perceptive and sensitive writer. They are useful not only in writing and speaking, but also in reading, listening, and problem solving.

In the following exercises, make sure you rehearse your solutions *orally* before you write them into the space provided. You may also want to refer to Unit Four, chapters 18 and 19.

Exercises

I

Combine the following sentences, using the cues in parentheses as your guide to linking the sentences. Answers are on p. 287.

1. The picketers left the streets.
   The police arrived. (when)

   ____

2. The angry bystanders knocked down the assassin.
   The angry bystanders tore him limb from limb. (-ing)

   ____

3. She was forty-one years old.
   She looked about twenty. (but)

   ____

4. He always quits.
   You need him. (just when)

   ____

5. Leonard Sly made much money in cowboy movies.
   Roy Rogers was known as Leonard Sly. (who)

6. Football is violent.
   North Americans love football. (even though)

7. Newspapers distort facts.
   Politicians charge this. (that)

8. Television manipulates feelings.
   Many people are not aware of this fact. (that)

9. Walter hates zucchini.
   He planted zucchini anyway. (although)

10. Scientists in the ancient world looked to the stars for guidance.
    Modern scientists may travel to the stars. (whereas)

2

Combine each of the following sets of statements into a single sentence using, where appropriate, the dependent clause cues on p. 55 and the transition words listed on pp. 174 and 182.

1. I don't get there by noon.
   Come looking for me.
   I may be in trouble.

2. The moon was full.
   We sat huddled under sleeping bags.
   The sleeping bags were full of down.
   The sleeping bags were very warm.
   It was time to turn in for the night.

3. The student cried out for mercy.
   The student threw herself at the soldier's feet.
   The student had been caught distributing anti-government propaganda.

4. Jill was lonely.
   Jill was disillusioned.
   Jill was bitter.
   Jill stumbled into the rest room.
   Her shoulders were sagging.
   Her shopping bags were heavy in her hand.

5. The moose sensed danger.
   The moose lifted its head.
   Its ears were stiff and straight.
   Its body was tense.
   It was ready to explode into action at the slightest sound.

6. Key glanced at first base.
   He went into his windup.
   Then he threw a hanging curve up in the strike zone that Wade Boggs, anticipating, unloaded over the right field wall.

7. The old train station was once the hub of the city.
   The old train station is now the dilapidated refuge of rats.

8. Matthew stumbled down the stairs.
   He gasped for air.
   He was horrified by the sight.
   Geoffrey and his friends were wrestling in the living room.

9. The chocolate sauce was rich.
   The chocolate sauce was dark.
   The chocolate sauce was unbelievably sweet.
   The chocolate sauce melted over my Death by Chocolate dessert.

10. Philosophy 101 is Monica's favourite course.
    Few students register for philosophy.
    Students think philosophy is a tough course.

3

This final set of exercises is more challenging. You may need to combine the given statements into two or more sentences. Turn to p. 288 to compare your answers with ours — which are only suggestions.

1. The City of Toronto boasts about the CN Tower.
   The CN Tower has a record.
   It is 555 metres high.
   It is the world's tallest free-standing structure.

2. The Toronto SkyDome is on a downtown site.
   It was completed in 32 months.
   It has a "first."
   The "first" is the world's first fully retractable stadium roof.
   The roof weighs 6 345 tonnes.
   That weight is equivalent to the weight of 2,376 family sedans.
   The SkyDome spans eight acres.
   It has only 575 parking spaces on its site.
   It can hold about 70,000 people.
   Toronto is the eleventh North American city operating a domed stadium.

3. Tiananmen Square is in Beijing.
   Beijing is in China.
   Three thousand students began a hunger strike in the square on May 13, 1989.
   The students erected a home-made, 10-metre-high replica of the Statue of Liberty.
   They called it the "Goddess of Democracy."
   This largely peaceful occupation of the square lasted for four weeks.
   Thousands of armed troops descended on the square.
   The troops first fired off tracer bullets and tear gas.
   Loudspeakers urged the students to leave.
   The soldiers opened fire directly on the crowds and charged them with bayonets.
   Hundreds of demonstrators were killed and hundreds were wounded.
   It was a Sunday morning, June, 4, 1989.
   It was a massacre.

4. Citizenship is an abstract term.
   For most, it means loyalty.
   For most, it means obedience.
   For most, it means conformity.
   For a few, it means thinking for themselves.
   For a few, it means acting independently.
   For a few, it means taking control of their own lives.
   Citizenship is often used as a passive term.
   It means playing one's part.
   That part is in the existing scheme of things.
   That part means no questions asked.

5. Citizenship can be an active term.
   It is the result of something.
   The something is struggle.
   It can mean the right to vote.
   It can mean the right to organize.
   It can mean the right to equality before the law.
   We enjoy these rights.
   These rights had to be won.
   Now citizenship means participation.
   It means involvement.
   This participation and involvement are at all levels of society.

6. Lawyers are professionals.
   Doctors are professionals.
   Business men are professionals.
   These professionals constitute fewer than ten percent of the Canadian workforce.
   These professionals occupy almost three-quarters of the seats in the House of Commons.
   These professionals occupy two-thirds of the offices in local party organizations.

7. There are blue-collar workers too.
   They comprise nearly fifty percent of the population.
   They hold fewer than ten percent of the positions either in local parties or in Parliament.
   Women are under-represented in Canada's political and economic institutions.
   Native people are under-represented in Canada's political and economic institutions.
   Minorities are under-represented in Canada's political and economic institutions.
   Such under-representation calls into question our nation's commitment to democracy.

8. Nursing is a discipline.
   The discipline is concerned with the promotion of the well-being of the individual in society.
   A nurse respects the dignity of each human being.
   A nurse respects the autonomy of each human being.
   A nurse respects the individuality of each human being.

9. Professional nurses provide a preventive service.
   Professional nurses provide an educational service.
   Professional nurses provide a restorative service.
   Professional nurses provide a supportive service.
   This service assists individuals, families and groups.

10. The RN performs acts requiring substantial specialized knowledge.
    The RN performs acts requiring skill.
    The RN performs acts requiring judgement.
    The RN assesses health needs.
    The RN plans nursing care.
    The RN implements nursing care.
    The RN evaluates nursing care.

____

____

____

____

____

____

After you have combined a number of sentences, you can evaluate your work. Read your sentences out loud. How they *sound* is important. Test your work against these six characteristics of successful sentences:

1. Meaning:	Have you conveyed the idea you intend?
2. Clarity:	Is your sentence clear? Can it be understood on the first reading?
3. Coherence:	Do the various parts of the sentence fit together logically and smoothly?
4. Emphasis:	Are the most important ideas and phrases either at the end or at the beginning of the sentence?
5. Conciseness:	Is the sentence wordy? Have you cut out all redundant or repetitious words?
6. Rhythm:	Does the sentence flow smoothly? Are there any interruptions in the development of the key idea(s)? Do the interruptions help to emphasize important points, or do they merely distract the reader?

If your sentences pass all six tests of successful sentence style, you may be confident that they are both technically correct and pleasing to the ear. No reader could ask for more.

grammar

Chapter 10 Subject-Verb Agreement

Chapter 11 Pronoun-Antecedent Agreement

Chapter 12 Tense Agreement

Chapter 13 Person Agreement

chapter

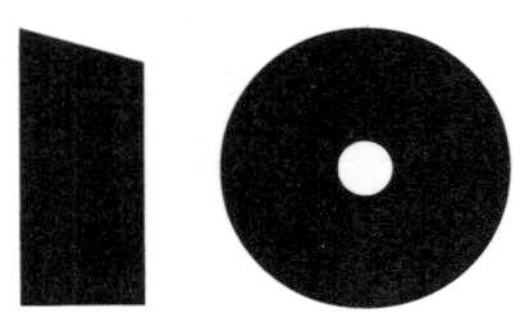

Subject-Verb Agreement

Errors in grammar are like flies in soup: they don't usually affect meaning any more than flies affect flavour. But, like flies, grammar errors are distracting and irritating. They must be eliminated if you want your reader to pay attention to what you say rather than how you say it.

One of the most common grammatical problems is failure to make the subject and verb in a sentence agree with each other. Here is the rule for subject-verb agreement:

> Singular subjects take singular verbs.
> Plural subjects take plural verbs.

Remember that *singular* words concern one person or thing . . .

The phone rings. Geoff watches TV.

. . . and *plural* words concern more than one person or thing:

The phones ring. Geoff and Tess watch TV.

The rule for subject-verb agreement will cause you no problem at all as long as you make sure that the word the verb agrees with is really the subject. To see how a problem can arise, look at this example:

One of the boys write graffiti.

The writer forgot that the subject of a sentence is never in a prepositional phrase. The verb needs to be changed to agree with *one*:

One of the boys writes graffiti.

If you're careful about identifying the subject of your sentence, you'll have no troubles with subject-verb agreement. To sharpen your subject-finding ability, review chapter 3, "Cracking the Sentence Code." Then do the following exercises.

Exercises

I

Identify the subject in each sentence. Answers begin on p. 289.

1. On the television right now is *Rocket*, your favourite rock video.

2. Unfortunately, large numbers of Canadians are bored by politics.
3. Elmo and his girlfriend long to visit Elvis Presley's Graceland Mansion.
4. Where are the invoices I asked for?
5. Do you know where your children are?
6. In order to compete with television, the print media are offering more service features.
7. One of the most popular comic strips, *Superman* was the invention of a Toronto cartoonist.
8. There are many reasons for joining a fitness club this year.
9. Is there anyone who hasn't heard of Elvis Presley?
10. The pressures of homework, part-time work, and nagging parents have forced many students to drop out of school.

2

Rewrite each of the sentences, following the procedure shown in the example.
Example: They are to let us know when they are able to fill the order.
He is to let us know when he is able to fill the order.

1. She thinks she will begin an investment course in the spring.
   They
2. That policy change affects the entire program.
   Those
3. His job has been in jeopardy since the last round of layoffs.
   Their
4. The woman is here because her husband wanted to emigrate.
   The women
5. They do their best work when they are unsupervised.
   He
6. They insist on having their way.
   She
7. Each of Cinderella's sisters was horrid in her own way.
   Both
8. This man's attitude isn't doing him any good.
   Those
9. The Toronto sports fan is delighted to be protected from the elements in the SkyDome.
   Toronto sports fans
10. Anyone who cares about his appearance should have a monthly facial.
    All those

3

Rewrite each of the sentences, following the procedure shown in the example.
Example: Jellybeans are my favourite snack.
My favourite snack is jellybeans.

1. Elmo's consuming passion in life is Elvis Presley artifacts and memorabilia. Elvis Presley artifacts and memorabilia

2. What he spends most of his money on is clothes.

3. Cigarettes are the one luxury I allow myself.

4. Huge meals and constant snacking were the cause of my obesity.

5. What Canada needs now is strong leadership and more jobs.

6. The reason for his failure was too many absences from class.

7. Disputes over wages and benefits are often the cause of strikes.

8. The differences between the Chinese and the Canadian attitudes towards the elderly are what she finds fascinating.

9. Something that he always enjoys is discussions about politics.

10. Garlic, a cross, and a stake through the heart are the only known antidote to a vampire attack.

So far, so good. You can find the subject, even when it's hiding on the far side of the verb or nearly buried under a load of prepositional phrases. You can match up singular subjects with singular verbs, and plural subjects with plural verbs. Now let's take a look at a few of the complications that make subject-verb agreement into such a disagreeable problem.

Six Special Cases

Some subjects are tricky: they look singular but are actually plural, or they look plural when they're really singular. There are six different kinds of these slippery subjects, all of them common, and all of them likely to trip up the unwary writer.

1. Multiple subjects joined by *or, either . . . or, neither . . . nor, not . . . but.* All the multiple subjects we've dealt with so far have been joined by *and* and have required plural verbs, so agreement hasn't been a problem. But watch out when the two or more elements of a multiple subject are joined by *or*, *either . . . or*, *neither . . . nor*, or *not . . . but*. In these cases, *the verb agrees in number with the nearest subject*. That is, if the subject closest to the verb is singular, the verb will be singular; if the subject closest to the verb is plural, the verb must be plural, too.

Neither the prime minister nor the cabinet ministers are responsible.

Neither the cabinet ministers nor the prime minister is responsible.

Exercise 4

Circle the correct verb. For 9 and 10, make up two sentences of your own.

1. Not the parents but the child (seems seem) to control the family.
2. Either "Miss" or "Ms" (is are) fine with me.
3. Onions, sad movies, or happiness (is are) likely to make her cry.
4. Either your friend or you (is are) lying about the accident.
5. Not cheap liquor but friendly people (is are) what I miss most about the States.
6. The oil company informed me that neither they nor their representative (is are) responsible for the damage to my car.
7. Neither the practical training nor the courses I took (was were) able to prepare me for the job.
8. According to a recent survey, not sexual incompatibility but disagreements over children (cause causes) the most strain in a marriage.

9. Either ________________________ or ________________________ .

10. Not ________________________ but ________________________ .

2. Subjects that look multiple but really aren't. Don't be fooled by phrases beginning with such words as *with*, *like*, *as well as*, *together with*, *in addition to*, *including*. These phrases are NOT part of the subject of the sentence. Cross them out mentally; they do not affect the verb.

> My typing teacher, ~~as well as my counsellor~~, has advised me to switch programs.

Obviously, two people were involved in the advising; nevertheless, the subject (teacher) is singular, and so the verb must be singular, too (has advised).

> All my courses, ~~including chemistry~~, are easier this term.

If you mentally cross out the phrase "including chemistry," you can easily see that the verb (are) must be plural to agree with the plural subject (courses).

Exercise 5

Circle the correct verb. Then make up two sentences of your own.

1. David Bowie, with the Tin Men, (is are) beginning a North American tour soon.
2. Margaret Atwood, like many contemporary Canadian authors, (write writes) novels with political themes.

3. My accounting assignment, not to mention my psychology and English homework, (is are) enough to drive me to drink.
4. The whole computer package, including disk drive, printer, and programs, (is are) too expensive for us.
5. In spite of the efforts of parents and educators, television, with its mix of adventure shows, comedies, and rock videos, (remain remains) the most popular pastime for young people.
6. My brother, as well as my parents, (want wants) me to move out.
7. The food he serves, along with the drinks he mixes, (is are) delicious.
8. This play, in addition to the ones she wrote in her youth, (is are) guaranteed to put you to sleep.

9. ________________, like ________________, ________________.

10. ________________, together with ________________, ________________.

---

3. Words ending in *one*, *thing*, or *body*. When used as subjects, the following words are always singular, requiring the singular form of the verb:

everyone	everything	everybody
anyone	anything	anybody
someone	something	somebody
no one	nothing	nobody

The last part of the word is the tip-off here: every*one*, any*thing*, no*body*. If you focus on this last part, you'll remember to use a singular verb with these subjects. Usually these words are troublesome only when modifiers crop up between them and their verbs. For example, no one would write "Everyone are here." The trouble starts when you sandwich a bunch of words between the subject and the verb. You might, if you weren't on your toes, write this: "Everyone involved in implementing the company's new policies and procedures are here." Obviously, the meaning is plural: several people are present. But the subject (every*one*) is singular in form, so the verb must be *is*.

Exercise 6

Circle the right verb. Then make up two sentences of your own.

1. Everybody on the fourth and fifth floors (was were) questioned by the police inspector.
2. No one who had seen the murderer (was were) found.
3. Everyone, including the victim's husband, (believe believes) the butler did it.
4. Anyone with information leading to an arrest (is are) entitled to a reward.

5. So far, no one but Miss Marple (seem seems) likely to try to claim the money.
6. Everything she had discovered, including the clue of the blood-stained Adidas, (is are) to be revealed tonight.
7. Until then, absolutely nothing in the victim's rooms (is are) to be touched.
8. Nobody (dare dares) question Miss Marple's explanation of the crime.

9. Something ______________________________.

10. Everybody ______________________________.

---

4. *Each, either (of), neither (of).* Used as subjects, these take singular verbs.

Either was suitable for the job.
Each wants desperately to win.

Neither of the stores is open after six o'clock. (Remember, the subject is never in a prepositional phrase.)

Exercise 7

Circle the right verb. Then make up two sentences of your own.

1. Neither of the boys (work works) very hard.
2. Either (is are) likely to be fired.
3. Neither of the proposals (interest interests) me.
4. Each of the contestants (hope hopes) to be chosen.
5. Either of the available seats (is are) very close to the stage.
6. I am sorry to say that neither (is are) ready to be used.
7. Each of the instructors (was were) eccentric in method and appearance.
8. Neither of his excuses (is are) believable.

9. Either ______________________________.

10. Each ______________________________.

---

5. Collective nouns. A collective noun is a word naming a group. Some examples are *company*, *class*, *committee*, *team*, *crowd*, *group*, *family*, *audience*, *public*, and *majority*. When you are referring to the group as a *unit*, use a *singular* verb. When you are referring to the *members* of the group acting *individually*, use a *plural* verb.

The team is sure to win tomorrow's game. (Here *team* refers to the group acting as a whole.)
The team are getting into their uniforms now. (The separate members of the team are acting individually.)

Exercise

8

Circle the correct verb. Then make up two sentences of your own.

1. The nuclear family (is are) the fundamental unit of society.
2. The electorate (seem seems) to be in an ugly, vengeful mood.
3. Your department (pride prides) itself on a high degree of efficiency.
4. The budget committee (fight fights) among themselves continually.
5. (Has Have) the jury reached a verdict?
6. Having waited for almost an hour, the crowd (was were) growing restless.
7. The office (give gives) a farewell party whenever anyone leaves.
8. The majority of immigrants (find finds) Canada a tolerant country.

9. The company ____.

10. A herd of water buffaloes ____________________________________.

---

6. Units of money, time, mass, length, and distance. These require singular verbs.

Four dollars is too much to pay for a hamburger.
Three hours is a long time to wait, and five kilometres is too far to walk.
Seventy kilograms is the mass of an average man.

Exercises

9

Circle the correct verb. Then write two sentences of your own.

1. Three hours (seem seems) to pass very quickly when I'm at the movies.
2. Patients who suffer from anorexia nervosa find that even 40 kg (seem seems) like too much weight.
3. Ninety-nine cents (seem seems) a fair price.
4. Twenty dollars (is are) all I need for tickets to the Beastie Boys.
5. Forty years in the desert (is are) a long time to delay one's gratification.
6. Twenty centimetres of snow in six hours (was were) enough to paralyze the city.

7. Five dollars an hour for babysitting (is are) not bad.
8. Seven hours of classes (is are) too much for one day.
9. Nine hundred and sixty-nine years ______________________________ .
10. One hundred kilometres ______________________________ .

In exercises 10 through 12, correct the errors in subject-verb agreement. Check your answers to each set before going on.

10

1. A group of unbiased men and women (is are) trying to solve the problem.
2. Anybody who really want to will succeed.
3. Over the last ten years, the number of couples who are living together has increased greatly.
4. Every one of the contestants (think thinks) winning a week in Lackawanna would be wonderful.
5. The amount of money generated by touring rock stars (is are) enormous.
6. If there is no bubbles, then you have patched your tire successfully.
7. Neither Peter nor I is a very strong swimmer.
8. The lack of things to write about cause the headaches.
9. Michael Jackson, along with his brothers, parents, pets, and retinue, have begun another world tour.
10. You'll find that not only ragweed but also animal dander makes you sneeze.

11

1. The source of all the problems were difficult to find.
2. Tai Chi, like yoga, teaches you to relax.
3. Neither university nor the community colleges appeals to me.

4. Only the first ten minutes of his lecture were interesting.
5. Nothing except junk foods appeal to my children.
6. Two thousand kilograms is simply too much for a four-cylinder engine to pull.
7. Every one of the applicants look good to me.
8. This afternoon the class are going to learn some propaganda techniques.
9. Absolutely everyone, my girlfriend and my mother included, not to mention my closest friends, have advised me not to pursue my musical career.
10. I'll bet neither you nor he are prepared to do battle with Hulk Hogan.

12

There's many good reasons for staying fit. The loss of strength, flexibility, and endurance that result from lack of exercise are very compelling factors, but everyone who joins the many health clubs in this city have individual reasons as well. The people I talked with says appearance or weight loss are their big motivation for working out. No one among the two hundred patrons of a local health club were there for the social aspects of the place, according to my poll. Either daily aerobics or weightlifting was what they wanted from their club, and the intensity of the workouts were clear evidence that they were serious. The manager of the club, along with all the members of his staff, were very careful to point out that supervised exercise is essential for best results, but neither he nor his workers was in favour of fad diets or sweat programs.

Complete the sentences in exercises 13 and 14 using present-tense verbs. After doing each set of ten sentences, check in the answer section to see whether your verbs should be singular or plural.

13

1. Neither my boss nor the receptionist
2. Everybody with two or more pets
3. Not the lead singer but the musicians
4. A flock of birds
5. Every one of his employees
6. Ten dollars
7. The whole family, including two aunts and six cousins,
8. The actors, as well as the director,
9. Either a Big Mac or a Whopper
10. No one among the hundreds present

14

1. The committee
2. The bill, including tip and taxes,
3. Part of the cost
4. Either Romeo or Juliet and the Nurse
5. A hike of fourteen or more kilometres
6. Each of the band members
7. A covey of birds
8. Fort Francis and Rainy River, together with Kenora,

9. The Canadian hockey audience

10. Each and every one of you

15

Write your own sentences, choosing your subjects as indicated and using present-tense verbs.

1. Use a collective noun as subject.

2. Use a compound subject.

3. Use *no one* as your subject.

4. Use *everything* as your subject.

5. Use *neither . . . nor.*

6. Use *not . . . but.*

7. Use a collective noun as singular subject.

8. Use a collective noun as plural subject.

9. Use your own weight as subject.

10. Use a compound subject joined by *or.*

16

Correct the following passage.

The rewards of obtaining a good summer or part-time job goes well beyond the money you earn from your labour. Contacts that may be valuable in the future and experience in the working world is a very important part of school-time employment. Even if the jobs you end up getting while attending school is not in the field of your future ambitions, there is many benefits that will show up later. For example, when scanning your résumé, an employer always likes to see that you know what working for other people are all about: arriving at the work site on time, getting along with fellow workers, taking instructions. Neither instinct nor instruction take the place of experience in teaching the basic facts of working life. These important considerations, in addition to the money that is the immediate reward, is what gives work its real value to those students who seek summer jobs or part-time employment. Everyone who has ever gone to school and worked during vacations are able to confirm these observations.

17

As a final check of your mastery of subject-verb agreement, correct the following sentences. (There are no answers provided for this exercise.)

1. All of his courses, including drafting and architectural history, is easier for him this term.
2. Either the class or the instructor were mistaken about the due date for the project.
3. Although you are unsure of your position on the issue, everyone else in my classes want to ban Pat Sajak from the airwaves.
4. The losing hockey coach, together with his hapless players, are often abused by the media.
5. Each of those outfits give Laszlo a seedy, disreputable look.
6. There is a buxom woman and two beefy gentlemen lurking in the parking lot waiting for you.
7. Did you know that a *clowder* of cats are what they call a whole bunch of them?

8. Twenty dollars only seem like a lot to pay for a Day-Glo velvet painting of Elvis.
9. Everyone who fear for the life of this planet are concerned about nuclear proliferation.
10. Either Margaret or Martin, accompanied by the kids, are going to the West Edmonton Mall this weekend.

chapter 11

Pronoun-Antecedent Agreement

The title of this chapter may be formidable, but the idea is really very simple. **Pronouns** are words that substitute for or refer to the name of a person or thing. The word that a pronoun substitutes for or refers to is called the **antecedent**.

> Bob has his own way of doing things.
>
> antecedent (Bob) — pronoun (his)
>
> This game is as close as it can be.
>
> antecedent (game) — pronoun (it)

The basic rule to remember is this:

A pronoun must agree with its antecedent.

You probably follow this rule most of the time, without even realizing that you know it. For example, you would never write . . .

> Bob has *its* own way of doing things.
> or
> This game is as close as *he* can be.

. . . , because you know that these pronouns don't agree with these antecedents.

There are three aspects of pronoun usage, however, that you need to be careful about. The first is how to use the relative pronouns — *which*, *that*, *who*, and *whom*:

Who and *whom* are always used to refer to people. *That* and *which* refer to everything else.

> The man *who* was hurt had to quit climbing.
> The women *who* were present voted unanimously.
> The moose *that* I met looked hostile.
> Her car, *which* is imported, is smaller than cars *that* are built here.
> The man *whom* the committee had decided to hire refused the job.

By the way, if you aren't sure whether to use *who* or *whom*, rewrite the sentence so you don't need either one: "The man the committee had decided to hire refused the job."

Exercise

I

Correct the following sentences where necessary. Answers begin on p. 292.

1. Is this the dog who bit the mail carrier that carries a squirt gun?
2. The path that I took led me past the home of a hermit, which lived all alone in the forest that surrounded our town.
3. The goal that came at 15:45 of the third period was scored by a player that I used to know in high school.
4. That can't be Janice O'Toole, the little girl that I used to bounce on my knee!
5. The building that we entered next was owned by the company who employed my father.
6. He is the man that I turn to whenever I feel depressed because of something my sister has said or done.
7. The open-concept office is one that makes sense to anyone who has worked in a stuffy little cubicle all day.
8. The four tests that we wrote today would have defeated anyone that wasn't prepared for them.
9. The wind whistled around the cabin, against whom they had propped their skis while waiting to see whether the skiers which they had passed earlier could catch up.
10. An advantage of the open-concept office is that it lets you see who is

working hard and who is taking it easy. It also allows you to spot people that you'd like to meet.

The second tricky aspect of pronoun-antecedent agreement concerns words and phrases that you learned about in chapter 10 — words and phrases ending in *one*, *body*, and *thing*:

everyone	everybody	everything
anyone	anybody	anything
someone	somebody	something
no one	nobody	nothing
none		
each (one)		
every one		

In chapter 10 you learned that when these words are used as subjects they are singular and take singular verbs. So it makes sense that the pronouns that stand for or refer to them must be singular.

> Antecedents ending in *one*, *body*, and *thing* are singular and must be referred to by singular pronouns: *he*, *she*, *it*, *his*, *her*, *its*.

Everyone is expected to do *his* duty.
Each of the students must supply *his* or *her* own lunch.
Every mother deserves a break from *her* routine.
No one can truly say in *his* heart that *he* believes otherwise.

Another problem involves sentences that are grammatically correct but sound awkward:

If anyone is at the door, he'll have to knock louder.
Everyone arrives on time, but he leaves early.

It is wrong to write

If anyone is at the door, they'll have to knock louder.
Everyone arrives on time, but they leave early.

So, in order to make the sentences sound better, you need to rewrite them. Here is one way:

Anyone who is at the door will have to knock louder.
Everyone arrives on time but leaves early.

In speech it has become acceptable to use plural pronouns with *one*, *body*, and *thing* antecedents. Although these antecedents are singular and take singular verbs, often they are plural in meaning, and in conversation we find ourselves saying

Everyone clapped *their* hands with glee.
No one has to stay if *they* don't want to.

This usage is acceptable only in conversation; *it is not acceptable in written Standard English*. Errors in pronoun-antecedent agreement are sometimes made because people are attempting to write "gender free" language — that is, to write without indicating whether the person referred to is male or female.

"Everyone is expected to do their duty" is incorrect, as we have seen; however, it does avoid making "everyone" male, as one of the grammatically correct versions seems to do: "*Everyone* is expected to do *his* duty." It also avoids the awkwardness of "*Everyone* is expected to do *his or her* duty."

There are two better ways to solve the problem.

1. Revise the sentence to leave the pronoun out.

Duty is expected of everyone.
or
Everyone is expected to perform dutifully.

Such creative avoidance of gender specific or incorrect constructions can be an interesting challenge. Method 2, however, is easier to accomplish:

2. Revise the sentence to make the pronoun plural.

You are all expected to do your duty.

Here are a couple of examples for you to study:

Problem: Each of the students has his or her assignment.
Revision 1: Each of the students has an assignment.
Revision 2: All of the students have their assignments.

Problem: Everyone will enjoy seeing his or her classmates again.
Revision 1: Everyone will enjoy seeing classmates again.
Revision 2: All graduates will enjoy seeing their classmates again.

Exercise

2

Choose the correct word from the pair in brackets. Check your answers before continuing.

1. No one I know would allow (his their) name to stand on the ballot.
2. Each of us prefers to answer the charges for (herself themselves).
3. Everyone wants to be considered an expert in (his their) own subject.
4. If we all try to do our best, each will find (her their) reward in a job well done.
5. Dogs and cats show (its their) affection for (its their) owners in vastly different ways.
6. All of the club members will have to contribute all (he they) can if no one is able to get (his their) parents to finance the trip.

7. Somebody is lying to cover up (his their) own guilt.
8. None of the pictures he took could be called great by (itself themselves), but together they made a stunning collection.
9. Each student must decide for (himself themselves) whether (he they) wants to be popular, successful, or happy, because it is unlikely that (he they) will be all three at once during the college years.
10. Ladies and gentlemen, whoever (he they) may be, must learn certain basic rules of behaviour so that no one can criticize (him them) in later life for ignorance.

Avoiding the third difficulty with pronoun-antecedent agreement depends on your common sense and your ability to think of your reader. If you try to look at your writing from your reader's point of view, it is unlikely that you will break this rule:

A pronoun must *clearly* refer to the correct antecedent.

The mistake that occurs when you fail to follow this rule is called **vague reference**:

> Sam pointed to his brother and said that he had saved his life.

Who saved whom? Here's another:

> Jackie felt that Helen should have been more careful with her car when she lent it to her because she was a good friend of her husband.

Who owns the car? Who has the husband?

In these sentences you can only guess about the meaning, because you don't know who is being referred to by the pronouns. You can make these sentences less confusing by using proper names more often and changing the sentences around. Try it on our examples.

Another type of vague reference occurs when a pronoun doesn't have an antecedent at all.

> He loves watching fast cars and would like to do it himself someday.
> (Do what?)
> Bicycling is her favourite pastime, but she still doesn't own one.
> (One what?)

How would you revise these sentences?

Be sure that pronouns have clear antecedents, with which they agree in number. That, in a nutshell (see "Clichés," p. 243), is the rule of thumb for pronoun-antecedent agreement.

Exercises

3

Correct the following sentences where necessary. In some cases, a perfectly correct answer of yours will differ from the answer we've given. That's because the reference was so vague that the sentence could be understood in more than one way.

1. Max is a good skater, which he practises daily.
2. He didn't hear her cry for help, which was due to his wearing earplugs.
3. That Mr. Cohen would be Stephen's teacher never occurred to him.
4. It seemed that every time he looked at the donkey he brayed.
5. Management refused to allow a cost-of-living clause, which is why the union walked out.
6. He told his brother he would soon get a job.
7. Whenever Ann and Carol met, she acted in a very friendly way so that no one would suspect that she hated her.
8. Joe told Henry that he was losing his hair.
9. Matthew threw his calculator on the floor and dented it.
10. This letter is in response to your ad for a waitress and bartender, male or female. Being both, I wish to apply for the position.

4

Correct the following sentences where necessary. Check your answers before continuing.

1. Anyone that has finished all his homework by now can't have done it properly.
2. This is a beaten team; none of the players cares any more whether he performs well.

3. Everybody I know is going, even if they can't get a date.
4. Each of my roommates finally left to find an apartment of their own.
5. I'd like to meet someone that is tall, dark, handsome, and rich; in fact, they don't even have to be tall, dark, or handsome.
6. Here everybody is allowed to find their own path to success, according to what they consider success to be.
7. The book tries to prove that nobody can rise above their own level of ability without the help of friends.
8. Constant nagging would make anyone lose their mind unless they learned to ignore it.
9. Somebody that has many friends will have to go; they will need friends if they hope to return.
10. Everyone likes to think that they're unique, but each of us is their own idea of perfect, so in fact we are all the same.

5

Correct these sentences where necessary. Then check your answers.

1. Each of the cars has their own faults, but nobody else wants this one, so I'll take it.
2. Every child is a product of their environment as well as their parentage.
3. They will get help from no one, since everybody has left in her own car.
4. The men which made up the team agreed that everybody would have to complete their assignment.

5. Writing is what she does best, although she hasn't been able to complete one lately.
6. She'll put her to bed now because she is short-tempered.
7. Everyone must get in their places for the game to begin.
8. Anybody that is without a partner will have to be sure he finds one which is about his height.
9. Neither the jacket nor the pants fits the way it should.
10. He said he wasn't trying hard enough and that anyone who said he was would get a punch on their nose.

6

Correct the following sentences where necessary. Check your answers before continuing.

1. Golf is a game that is good for anyone that wants to enjoy competition in the outdoors without getting their body sweaty or hurt.
2. Each person that wants to come on our annual ski trip to the Gatineau Hills must pay their money well in advance.
3. We have tried to convince every student to see their teachers regarding their evaluations.
4. Everyone seems to think that age will never affect them, but at about thirty, they start to realize that time is, indeed, passing.
5. Is there anyone that is so sure of victory they never contemplate an excuse for defeat?
6. We are trying to find a comfortable chair for an elderly lady which is well-padded and has curved legs.

7. They'll try to find accommodations for the tourists, even though they don't really know what they want.
8. We'll try to choose someone whose intelligence and creativity are so outstanding that they won't need any supervision.
9. I remember the old days when anyone that had a computer wore horn-rimmed glasses, understood calculus, and didn't know if their shoes were tied.
10. Deborah told Dorothy that she had an excellent chance of making the team if she just did everything she told her to do when she spoke to the coach.

7

Correct the errors in this passage. All three kinds of pronoun-antecedent agreement errors are represented in this exercise. Part of the challenge in this exercise is to make the passage free of gender-specific pronouns.

Anyone that has competed in a triathlon (a three-part race consisting of swimming, cycling, and running) knows that proper training is an absolute necessity, not only to their success, but also to their survival. Swimming is one of the toughest contests, because it demands cardiovascular fitness as well as strength, and it makes demands on the whole body. While each of the three segments has their own challenges, the cycling part of the triathlon is the event that separates the serious athlete from the part-time fitness buff. Here he will find he can't summon enough energy after his swim to stay close to his opponent if he has trained harder than he. The serious athlete will begin to assert their dominance now, and by the end of the bike ride, anyone that has achieved a high level of physical efficiency through their training will still have a chance of a high placing. For the competitor in a triathlon, survival is often the primary goal. The body's reserves are called upon, and only the dedicated, well-trained athlete will be able to do it. For most, reaching the finish line is a personal test, and the only competition is with one's pιevious finish times. The person that still has winning on their mind after the swim, the cycle race, and the run has physical and mental reserves beyond the ordinary.

8

Correct the following sentences where necessary. (No answers are provided for this exercise.)

1. Each of the teachers behaved as if they do could no wrong, so they had a terrible time deciding which of them they should choose as tutors.
2. When it comes to dessert, anything is fine as long as they are sweet and fattening.
3. If anyone here feels it's any of their business, they had better speak up now before the final commitment is made.
4. No one wants their name published in the paper during a trial, unless they're lawyers.
5. Every good student deserve to have their accomplishments recorded so they can hire them when they graduate.
6. Feeling very lonely, Doris longed for someone that would sit with her on a cold night in front of a fire and give her their sympathy.

7. There is one city, in my opinion, who anyone that enjoys theatre should visit when they go to Europe, and that's London.
8. Anyone that would write a sentence like number 7 on this page should turn in their typewriter and become a bricklayer.
9. Just about everyone I know loves to play tennis whenever they can, but none of them enjoy themselves on the squash court.
10. They are the ones that tried to buy a car just when they brought out the new models.

Tense Agreement

Verbs are time markers. The different tenses are used to express differences in time:

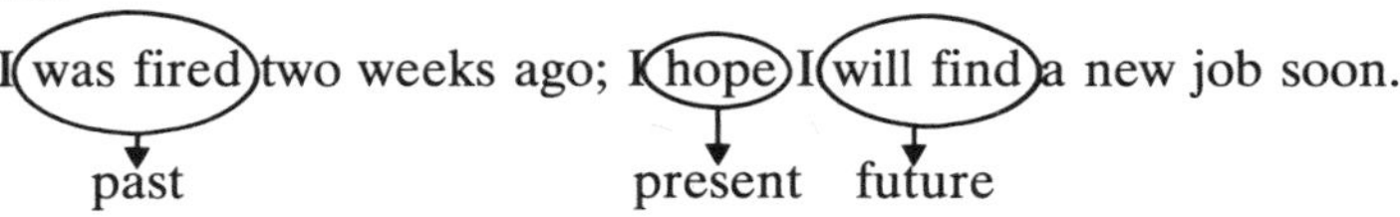

I was fired two weeks ago; I hope I will find a new job soon.
past
present
future

Sometimes, as in the sentence above, it is necessary to use several different tenses in a single sentence to get the meaning across. But usually, whether you're writing a sentence, a paragraph, an essay, or a report, you will use *one tense throughout*. Normally you will choose either the past or the present tense. Here is the rule to follow:

Don't change tense unless meaning requires it.

Readers like and expect consistency. If you begin a sentence with "I kicked and screamed and protested," the reader will tune in to the past-tense verbs and expect any other verbs in the sentence to be in the past tense too. Therefore, if you finish the sentence with ". . . but he looks at me with those big blue eyes and gets me to take him to the dance," the reader will be abruptly jolted out of one time frame and into another. This sort of jolting is uncomfortable, and readers don't like it.

Shifting tenses is like shifting gears: it should be done smoothly and when necessary — never abruptly, out of carelessness, or on a whim. Avoid causing verbal whiplash: keep your tenses consistent.

Wrong: He kicked a stone from his path as he rambles up the winding driveway.

Right: He kicked a stone from his path as he rambled up the winding driveway.

Also right: He kicks a stone from his path as he rambles up the winding driveway.

Wrong: She hesitated but then began to climb the steps. Suddenly she hears a low groan.

Right: She hesitated but then began to climb the steps. Suddenly she heard a low groan.

Also right: She hesitates but then begins to climb the steps. Suddenly she hears a low groan.

Exercises

Most of the following sentences contain unnecessary tense shifts. Use the first verb in each sentence as your time marker, and change the tense(s) of the other verb(s) in the sentence to agree with it. If you get exercise 1 entirely correct, skip ahead to exercise 4. Answers begin on p. 295.

1

1. He goes home and told her what happened.
2. She was so tired that she goes right to sleep.
3. The plane was chartered, the bags were packed, and the champagne is on ice.
4. The referee stands there, blinking, unable to believe what he was seeing.
5. The goalie must not move from his stand until the penalty kicker makes contact with the ball.
6. Pat asked Andy if they wanted to bring Maggie.
7. First you will fry the onion; then you brown the meat.
8. As soon as you rub the lamp, a genie appeared.
9. "Safety colours" are bright and will attract immediate attention.
10. When Bon Jovi came on stage, the crowd goes crazy.

2

1. First, comb your hair into spikes; then you will coat your head with glue.
2. The guy walked over and punched me in the stomach.
3. The Peter Principle states that every person will rise to his or her level of incompetence.
4. The couple next door had a boa constrictor that keeps getting loose.

5. He began by asking a rhetorical question that he proceeds to answer.
6. She didn't say anything; she just storms out of class.
7. While our team suffered one defeat after another, the Russians rejoice.
8. The town seemed fast asleep as he drove along Main Street.
9. The new employee was too inexperienced to do the job in the time she's given.
10. If you'll be still for a minute, I would explain everything.

3

1. Prejudice is learned and will be hard to outgrow.
2. He used to get into trouble when he drinks.
3. If you will just keep your eyes and ears open, you learn something new every day.
4. After I had already put the car away, I realize Ann is still waiting for me at school.
5. The guard didn't say anything. He just stands there and stares at us.
6. We came in early and ate all the steaks.
7. In the movie, King Kong climbs the Empire State Building and got buzzed by small planes.
8. Her argument became silly when she goes on to suggest that watching television weakened the genes.
9. We were embarrassed when Elmo gets up and says that two of our favourite musicians are eunuchs.

10. In the dead of night, while coyotes howled in the distance, someone — or some *thing* — is prowling in the dark recesses of the cave.

4

Correct the faulty tense shifts in the following sentences.

1. In 1897, Bram Stoker published his novel *Dracula* and gives the world one of its most enduring horror stories.
2. The story is based on numerous legends of the undead who remain immortal because they preyed on the blood of the living.
3. The Count himself is modelled on Prince Vlad V of Wallachia (1431–1476) who has a penchant for impaling his enemies on spikes.
4. There is no historical evidence, however, to suggest that this Vlad the Impaler drank their blood after he skewers them.
5. Stoker's novel depicts a loathsome but powerful count who leaves Transylvania for England, where red-blooded victims abounded.
6. He takes pleasure in sucking the life from pure young maidens who become, in their undead state, craven creatures who used a kind of lurid sexuality to seduce their own victims.
7. Like the Count, these creatures lay in their coffins during the day, gorged with blood, and roam during the night to satiate their blood lust.
8. Only the old magic — garlic, crosses, stakes through the heart — can overcome the horrible power of Count Dracula.
9. Told in epistolary fashion (that is, in letters, diaries, and journals sup-

posedly pieced together), *Dracula* is, of course, a grotesquely sensational tale that was wildly improbable.

10. Nonetheless, that the story was rooted in archetypal fears and retains a powerful hold on our collective imagination is attested to by the fact that Stoker's novel has never been out of print.

5

Correct the faulty tense shifts in the following paragraphs.[1] Then compare your answers with the author's version.

The winters of my childhood were long, long seasons. We live in three places — the school, the church and the skating-rink — but our real life is on the skating-rink. Real battles were won on the skating-rink. Real strength appears on the skating-rink. The real leaders show themselves on the skating-rink.

School was a sort of punishment. Parents always wanted to punish children and school is their most natural way of punishing us. However, school is also a quiet place where we can prepare for the next hockey game, lay out our strategies. As for church, we found there the tranquillity of God: there we forget school and dream about the next hockey game. Through our daydreams it might happen that we will recite a prayer: we would ask God to help us play as well as Maurice Richard.

We all wear the same uniform as he, the red, white and blue uniform of the Montreal Canadiens, the best hockey team in the world; we all combed our hair in the same style as Maurice Richard, and to keep it in place we use

---

[1] *Exercises 5, 6, and 7 are adapted from "The Hockey Sweater" by Roch Carrier, translated by Sheila Fischman in* The Hockey Sweater, *Anansi Press, Ltd. Reprinted by permission.*

a sort of glue — a great deal of glue. We laced our skates like Maurice Richard; we tape our sticks like Maurice Richard. We cut all his pictures out of the papers. Truly, we know everything about him.

6

Correct the faulty tense shifts in this continuing passage. Then compare your version with the author's version.

On the ice, when the referee blew his whistle the two teams would rush at the puck; we are five Maurice Richards taking it away from five other Maurice Richards; we were ten players, all of us wearing with the same blazing enthusiasm the uniform of the Montreal Canadiens. On our backs, we all wear the famous number 9.

One day, my Montreal Canadiens sweater becomes too small; then it got torn and has holes in it. My mother says, "If you wear that old sweater people are going to think we're poor!" Then she does what she did whenever we needed new clothes. She starts to leaf through the catalogue the Eaton company sent us in the mail every year. My mother was proud. She doesn't want to buy our clothes at the general store; the only things that were good enough for us are the latest styles from Eaton's catalogue. My mother didn't like the order forms included with the catalogue; they were written in English and she didn't understand a word of it. To order my hockey sweater, she did as she usually did; she takes out her writing paper and writes. . . .

7

The continuing passage is written in the present tense. Rewrite the passage, changing the verbs to the past tense where necessary. Your first sentence will begin, "Monsieur Eaton was quick to answer. . . ." Compare your version with the one given in the answer section.

Monsieur Eaton is quick to answer my mother's letter. Two weeks later we receive the sweater. That day I have one of the greatest disappointments of my life! I would even say that on that day I experience a very great sorrow. Instead of the red, white and blue Montreal Canadiens sweater, Monsieur Eaton sends us a blue and white sweater with a maple leaf on the front — the sweater of the Toronto Maple Leafs. I always wear the red, white and blue Montreal Canadiens sweater, all my friends wear the red, white and blue sweater; never has anyone in my village ever worn the Toronto sweater; never have we even seen a Toronto Maple Leafs sweater. Besides, the Toronto team is regularly trounced by the triumphant Canadiens. With tears in my eyes, I find the strength to say:

"I'll never wear that uniform."

8

Test your mastery of verb tense agreement by correcting the following sentences where necessary. (There are no answers provided for this exercise.)

1. He goes and told me the whole seamy story.
2. Two things we can't avoid were death and taxes.
3. They come in and ate up all of the anchovy-pineapple pizza.
4. Grandma and Grandpa jumped out of the car, ran up the steps, grab the kids, and give them a big hug.
5. Elmo often reminds Dee Dee that without him she will still be working at the Dairy Queen.

6. Watching television for nine hours a day exposed young children to more violence than is good for them; it will turn them into "vidiots."
7. My long-lost uncle finally returned home and give us all a share in his gold mine.
8. Before the doctors decided to operate, they review the case thoroughly.
9. Def Leppard and Mötley Crüe are heavy metal groups who rely on huge amplifiers and sensational stage shows.
10. Anorexia nervosa is a condition in which a person starves herself and loses an excessive amount of weight.

chapter 13

Person Agreement

There are three categories of "person" that you can use when you write or speak:

> **first person**: I, we
> **second person**: you (singular and plural)
> **third person**: he, she, one, someone, they

Here is the rule for person agreement:

Do not mix "persons" unless meaning requires it.

In other words, you must be consistent: if you begin a discussion in second person, you must use second person all the way through. Look at this sentence:

> If *you* wish to succeed, *one* must work hard.

This is the most common error — mixing second-person *you* with third-person *one*. Here's another example:

> *One* can live happily in Winnipeg if *you* have a very warm coat.

We can correct this error by using the second person throughout . . .

> *You* can live happily in Winnipeg if *you* have a very warm coat.

. . . or by using the third person throughout:

> *One* can live happily in Winnipeg if *one* has a very warm coat.
> or
> *One* can live happily in Winnipeg if *he* has a very warm coat.

These last three sentences raise two points of style that you should be aware of:

1. Although these three versions are equally correct, they sound somewhat different from one another. The second sentence, with its two *one*'s, sounds the most formal — even a little stilted. Don't overuse *one*. The sentence in the second person sounds the most informal and natural — like something you would say. The third sentence is between the other two in formality and is the one you'd be most likely to use in writing for school or business.

2. As you will have noted from the examples in chapter 11, the pronoun *he* is generally used to represent both sexes. If this usage bothers you, you can sometimes substitute *he or she*:

> A person can live happily in Winnipeg if he or she has a very warm coat.

But if *he or she* occurs too frequently the sentence becomes very awkward:

> A student can easily pass this course if he or she applies himself or herself to his or her studies.

You can fix sentences like these by switching the *whole sentence* to plural:

> Students can easily pass this course if they apply themselves to their studies.

Exercises

1

Choose the correct word from the brackets for each of the following sentences. Check your answers on p. 297 before continuing.

1. One who works hard will usually succeed, even if (you they he) may be without talent.
2. A great burden is lifted from one's shoulders by the realization that (you he they) will be accepted.
3. Any girl could be popular if (you one she) would use Beautifem Products!
4. You'd do better if (you one he) were to try harder.
5. If one reads the instructions, (you I one) will have no more difficulty.
6. Anyone who helps will get (your their his) reward.
7. No member of this team needs to feel that (you she) didn't try as hard as (you she) could.
8. A survey of the problem shows that (he it) could have been solved earlier if corrective measures had been taken.
9. When we came up for air, (you we he one) couldn't see land!
10. If you get pneumonia, (one you he) should rest completely and follow a doctor's orders.

Correct the following sentences where necessary. Check your answers to each set of ten before going on.

2

1. You mustn't upset the instructor if one wishes to leave class on time.
2. Anyone going to the class party can pick up your tickets now.

3. Men who don't think women are their equals may have to get used to living on your own.
4. Canadians don't seem to realize that the situation may get out of hand if you don't vote wisely.
5. One must try to control your temper when you feel frustrated or angry.
6. When he pushed me into the water, I pulled him in after me.
7. Everyone is going to get what they deserve.
8. If one is convicted on that charge, a fine is the least of your worries.
9. After we had driven about 300 km, you could feel the sleepiness begin to weight our eyelids.
10. One who is unable to cope with pressure must expect to be replaced when he has demonstrated his incompetence.

3

1. A great way to develop one's skills is to push yourself to the limit.
2. Everyone who wants more from life must stand up and shout your name as loudly as you can.
3. Canadians who travel abroad should remember you're representing your country.
4. Following one's hunch can lead to disaster — or to an easy solution to your problem.
5. Once you have been elected to Parliament, one should always remember that he is in the public eye.

6. In this country, one receives more acclaim as a hockey player than you do as a symphony conductor.
7. Anyone who drives one of those things should be aware of the risk you're taking.
8. You'll never find a place to live that's perfect for your life style, even if you search from here to Yellowknife.
9. Can one really be happy if you don't own an electric pencil sharpener?
10. Why must people always want something they don't have, even when you have more than you'll ever need?

4

1. I enjoy living in the country, because there one doesn't have to deal with traffic or pollution, and you can always get to the city if you want to.
2. One never really knows whether she's joking or not, do you?
3. I collect art because you can always get your money back on the investment, and one can sometimes make a killing.
4. No one can help him, because if you try one is quickly and rudely rebuffed.
5. Americans who vacation in Canada should take the opportunity to add to your collection of china at bargain prices.
6. A graduate from high school who can't construct a proper sentence ought to be ashamed of yourself.
7. One can't go around picking up after one's sloppy relatives all day, can you?

8. When we left the hotel's air-conditioned comfort, the heat knocked you over.
9. Canadian history may seem dull to one who doesn't know much about it, but to one who is fascinated by the unusual and the eccentric it can be a gold mine of wonderful stories.
10. An expert wine taster will find this a very acceptable vintage, and even one who knows little about wine will enjoy yourself with a bottle or two.

5

This exercise will test and reinforce your understanding of both tense agreement and person agreement. Correct the following sentences where necessary.

1. When you're bright, talented, and rich, one doesn't really have to try very hard to impress one's elders, especially if you were also handsome.
2. Two years ago we went for a long canoe trip in Killarney Park. We are amazed by the beauty of the country, especially the spectacular mountains. You learn quickly why the Group of Seven painted many of their most famous pictures there.
3. You can't beat a charcoal grill for preparing great hamburgs in the summertime. One got so tired of pan-fried meat patties all winter long.
4. Now that spring is here, we are looking forward to doing all the outdoor things that we missed in the winter. You really don't get out as much as one should when it's cold, but we were going to make up for that now.
5. You can't truly enjoy a sport unless you know the basic rules. How can one understand the game unless you know what's going on?

6. One mustn't push him too far, because he will either lose his temper or become hysterical, and that isn't what you want.
7. Our opinion is that there is not a better spot in town to meet for a quiet, inexpensive lunch. We get good service, which you don't find very often, and one finds the bill tolerable as well.
8. It was as though she had turned on a light: suddenly we all get the idea. You can't wait to get your hand in the air to tell the others what you had discovered.
9. Finally we were out of debt. Years of hard work and sacrifice had left one tired and somewhat bitter, but the feeling of accomplishment at that moment made you feel it was all worth it.
10. I can hardly believe I climbed it. Often one gets so tired that you want to give up.

In the following passages, choose the right word from those in brackets.

6

People who get married while (they're one is) still in college may have an especially hard time completing (your their one's) studies. If both spouses are in school, (they he or she one) may not have enough money for an apartment, and they may have to live with (one's your their) parents for a while. Students whose spouses work may find (oneself themselves himself) studying on weekends while (their his or her one's) spouses rest or socialize. The wife who supports a student husband, along with the husband who supports a student wife, may find that the responsibility weighs heavily on (him her them). Anyone in such a situation would be likely to feel at the end of (their your his) wits sometimes, so students whose marriages are shaky may find that (one is they are you are) having a very hard time of it and that (you their one's) schoolwork is suffering. On the other hand, these various demands may strengthen a marriage, and a student who marries may find that (their one's his or her) motivation to succeed at school has increased. Some married students may even find (themselves himself oneself) studying more, using the time (they he one) would otherwise have spent dating.

7

A woman who enjoys baseball may have difficulty explaining (their one's her) passion to those who find the game a bore. Each February, the die-hard fan begins to sharpen (their one's her) listening and watching skills by tuning in to spring training games. If you have ever seen one of these fanatics watch a baseball game, (one you he) can't help but notice the alertness and intensity with which (one they she) follows the play. It is this single-minded dedication that the non-fan finds (himself themselves oneself) unable to comprehend. How can one be so interested in something that (one they you) must watch for three hours to see almost nothing take place? How can (one they you) get excited by a no-hitter, which, by definition, means that nothing has happened during the game? Baseball fans maintain that the game to which (one is they are) addicted has many more pleasures than mere action. They cite fielding plays and the strategy of pitcher versus hitter matchups in defence of the game that (he one they) would rather watch than any other. Those for (which whom who) these pleasures hold little appeal might enjoy watching golf or lawn-bowling.

8

As a final test of your mastery of person agreement, correct the following sentences. (There are no answers provided for this exercise.)

1. From the hilltop, one could see for miles if your eyes were sharp enough and there was no haze.
2. You will soon see the reason for my enjoyment of flying, because my friend has agreed to take us up in his plane.
3. One's self esteem is often tied up with his duty to other people for whom you really have no affection.
4. Anyone who thinks that splitting wood is easy can line up right here to get your axe and have a turn at my wood-pile.
5. Each person here who drives your car too fast will not pass your driving test, regardless of how well you did on the exam.

6. Aiming too high is a common fault one must learn to overcome if you are ever to succeed as a manager.
7. On the other hand, you can aim too low, and the results of that will equally ensure your failure.
8. If one works hard, keeps his or her nose clean, and takes on every job you can handle, regardless of how dirty it is, one's advancement in this corporation is assured.
9. Everyone would prefer to be healthy and fit, so why do so many people over-eat and under-exercise your way to sickness?
10. One who enjoys the finer things of life, such as symphonic music, classic art, good wine, and expensive cars, shouldn't allow yourself to miss the upcoming concert by the Puketones.

9

Think of the most important experience you've ever had. (If you don't like important, try thrilling or frightening.) Write an account of this experience, telling your story in the third person (that is, instead of using *I*, use *he* or *she*). When you've completed your work, reread it carefully. Check your spelling. Check your sentence structure. Check carefully subject-verb, pronoun-antecedent, tense, and person agreement.

4

punctuation

chapter 

The Apostrophe

Although it is very easy to use correctly, the apostrophe is one of the most misused gadgets in English. In fact, correct use of apostrophes is one of the best indicators of a careful writer. One large government corporation gives prospective employees a five-part grammar test, and three of the sections test the applicant's ability to use the apostrophe correctly. Clearly this employer doesn't consider the apostrophe a frill.

In many sentences, an apostrophe is needed to enable the reader to understand what you're trying to say. Here's an example:

> The teacher began class by calling the students names.
> The teacher began class by calling the students' names.

The apostrophe is used for two distinct purposes: to indicate contraction and to indicate possession.

Contraction

The rule about where to put apostrophes in contractions is one of the rare rules to which there are no exceptions. It *always* holds.

> When two words are shortened into one, and a letter (or letters) is left out, the apostrophe goes in the place of the missing letter(s).

they are	they're	you would	you'd
there is	there's	cannot	can't
we are	we're	is not	isn't
we will	we'll	who is, who has	who's
it is, it has	it's	will not	won't (Note the slight spelling variation here.)

Exercises

Check your answers to each set of ten before going on to the next. Answers for this chapter begin on p. 300.

1

Make these sets of words into contractions.

1. there is
2. did not
3. they will
4. it is
5. do not
6. it will
7. it has
8. we are
9. you are
10. he is

2

Make these sets of words into contractions.

1. she will
2. we have
3. I am
4. will not
5. who is
6. should not
7. they are
8. who has
9. you will
10. has not

3

Place apostrophes correctly in these words.

1. cant
2. youre
3. theyll
4. wouldnt
5. whos
6. wont
7. itll
8. theyre
9. weve
10. youve

4

Correct these sentences by placing apostrophes where needed.

1. Theyll have to stay home because theyre still sick.
2. Its been a long time since theyve had a good holiday.

3. Were many kilometres from where we were then.
4. Youre not going to try your luck again, are you?
5. Its been so long since someone wholl stand up for what is right has run for office.
6. Youre going to class because its good for you; youll never get far unless youve got your education.
7. Lets see if theyre up to the standards weve set.
8. Well have to do better if were to succeed.
9. Theyve finally done what shes suggested.
10. Since youve been in Europe, weve adopted the metric system in Canada.

5

If you've had no difficulty with exercises 1 through 4, skip this exercise and go on to "Possession." If you have had problems, review the rule for contraction, study your errors carefully to be sure you understand why you were wrong, and do exercise 5. Then check your answers.

Make the bracketed words into contractions.

1. (Who is) the girl (I have) been seeing you with?
2. (There is) a faster way to get there, but (we have) missed the turn.
3. (It has) been impossible to talk to you because (you have) already made up your mind.
4. (I have) found (they are) not very friendly unless (there is) a chance of making some money.
5. Hockey is our most popular sport, so (you will) be surprised to learn that it (is not) our official national sport.
6. We (could not) get here faster; (I am) not very good at reading maps.
7. Sam (will not) be a good accountant as long as (he is) unwilling to work after hours.
8. Money has been my biggest problem, but (I have) also had difficulties with my son, as (you are) aware.

9. (You will) find that his favourite food is fish; (he is) a fairly normal cat.
10. (We are) all here, but (we will) have to wait until (he is) sure we (have not) brought someone who (does not) belong.

Possession

The apostrophe also shows ownership or possession. Here's the rule that applies in most circumstances:

> 1. Add *'s* to the word that indicates the *owner*.
> 2. If the resulting words ends in a double or triple *s*, erase the last one, leaving the apostrophe in place.

Examples:

person + 's = person's
people + 's = people's
women + 's = women's
sisters + 's = sisters'~~s~~
teacher + 's = teacher's
Archimedes + 's = Archimedes'~~s~~

clerk + 's = clerk's
Pamela + 's = Pamela's
Marx + 's = Marx's
mother-in-law + 's = mother-in-law's
teachers + 's = teachers'~~s~~
goodness + 's = goodness'~~s~~

When you're forming possessives, you must be careful to determine first whether the *owner* is singular or plural. For example:

the student's names (The names belong to a *student*.)
the students' names (The names belong to two or more *students*.)

If you remember that possession indicates belonging to, you can figure out where to put the apostrophe by "translating" your sentence like this:

Incorrect: The policeman asked Elmo for his drivers licence.
1. Translation: the licence belongs to a *driver*
2. Add *'s*:

Correct: The policeman asked Elmo for his driver's licence.

Incorrect: The college finally met the librarians demands.
1. Translation: the demands belonged to — the *librarian*? or the *librarians*? Here's where you have to decide whether *one* or *more than one* is involved.
2. Add *'s*:

Correct: The college finally met the librarian's demands. (Only one librarian was involved.)

Also correct: The college finally met the librarians' demands. (More than one librarian was involved.)

Possession does not have to be literal. The owner does not have to be a person or thing. Ideas or concepts can be "owners," too:

day's work (the work of, or belonging to, a day)
at arm's length (the length of, or belonging to, an arm)
two cents' worth (the worth of, or belonging to, two cents)

You should know that there are alternatives to the second part of the rule given in the box above. Many writers prefer to keep the final *s* when forming possessives of one-syllable words ending in "s" and of some proper names. In these words, the *'s* represents a pronounced sound, and the *s* after the apostrophe is retained to reflect that sound:

boss's temper
class's decision
Brutus's betrayal
Yeats's poem

Note that the following words, called **possessive pronouns**, are already possessive in form and so do not take the *'s*:

my/mine	its
your/yours	our/ours
her/hers	their/theirs
his	whose

As you learned in chapter 2, in the section on sound-alikes and look-alikes, four of these words are often confused with contractions that sound like them. The possessives are at the left in the following list, the contractions at the right. Remember, when you need to decide which word to use, you can separate the contraction into its two root words and try them out in the sentence. Better yet, you can memorize these words.

their:	they own something	they're = they are
your:	you own something	you're = you are
whose:	"who" owns something	who's = who is, who has
its:	it owns something	it's = it is, it has

They're going to try *their* luck at cards.
You're losing *your* hair.
Who's been sleeping in *whose* bed?
It's obvious the car has a hole in *its* muffler.

Exercises

6

Make the following words possessive (owner words).

1. wagon
2. sea
6. horse
7. men

3. everybody
4. love
5. Alice
8. Ross
9. congress
10. agents

7

If you got any of the words in exercise 6 wrong, go back over the possession rule. When you're satisfied you know the rule and how to apply it, make these words possessive.

1. saleswoman
2. nurses
3. its
4. candy
5. someone
6. Joneses
7. Niagara Falls
8. women
9. stewardesses
10. lady

8

Make the following words possessive.

1. she
2. Bess
3. they
4. you
5. babies
6. history
7. one
8. actress
9. chairperson
10. ladies

9

Make the bracketed words in the sentences possessive.

1. He gave one (month) notice before leaving (they) office.
2. All of the (children) work was better than (you).
3. The (dog) collar was around (it) neck.
4. (George) hobby is spending his (wife) money.

5. In (it) purest form, gold is very soft, and a (jeweller) joy to work with.
6. (Phyllis) essay was on (Dickens) *Great Expectations*.
7. (Fishermen) time is wasted if (they) luck is bad.
8. When the (spray) effect wore off, our (trees) trunks became infested with beetles.
9. Canadian (authors) books aren't often recommended by our (school) curriculum planners.
10. After a (moment) pause, I accepted a (week) pay instead of the time off I was entitled to.

10

Correct these sentences by adding apostrophes where necessary.

1. Hikers equipment is on special during the weeks sale at Browns Sporting Goods.
2. Womens liberation is a touchy topic for Gails sister, whos lost a job to a man.
3. The waitress tip ended up in the busboys pocket.
4. Virtue is its own reward, according to people whose consciences are clear.
5. The mens room is down the hall, but its door isn't marked.
6. Gordie Howes records may eventually fall, but his careers achievements will never be surpassed.
7. Americas wealth has some Canadians wondering whether our countrys independence is worth maintaining.
8. Its coat shone like gold in the suns dying rays.
9. Scholars aims and athletes goals can both be achieved at college.
10. Mens and womens traditional roles are being questioned as this generations leaders refuse to take any of yesterdays values for granted.

Review Exercises

The following exercises will test and reinforce your understanding of both contraction and possession.

11

Choose the correct word from those in brackets. Check your answers before going on.

1. (Its It's) been a long time since (its it's) last overhaul, but I think (its it's) all right for another (week week's weeks') driving.
2. (They're There Their) your new relatives, so (its it's) silly not to try to get along with them.
3. (Your You're) in real trouble if the (police's polices') check turns up anything on (your you're) record.
4. (Betty's Bettys') dream is to make a career of her part-time work at (Children's Childrens') Aid.
5. (Who's Whose) going to win the game is (anybodys' anybody's) guess.
6. (They're Their There) real triumph is in achieving (they're their there) goals in spite of the handicaps that (they're their there) facing.
7. (Its It's) been a long time since (your you're)(son's sons') wife had her baby.
8. (Todays Today's Todays') music is returning to the (melodies melodies') and themes of (its it's) roots.
9. When (your you're) smiling, (its it's) as though the people you meet have known you all (they're their there) lives.
10. The (boys boy's boys') won the (cheaters cheater's) money in (Gords' Gord's) (fathers father's fathers') poker game.

12

To test your mastery of the apostrophe for both possession and contraction, correct the following sentences.

1. Philips best friend, whose a Junior A goaltender, came out to coach theyre teams goalie.
2. Blondies the name of my dogs first puppy. Were going to keep her when the rest of the litters old enough to sell.
3. Everybodies favourite mens store is Peebles, where, in a weeks time, youll be able to save hundreds in theyre fall sale.
4. While Nans boyfriends car was being repaired, Kevin rented a car and invited her to his schools formal. Its been a long time since shes been out in anyone elses company.
5. We shouldve had youre spaghetti sauce; its bound to be better than theirs. Well know better next time were invited to Gords parents place.
6. Didnt you see the U.S. Navies commercial on television? Its intended to make youre parents want a sailors uniform on you.
7. Apostrophes dont seem very significant until youve lost fifty percent of youre papers value for leaving them out.

8. Joannes dreams concern her longings for lifes better things: fast cars, boys admiration, parents approval, glamorous homes, and large bank accounts.
9. The parties over. Its time to call it a day. Were finished with our nights fun and dreading tomorrows dawn.
10. The ladies going to mend her ways and try to find out if its true that virtues reward is a long life. Unfortunately, Las Vegas call is very strong and theres some doubt about her ability to resist its summons back to the fast lane.

13

Make words 1 through 5 possessive. Form the contraction for numbers 6 through 10.

1. boys
2. knife
3. audience
4. it
5. secretaries
6. they are
7. who is
8. you are
9. it is
10. could not

Now write five sentences, each containing one of the possessives and one of the contractions.
Example: The *boys'* shorts are so flimsy that *they're* falling apart.

14

Make words 1 through 5 possessive. Form contractions for numbers 6 through 10.

1. gentlemen
2. typist
3. anyone
6. will not
7. it has
8. there is

4. enemy
5. enemies
9. has not
10. should not

Write five or more sentences, each containing at least one of the possessives and one of the contractions.

____

____

____

____

____

15

Correct the apostrophe errors in this paragraph. (No answers have been provided.)

Gladys decided that she should buy a dog for its ability to protect her and her apartment. There had been several break-ins at neighbours houses, and she felt that a dogs bark might discourage thieves who had they're eyes on her possessions. Gladys reputation for thoughtful consideration was well deserved, and she began to do research into the various breeds characteristics and the breeders reputations. A weeks work convinced her that she could never accumulate enough knowledge about every type of dog, so she narrowed her choice down to three who's characters seemed to suit her: the Doberman, the Bouvier, and the German Shepherd. Of the three, the Dobermans reputation for violence impressed her the most, but the Bouviers extreme loyalty and the Shepherds intelligence were factors she had to consider. Finally, after talking to the various breeders and getting they're sales-pitches, she realized that its a gamble any way you buy a dog, and one animals individual characteristics may well outweigh the breeds traits. In the end, Gladys decision was to go to the Humane Society and choose a dog for it's cuteness, in the hope that eventually it could be trained to protect it's mistress.

---

chapter 15

Question and Exclamation Marks

The Question Mark

Everyone knows that a question mark follows an interrogative, or asking, sentence, but we all sometimes forget that it does. Let this chapter simply serve as a reminder not to forget!

> The question mark is the end punctuation for all interrogative sentences.

The question mark gives the reader an important clue to the meaning of your sentence.

There's more?

is vastly different in meaning from

There's more!

and that difference is communicated to the reader by the punctuation alone.

The only time you don't end a question with a question mark is when the question is part of a statement.

Are you going? (question)
I asked whether you are going. (statement)
Do you know them? (question)
I wonder whether you know them. (statement)

Exercises

I

Put a check next to the sentences that have correct end punctuation. Turn to p. 303 to check your answers before going on.

1. _____Why do I have to be the one to go.
2. _____Jim wanted to know whether the class picture is ready for the yearbook?
3. _____Is there intelligent life on Mars?
4. _____Some people wonder whether there is intelligent life on earth.
5. _____Can't you make him be quiet?

6. ____There is some question as to whether Jason is capable of passing typing?
7. ____How do they get the whipped cream inside the cake without leaving a hole in the cake.
8. ____If chess is such a good game, why do so few people play?
9. ____There is still a chance, isn't there?
10. ____If they get a new centre, they could have a winning season.

2

Put a check next to the sentences that have correct end punctuation. Check your answers before going on.

1. ____Who's at the door?
2. ____I'm a better actress than she is, don't you think?
3. ____Haven't you done enough damage for one day.
4. ____I question the fairness of the marking in this course?
5. ____The others can do it, so why can't I?
6. ____I wonder whether they will arrive on time.
7. ____Jill asked about the price of a new car?
8. ____If ever there was a time for action, it's now?
9. ____Although I've talked it over with the teacher many times, and thought about it often, I still don't understand why sociology is so important in a business course?
10. ____Have you ever considered all the different types of people you'll have to deal with every day in that line of work.

3

Supply the correct end punctuation for these sentences. Then check your answers.

1. I'd like to help, but I don't know what I could do
2. Kim will be in real trouble if you don't admit you were wrong
3. Why is there always a cop around when I'm speeding, but never when I need help
4. Cut the lawn this morning, or you'll have to stay home tonight
5. It's a tough way to make a living, isn't it
6. It's not so bad if you keep up to date and don't let the marking get you down
7. If there were a different course available, I'd take it
8. When will the weather clear up so we can start our trip
9. Can't we go any faster in this old wreck
10. Take a look around you sometime and see for yourself whether I'm right

---

The Exclamation Mark

The exclamation mark can be a most valuable piece of punctuation for conveying your tone of voice to the reader. There is a distinct difference in tone between these two sentences:

There's a man behind you.

There's a man behind you!

In the first case, a piece of information is being supplied, possibly about the line-up at a grocery-store check-out counter. The second sentence might be a shouted warning about a mugger in the back seat of a car.

> Use an exclamation mark as end punctuation in sentences requiring extreme emphasis or dramatic effect.

The only way that the exclamation mark can have any punch or drama is if you use it sparingly. If you use an exclamation mark after every third sentence, how will your reader know when you really mean to indicate excitement? The overuse of the exclamation mark is a result of too much comic-book reading. The writers of comics use the exclamation mark after every sentence to try to heighten the impact of their characters' words. Instead, they've robbed their exclamation marks of all meaning.

Practically any sentence may have an exclamation mark after it, but remember that the punctuation changes the meaning of the sentence. Read the following sentences with and without an exclamation mark, and picture the situation that would call for each reading.

He's gone	Don't touch that button
The room was empty	There she goes again

Exercises

4

Insert the correct punctuation in these sentences.

1. Take that, you monster
2. Why, you've been hit
3. Stifle it, Edith
4. Oh, Henry, it's beautiful
5. Does this mean we're engaged
6. Heavens above   Who was that masked man
7. We have the winning number
8. All right, I quit
9. What do you care, you heartless creature
10. Overtime   Are you serious

5

Supply the correct end punctuation for these sentences. In many cases, the punctuation you use will depend on how you want the sentence to be read. Notice the extent to which different punctuation can change the meaning of a sentence.

1. Why is everything always so difficult for me
2. Why, it's my long-lost brother
3. I dare you
4. Could they have known about Carol and me before they saw us at the drive-in
5. There's another way
6. You aren't paying attention to what I'm saying, are you
7. Where Wilson goes, trouble is sure to follow
8. How he manages to get dates with such gorgeous women, I can't imagine
9. When you say there's going to be trouble, what do you mean
10. They descended on the newly opened department store with the battle cry, "Charge it "

6

Provide these sentences with appropriate end punctuation — an exclamation mark, question mark, or period.

1. Who can we turn to now that the deadline has passed
2. There's a fly in my soup
3. Help   Where are the lifeguards when you need them
4. I wonder where the twins went
5. Can't we go outside to play   Absolutely not
6. The sky is falling
7. Where once there was hope, now there is only fear
8. Has the winner been declared   Hooray
9. I can't believe it   The thing actually flies
10. What good will that do   Why don't you try another brand

7

Correct the punctuation in the following sentences.

1. She isn't sure whether or not there's a game tonight?
2. Why can't she do the right thing and tell him how she feels about him.
3. "Slide." The whole team was screaming in unison.
4. Is there life after high school's long days of boring classes and nights consumed by homework.
5. What good will it do if I continue to be pleasant to those who take such delight in making me look foolish.

6. We wondered how to behave after the boss had burst into tears and gone home?
7. The team questions the meaning of life as it relates to curling?
8. Despite the head-first slide into third, the umpire bellowed, "Out."
9. Oh joy. You've bought me a pair of Bermuda shorts. Be still, my beating heart.
10. Why can't the sports fans who yell so loudly about the mistakes of their heroes try to put themselves in the same position as those they criticize and try to be a little more forgiving.

8

Supply the punctuation in this passage.

When Tony Fernandez, the leadoff hitter, came to the plate, I was ready my first pitch, a slow curve, caught the outside corner "Strike one" howled the umpire why was I pitching to Tony Fernandez what was an English teacher doing on the mound in the SkyDome who was that rag-tag collection of players surrounding me the answers make one of the strangest chapters in baseball history undefeated in our recreation league, we had challenged the semi-pro team in our community, defeated it, and gone on to beat three other professional teams from nearby cities then *Sports Illustrated* printed a story about our exploits it was unbelievable the magazine article attracted international attention we were stars it was inevitable that the Blue Jays would want to take advantage of the publicity we were getting, so they invited us to play at the Dome and paid our transportation to Toronto.

I struck out Fernandez with my slider, took care of McGriff on three pitches, and got Gruber with an overpowering fastball hey this was easy the second and third innings were repeats of the first all nine batters striking out my teammates were getting restless, so in the fourth and fifth, I allowed a couple of easy ground balls and gave the outfielders their turn with a couple of easy fly balls in the sixth then I went back to work and struck out the side in the seventh, eighth and ninth meanwhile, I had driven in the only run with a hard-hit double down the first-base line the crowd went berserk "Sar-ah" they chanted over and over after the game, the Blue Jay management asked me to sign up as a free agent, but I said, "Thanks, but grammar is my game"

9

Supply appropriate punctuation for this paragraph.

Why you little sneak. I'll pull your ears off. Can't you even do as you're told when you know you'll be found out if you cheat. Haven't you the decency to admit your guilt. You should be expelled. If I have my way, you'll wonder what hit you. When the principal is finished with you, some of that confidence will be gone, believe me. If I ever hear of a repetition of this behaviour, it'll be the end of your career at this obedience school. Now, I'll give you one more chance to do it right. Fetch, Rover.

10

Supply correct end punctuation for the sentences in this paragraph. Use question and exclamation marks wherever the meaning of the sentence makes them appropriate. (No answers are provided.)

Who says there are no gentlemen left in the world. Why only the other day, I was walking down the street and noticed a lady in distress. Her coat was caught in a doorway, and she was tugging desperately to get it free. Suddenly it ripped, and she staggered out onto the road, right into the path of an oncoming truck. With true gentlemanly courtesy, I called out, "Excuse me, ma'am. There's a truck coming." Alerted by my words, she whirled around and dove out of the way. The truck missed. As I approached, she looked up from the pavement questioningly. I asked if she was hurt. She told me that she wasn't, but that she felt awfully weak. As I walked away, I suggested that she get up from the road before another truck came along. Her reply shocked me. Hadn't I been a perfect gentleman. Hadn't I done everything that might be expected. What is the world coming to, that such ingratitude should be displayed towards someone trying to help. Just see if I behave like a gentleman again. Ever.

chapter 16

Quotation Marks

Quotation marks (" ") are used to set off direct speech (dialogue), quoted material, and some titles. Quotation marks come in pairs; there has to be a set to show where the dialogue or quotation begins and a set to show where it ends. You must be absolutely sure that whatever you put between them is *exactly* the way it is stated in the source you are using. The only other thing you need to know about quotation marks is how to punctuate what comes between them.

Dialogue

When you quote direct speech, include normal sentence punctuation. If the speaker's name is also included in your own sentence, set it off with commas. The comma or the end punctuation mark comes *inside* the final set of quotation marks.

> "Did you," Tim asked in a rage, "drink all of my Black Label?"
>
> "No, there are a couple of swigs left," I said.

Be careful that you put quotation marks only around direct speech (someone's exact words). Don't use quotation marks with indirect speech:

> Tim, in a rage, asked me if I had drunk all his Black Label. (These are not Tim's exact words, nor is the sentence a question.)

Quoted Material

When you quote a *short* written passage (three lines of print or less), you can work it into your own sentence. Again, include normal sentence punctuation within the quotation marks.

> "Marriage," wrote Dr. Johnson, "has many pains, but celibacy has no pleasures."
>
> "The medium is the message," Marshall McLuhan points out in his book *Understanding Media*.

If your own introductory words form a complete sentence, use a colon:

Dr. Johnson made an interesting statement on wedded life: "Marriage has many pains, but celibacy has no pleasures."

Marshall McLuhan captured the imagination of a generation brought up on television: "The medium is the message."

A *long* written passage (more than three lines of print) should be single-spaced and indented from both margins on your page so that the quotation stands apart from your own text. An intended quotation is not enclosed in quotation marks.

Titles

Titles of whole books or volumes are *underlined*; titles of parts of those books or volumes are placed in quotation marks. Thus, books, names of magazines, pamphlets, newspapers, plays, and films are underlined. Titles of single articles, essays, stories, or poems should be placed in quotation marks.

"The Bear on the Delhi Road," by Earle Birney, in <u>Fifteen Canadian Poets</u>

"I Am Jane's Pancreas," in <u>Reader's Digest</u>

Exercises

1

Place the quotation marks correctly in these sentences, and insert the necessary punctuation. The answers for this chapter begin on p. 305.

1. Who was the lady I saw you with last night? asked the straight man.
2. Groucho replied That was no lady; that was my wife!
3. That's a really good price said Georgia as she eyed the floor-length mink.
4. John inquired if the trains were always this late.
5. Put that gun down, yelled the officer, or I'll shoot!
6. The coach asked his best player Why don't you wear a face mask?
7. The time has come, the Walrus said, to speak of many things.
8. Leave me alone, Sandra, Sarah pleaded.
9. The teacher questioned the class about who said that today's class was cancelled.
10. I'd like to help, said David, but I'm far too busy just now.

2

1. Trying desperately to catch up, Paul gasped Wait for me!
2. Referring to the chapter called Punctuation, Nell said This book is really helpful in improving my writing.
3. I said that I'd like to meet her.

4. Put yourself in my place and you'll understand why I feel hurt Stephen said.
5. I cannot believe exclaimed Debbie that you really did it!
6. Is there hope? asked Judy. Can we still get back?
7. Nancy wants to know whose dog won the ribbon.
8. Brian finally asked When do we eat?
9. The reply was When you cook some food.
10. In frustration and anger, Sheila told the entire company she was quitting. I've had enough she yelled.

3

1. Considering your record, intoned the principal, I'm inclined to suspend you for a month.
2. Go ahead replied Percy. I'm not afraid to stand up for something I believe in, he added.
3. Television is a vast wasteland Newton Minnow said, and many have added that it is also potentially dangerous.
4. Lights! Camera! Action! These three words, so often said by Hollywood directors, have entered the language as a synonym for an exciting beginning.
5. Carefully and deliberately, John turned to his tormentor and spoke. I don't want to play this game any more.
6. Say you love me, he pleaded. OK, she replied, You love me.
7. I challenge you, sir, to a duel, François cried. You have the choice of weapons.
8. The only thing I'd like to say is that we'll all have to improve 100 percent if we're going to win the next one.
9. Ridiculous! Brigit snorted nervously. I've never seen him before in my life.
10. Put that out said the waitress pointing to a sign that said No Smoking.

4

1. This, cried the carnival salesman, is genuine simulated leather.
2. I suggest that the victim then tried to defend himself with this feather, cried the prosecuting attorney dramatically.
3. There was an uproar in the courtroom. How could he defend himself against a 12-gauge shotgun with a feather? was the most common question.
4. Well, suggested the prosecutor, since he couldn't reach the banana in time, the feather was the best he could do.
5. At this, the defendant leaped to his feet and admitted that he was, indeed,

guilty. How did you know about the banana? he muttered as he was led away.

6. Elementary, my dear Winston, laughed the lawyer, misquoting the great Sherlock Holmes who had said much the same thing.
7. Draw! Slap leather! yelled the gunfighter. With great calm, the sheriff replied Huh?
8. Jordan admitted that it was a terrific idea, but added that he was too tired to attend.
9. Can you find the relevant passage? asked the teacher as she leafed through Leacock's short story My Banking Career.
10. Oh! said Miss Manitoba. This is such a thrill and honour that I don't know what to say or anything.

5

Now, try this final test of your ability to place quotation marks appropriately, and to insert the necessary punctuation with them. (There are no answers provided for this exercise.)

1. Sink the Bismarck! became the cry of the Royal Navy.
2. I wish that you'd let me tell them how angry I am.
3. Let's just drop the subject, Charles said Diana. I'm afraid this is going to lead to an argument.
4. After the first date, Gordon swore Never again!
5. Foster Hewitt's words have echoed down through the years as the ultimate expression of hockey achievement He shoots! He scores!
6. Barbara enjoys many winter sports, but often says her favourite is après-ski.
7. Finally! I cried. The end is in sight at last!
8. It's a nice little vintage, the connoisseur sniffed importantly, I suspect you'll be rather amused by its pretensions.
9. What did he say whispered Joan. Did you understand any of it.
10. Smoking is very good for you coughed Jon. Seeing the smoke come out of your mouth reaffirms that you're still alive and breathing. Why else do you suppose people don't enjoy smoking in the dark he added.

---

chapter 17

The Colon

The colon functions as an "introducer." When a statement is followed by a list or by one or more examples, the colon between the statement and what follows alerts the reader to what is coming.

> We have only two choices: for or against.
>
> There are three things I can't stand: brussels sprouts, cats, and Sylvester Stallone's films.
>
> One person prevented her rise to wealth and fame: herself.

The statement that precedes the colon must be a complete sentence (independent clause). Therefore, a colon can never come immediately after *is* or *are*. For example, the use of the colon in the sentence

> Two things I cannot stand are: cats and brussels sprouts.

is incorrect because the statement before the colon is not a complete sentence.

The colon, then, follows a complete statement and introduces a list or example that defines or amplifies something in the statement. The information after the colon very often answers the question "what?" or "who?"

> There is a new danger to consider: (what?) inflation.
>
> He peered into the clear water to see his favourite friend: (who?) himself.

The colon is also used after a complete sentence introducing a quotation.

> Irving Layton is not fond of academic critics: "There hasn't been a writer of power and originality during the past century who hasn't had to fight his way to acceptance against the educated pipsqueaks hibernating in universities." (Layton, in a letter to *The Montreal Star*)

The uses of the colon can be summed up as follows:

The colon follows an independent clause and introduces one of three things: examples, a list, or a quotation.

Exercises

1

Put a check next to the sentences that are correctly punctuated. Check your answers on p. 306 before going on.

1. _____Two of the most common causes of failure are laziness and lack of self-discipline.
2. _____Only one thing was needed a boat.
3. _____He tried three different tactics: phone calls, flowers, and flattery.
4. _____On the list we must include: chips, mix, ice, and peanuts.
5. _____The instructor's first words were not encouraging: "Half of you are going to fail, and the other half won't get jobs."
6. _____Three qualities of a good quarterback are: leadership, intelligence, and physical strength.
7. _____There are two things that every ambitious person strives for: money and power.
8. _____The pond is: deep and cold.
9. _____Dogs have many qualities that make them superior to cats; loyalty, intelligence, working ability, and friendliness.
10. _____Let me give you an example, Louis Riel.

2

Put a check next to the sentences that are correctly punctuated. Check your answers before going on to exercise 3.

1. _____I'd like to help: but I can't.
2. _____I'll take the following volunteers, John, Susan, David, and Colin.
3. _____We'll have to go back to get: tent poles, matches, and paddles.
4. _____Two very good centres were Beliveau and Apps.
5. _____The debate will be lively if they choose a certain topic: religion.
6. _____No one wants to go with him, for two very good reasons money and time.
7. _____He's involved in all types of athletics: skiing, hiking, hockey, and football, to name a few.
8. _____My boss is so mean she must be: bitter or crazy.
9. _____She won more medals at the Games than we expected: two gold and a bronze.
10. _____They were unlucky twice: when they bought that car and when they sold it.

3

Insert colons in the following sentences where necessary, and then check your answers. If you find you've made any mistakes, review the explanation, and be sure you understand why your answers were wrong.

1. You'll succeed only if you win the lottery or marry money.
2. They finally realized there was only one course open to them obedience.
3. Gary had trouble with his canoe it tipped over and then sank.
4. There is someone who can save us, though, Captain Canuck!
5. He tossed and turned all night and found the same images recurring in his dreams a river and a wolf.
6. His body was beyond the point of exhaustion, but he tried to force himself on by thinking of one thing victory.
7. They tried to make ends meet by making their own candles, soap, and butter.
8. I have a very large garden, but it grows only two things tomatoes and weeds.
9. She has one goal that she is determined to achieve the world record.
10. Two issues remained to be settled wages and benefits.

4

Correct the incorrectly punctuated sentences in exercise 1.

5

Correct the incorrectly punctuated sentences in exercise 2.

6

As a test of your ability to use colons, put a check before sentences that are correctly punctuated, then go back and correct the ones that are wrong. (There are no answers given for this exercise.)

1. _____Several exercises are particularly beneficial for the heart: cycling, swimming, walking.
2. _____Two of my favourite desserts are: apple pie and strawberry custard.
3. _____In order to win, you'll have to make him tired: he's not in very good shape.
4. _____Many breeds of dogs work for their living: collies, shepherds, and huskies are three of them.
5. _____Parents ask such interesting questions: "Who do you think you are?"
6. _____Jeff has everything one could want in life except one thing: happiness.
7. _____There are many places I would like to go besides Japan, Australia, and Greece.
8. _____He is trying to become what he has always admired: an Olympic figure skater.
9. _____Instead of lasagne, let's serve: spaghetti, a salad, and crusty bread.
10. _____You should come with us because we're: fun, lively, wealthy, and youthful.

---

chapter 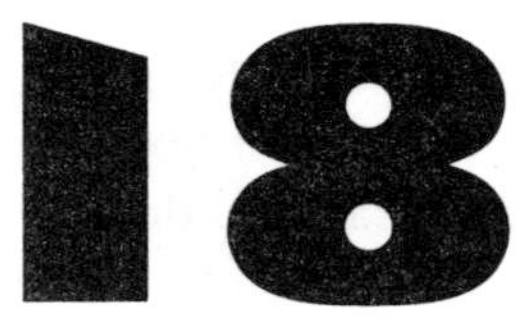

The Comma

The comma is the most frequently used and the most frequently misused punctuation mark. The omission of a necessary comma can distort the meaning of a sentence. Unnecessary commas ("comma-itis") can distract the reader and give the sentence a jerky quality. Perhaps nothing is so sure a sign of a competent writer as the correct use of commas, so it is very important that you master them. This chapter presents four rules that will give you a good indication of when you should use a comma. If the sentence you are writing is not covered by one of the four rules, remember this:

> When in doubt, leave the comma out!

Four Comma Rules

In this section we will present the four most helpful rules for using the comma. Here's the first rule:

> Use commas to separate items in a series of three or more.

Required subjects are math, English, bookkeeping, and business law.

Walk up the hill, turn left, go two blocks, and you'll be there.

Henry went to the show, Joan went home in tears, Norah and Phil talked until dawn, and I went upstairs to bed.

The comma before the *and* at the end of the list is optional; use it or leave it out, but be consistent.

Exercise

1

Insert commas where necessary in the following sentences. Check your answers on p. 307.

1. Careful investment of money and time can lead to wealth fame and happiness.
2. Cats and dogs make the best pets.
3. Does anyone remember John Paul George and Ringo?
4. Country-music fans and rock fans sat side by side and enjoyed the music.
5. Cutting the lawn washing the dishes and doing the shopping are my least favourite activities.
6. MacDonald Laurier Borden and Pearson are four dissimilar men who have at least one thing in common.
7. He is an all-round athlete who enjoys many sports: skating skiing cycling riding and hunting.
8. She has strong ambition a cool head good health and an inquiring mind; everyone hates her.
9. He really wants to get married, but he can't decide between Monika and Kim.
10. Many people see Canada as a land where only French is spoken ice and snow are year-round hazards and violent hockey is the only pastime.

Here is the second rule:

> Use comma(s) to separate from the rest of the sentence any word or expression that is not *essential* to the sentence's meaning or that means the same as something else in the sentence.

Writing business letters isn't difficult, if you're careful.

The phrase "if you're careful" is not essential to the meaning of the sentence, so it's separated from the rest of the sentence by a comma.

Stephen Leacock, one of the world's great humorists, was a professor of economics at McGill.

The phrase "one of the world's great humorists" means the same as "Stephen Leacock." The two expressions refer to the same person, so the second is set off by commas. When a nonessential word or phrase occurs in the middle of a sentence, rather than at the beginning or the end, be sure to put commas *both* before and after it.

If it were up to me, Judy, I'd hire you right now.

The word "Judy," the name of the person spoken to, is not essential to the meaning of the sentence, so it's set off by commas.

Exercise

2

Insert commas where necessary in the following sentences. Check your answers before going on.

1. He is you know one of our best teachers.
2. Sandy Wilson a B.C. film-maker made *My American Boyfriend.*
3. You'll have to do better than that Steve if you want to join us.
4. Despite her reputation, she is we have found out fairly bright.
5. Listening to music is a perfect way to relax after a tough day at school.
6. One of my favourite performers is Gordon Lightfoot the former Presley imitator from Orillia.
7. Where will you go now Heather?
8. Hockey seats despite the huge increase in prices are still always sold out in Toronto and Montreal.
9. The bride in a departure from tradition wore a yellow pant suit.
10. We tried all of us to be of some help.

The third rule is as follows:

> Place a comma between independent clauses when they are joined by these transition words:
>
> | | | |
> |---|---|---|
> | and | nor | for |
> | or | but | yet |
> | so | | |

It was a good party, but last year's was better.
I'm not speaking to her, so you'll have to tell her.
I can't make it to class, yet I feel I should go.
Ross is a good student, for he studies hard.

Be sure that the sentence contains two independent clauses rather than a single subject and a multiple verb (see p. 35 for more explanation of this).

We ate very well in Paris and gained 3 kg each. (Here, We is the subject, and there are two verbs: ate and gained. No comma is needed between two verbs with a single subject.)

We ate very well in Paris, and each of us gained 3 kg. (This sentence has two independent clauses — we ate and each gained — joined by an *and*. The comma is required here.)

Exercise

3

Insert commas where necessary in the following sentences. Then check your answers.

1. He and I are good friends yet we sometimes argue.
2. Now we'll have to try bribery or we can resort to force.
3. We can't win this game nor can we afford to lose it.
4. The car swerved wildly but it narrowly missed the crossing guard.
5. She tried and tried and soon her efforts paid off.
6. I'd like to buy a house as an investment but I can't afford the down payment right now.
7. My part-time job isn't very rewarding so I'm coming back to school next fall.
8. There are not many dangers so we must conquer our fear of failure.
9. This is her last semester so she's concentrating on school for a change.
10. Clutching his wounded shoulder he fell through the air but he managed to land on his feet.

Finally, here is the fourth comma rule:

> Put a comma after any word or group of words that comes before an independent clause.

Charley, you aren't paying attention. (The second rule applies here, too.)
Though tattered and torn, the book was worth a fortune.
Wherever you go, remember me.
If that's all there is, we'd better buy more.
'Until he got his promotion, he was quite friendly.

Exercise

Write out the four comma rules on a sheet of paper. Then do the exercise.

4

Insert commas where necessary in the following sentences. Check your answers when you're done.

1. In the end quality will win.
2. John if you don't quiet down you'll have to leave.
3. If there were any justice I'd have been rewarded for what I did.

4. Well I don't believe it!
5. When the sun came up in a clear blue sky we all sighed with relief.
6. Adorned with blue bows her shoes clashed with her green outfit.
7. Moved beyond words he was able only to gesture his thanks.
8. Carefully placing one foot in front of the other she managed to walk along the white line for several metres.
9. Falling staggering to his feet then falling again he stumbled painfully towards the finish line.
10. Where a huge hardwood forest had stood now there was only blackened ground.

One final note about the comma, before you try your hand at the review exercises: never place a *single* comma between a subject and its verb:

> *Right*: Adam and Liz are going into business.
> *Never*: Adam and Liz, are going into business.

Two commas between a subject and its verb are all right, however, *if* they are setting off nonessential material:

> Adam and Liz, both recent graduates, are going into business.

Exercises

Insert commas where necessary in the following exercises. Check your answers to each set of ten and make sure you understand any mistakes before you go on to the next exercise.

5

1. The job interview isn't so bad if you're prepared relaxed and confident.
2. With a shout of glee the boys ran to the heavily laden Christmas tree.
3. There is something wrong here but I haven't yet determined what it is.
4. In the end they'll be caught so all we have to do is wait.
5. George Washington the first president of the United States was an officer in the British army before the American Revolution.
6. Charlottetown Quebec and Kingston were the sites of conferences that eventually led to Confederation in 1867.
7. Well Mrs. O'Hara if that's the best you can do it's out of my hands.
8. The Great Lakes form an inland passageway by which the great seagoing ships reach the heart of the North American continent.
9. A good dictionary used properly can be an important tool for developing a mature vocabulary.
10. If there were any point in complaining I would have protested long ago but I don't think anything can change their course of action now.

6

1. My world is made up of handsome men fast cars loud music expensive clothes and other dreams.
2. The movie despite some excellent action sequences was a failure because of the terrible script.
3. If starvation and lack of recognition made great artists Canada would be a land of Picassos.
4. The letter of application is the most important document you will ever write yet you have spent only an hour composing it.
5. Wrapping the watch in a handkerchief he produced a mallet and smashed the expensive timepiece to smithereens or so it appeared.
6. The retirement of Bobby Orr from hockey was the end of an era for the game but those who saw him play will never forget it.
7. In the 1960s blue jeans became a uniform for the young but now they are popular only as very casual attire and a much more fashionable look has emerged.
8. Despite some early problems the National Gallery in Ottawa has become one of the most interesting and exciting exhibits in North America don't you think?
9. There you've gone and broken it again!
10. Doing punctuation exercises is tedious work but is cleaner than tuning the car.

7

1. Your fall order which we received last week has been filled.
2. An excellent pool is available for those who like to swim and for those who play golf there is a beautiful eighteen-hole course.
3. John realizing his position resigned.
4. Inside the piano was going at full blast.
5. What you hear what you read and what you think all help to form your intellectual background.
6. Quickly girls or we'll be late.
7. Ever since I have been a regular threatre goer.
8. A few days after they sailed the boat sprang a leak.
9. A fine fellow a member of the yacht club was drowned.
10. Antonio's grandmother was very short black haired and extremely thin.

8

1. When you enter the store go to the counter on your left ask for Ms Bertrand and tell her that you want to see the latest prints.

2. These cold wet grey days are not good for the crops.
3. The thick syrup boiled over and spilled on the stove on the table and on the floor.
4. Alice was neither wife nor mother.
5. Conflicts have occurred between students and faculty students and administration and faculty and administration.
6. However capable he was he failed miserably in this case.
7. Oh excuse me. I didn't hear you come in.
8. Nearby an old oak lifted its gaunt limbs to the sky.
9. Mr. Smith the head of the department despite his vast knowledge of his subject couldn't change a light bulb if his life depended on it.
10. I dressed you will be amazed to learn in two minutes flat and was out the door before his knock had stopped echoing.

9[1]

1. After they had eaten Big Tom pushed the cracked and dirty supper things to the back of the table and took the baby from its high chair carefully so as not to spill the flotsam of bread crumbs and boiled potatoes from the chair to the floor.
2. He undressed the youngster talking to it in the old dialect trying to awaken its interest.
3. He stood for long minutes at the side of the bed staring trying to diagnose the child's restlessness into something other than what he feared.
4. For long minutes after the baby was asleep he talked on letting the victorious words fill the small cabin so that they shut out the sounds of the Northern Ontario night: the buzz of mosquitoes the far-off bark of a dog the noise of the cars and transport trucks passing on the gravelled road.
5. The trailer residents were not yet awake so he sat down on the wooden walk leading to the shower room his baskets resting on the ground in a half circle behind him.
6. This done he stood and watched the headlights of the cars run along the trees bordering the road like a small boy's stick along a picket fence.
7. Big Tom followed behind all the anguish and frustration drained from him so that there was nothing left to carry him into another day.
8. He was becoming worried about the baby and her presence while it might not make the baby well would mean that there was someone else to share his fears.
9. The child was feverish its breath noisy and fast.

[1] *The sentences in this exercise are adapted from "One-Two-Three Little Indians," by Hugh Garner, Copyright © Hugh Garner. Reprinted by permission of McGraw-Hill Ryerson Limited.*

10. One by one as he waited the lights went out until only the sign lit up a small area at the gate.

10

1. Despite the negative feelings of some and the outright often violent hostility of others the project will proceed on time.
2. Put the casserole in the oven at four o'clock but make sure the roast is cooked before you do.
3. Josey whom you know from last summer has been asking for your address but I thought I should ask your permission before I send it.
4. Prowling around the old cemetery we came upon the grave of a young child who died during a flu epidemic.
5. Art is something I know little about except that oils watercolours and pastels require different skills and techniques.
6. Flattery the old saying goes will get you nowhere but this has not been my experience.
7. Robert collects coins listens to some types of music and skis when he can but otherwise devotes all of his time to his appearance.
8. Computers and robots are certain to be part of everyone's future unless there's a nuclear holocaust in which case no one has a future.
9. Certain to feel better after a good meal I left the party and went to a nearby steak house.
10. Before I left however I managed to offend the host insult the hostess and humiliate the guest of honour.

11

One of the teachers at our school a mild-mannered man under most circumstances burst into my office one day last spring and he spent twenty minutes pouring out his frustration into my startled ears. Having spent several hours preparing for a class on stress management he had been confronted by a student who asked if they were going to do anything important in class that day. Teachers are asked this question on a regular basis and every time it happens they wince. Most however are able to control themselves and make some sarcastic comment. This teacher had been asked once too often I'm afraid. He ranted raved and roared despite my best efforts to calm him down but gradually he ran out of steam and finally collapsed into a quivering blob. Seeing that he was now more or less under control I told him that most teachers have developed defence mechanisms to counteract the trauma of being asked that question. My favourite response is to ask why today's class should be any different from all the other classes in the term; since we have done nothing of importance in any other class it seems unlikely that we would be doing anything significant now. Some students take this as sarcasm but others assume that I'm giving them permission to skip. The teacher in my office found my reassurance helpful I'm sure because he smiled as he left my office on his way to teach another class on how to handle stress.

12

In this paragraph, we have incorporated many of the kinds of comma errors most often found in student writing. Remove all unnecessary commas and insert commas where they should go. This might be a good time to review the four rules . . . and to remind yourself of the first comma commandment: "When in doubt, leave the comma out!"

The Canadian appetite, for sports entertainment, seems insatiable. In the past, three sports dominated the year for the sports fan but now thanks to specialty television, some very unusual and exotic competitions are finding fans, in this country. Australian-rules football a game that belies its name by seeming to have no rules is gaining in popularity, though purely as a spectator sport. Triathlons, biathlons, marathons, mini-marathons, and a host of similar endurance events, are now avidly watched, by the armchair athlete and enthusiastically entered, by the physically fit. Sumo wrestling while not accessible to most of us, as a participatory activity, seems to have a devoted following and even darts and lawn bowling, have their supporters. And then there is, golf. To some watching golf on television, is as exciting as watching paint dry, but during inclement weather when they can't be on the course themselves, golfers follow their heroes' every televised step and agonize with them, over every shot for hours. The challenge, for Canadian jocks of both sexes, and all ages is to tear themselves away from these various spectator entertainments in order, to play their favourite sports.

13

Correct the punctuation in this paragraph by adding commas in appropriate places. No answers are provided for this exercise.

Have you ever had days when nothing goes right? Despite my generally high level of intelligence and reasonable manual dexterity I seem to have more than my share of such days. In fact now that I think of it most days seem to have at least a small element of disaster in them. Last Tuesday I think it was I went out and bought a new telephone. At the store I was convinced the grey was a perfect match for the kitchen where it was to go. The brown blue and white all had their appeal but the grey was definitely the best match. Naturally when I arrived home it was made very clear to me that brown any shade of brown would have been a better choice. However it didn't really matter because the phone jack didn't match the ones in the house so the thing wouldn't work anyway. Not one to despair easily I leaped back into the car and journeyed the fifteen kilometres back to the phone store neatly hitting the rush hour traffic just at its peak. Once in the store I sought out the young lady who had sold me the phone. She would be delighted to change the instrument but there would be a standard $14 fee to exchange colours. Whimpering softly I fled.

chapter 19

The Semicolon

The colon and semicolon are often confused and used as if they were interchangeable. They serve very different functions, however, and their correct use can dramatically improve a reader's understanding of your writing. Here is one function of the semicolon:

> The semicolon can replace the period; in other words, it can appear between two independent clauses.

You should use the semicolon when the two clauses (sentences) you are joining are closely connected in meaning or when there is a cause-and-effect relationship between them.

> I'm too tired; I can't stay awake any longer.
> There's a good movie on tonight; it's a Canadian film called *In Praise of Older Women*.

A period could have been used instead of the semicolon in either of these sentences, but the close connection between the clauses prompted the writer to use a semicolon.

Certain connecting or transition words are sometimes put between independent clauses to show cause and effect or continuation of an idea. Words used in this way must be preceded by a semicolon and followed by a comma.[1]

> Put a semicolon in front of these words and a comma after:
>
> | | | |
> |---|---|---|
> | ; consequently, | ; besides, | ; furthermore, |
> | ; however, | ; for example, | ; in fact, |
> | ; therefore, | ; nevertheless, | ; thus, |
> | ; moreover, | | |

> We had hiked for two hours; consequently, we were glad for the rest.
> There are only two of us; however, we're both pretty big.
> The sun was very hot; therefore, we stopped at an ice-cream store.

[1] *Sometimes the words listed in the box are used in sentences as nonessential expressions rather than as connecting words. They are then separated from the rest of the sentence by commas.* *See chapter 18, p. 173.*

Note that the semicolon and transition word are used *together* to connect the two independent clauses.

Sometimes semicolons should be used in a list instead of commas:

> To make a lengthy, complex list easier to read and understand, put semicolons between the items instead of commas.

Here's an example:

> A few items are necessary: matches to start a fire; an axe or hatchet to cut wood; cooking utensils and eating implements; and, of course, the food itself.

Exercises

1

Put a check next to the sentences that are correctly punctuated. Check your answers on p. 312 before continuing.

1. _____He sat down in a convenient bar; he was very thirsty.
2. _____He sat down near a refreshing stream; for he was very tired.
3. _____My cats get along fine with the dog; it's each other that they hate.
4. _____It's a beautiful day; just right for a long walk.
5. _____Six of the Indian nations joined together in a loose union, they were called Iroquois.
6. _____The lawn, a little ragged, needs to be cut, the hedge, shrubs, and ivy need to be trimmed, the flowers need to be watered, and, not least of all, the gardener needs to be paid.
7. _____I'd like to help, however, I'm supposed to rest all day.
8. _____We reached Canoe Lake in time to meet the others; in fact, we arrived a little ahead of schedule.
9. _____Winnipeg is my favourite city; someday I'm going to move there.
10. _____Winter is something only Canadians really understand; it has shaped this country more than the railways, the politicians, and even the founding peoples.

2

Put a check next to the sentences that are correctly punctuated. Then check your answers.

1. _____It's far too expensive; besides, we don't really need one.
2. _____There are only a few who could catch him; and I'm sure she isn't one of them.
3. _____Coffee prices are ridiculous, yet I still must have my morning cup or two.

4. _____She wants to be an Olympic gymnast; consequently, she spends six hours a day in training.
5. _____We'll have to go soon; for it's getting late.
6. _____The weather is bad; I have a cold; the electricity is out; and, to top it all off, my in-laws are coming for dinner.
7. _____If ever there were a time to act; it is now.
8. _____Some people are skilled in many fields; Gary, for example, is both a good plumber and a great cook.
9. _____She disobeyed the rules; so, she will have to be punished.
10. _____She is always late, however, she's worth waiting for.

3

Correct the faulty punctuation in exercise 1.

4

Correct the faulty punctuation in exercise 2.

5

Insert commas and semicolons where necessary in these sentences. Then check your answers carefully.

1. There seems to be no end to the work that must be done furthermore there isn't enough time in which to do it.
2. There must be a way or we're finished before we've begun.
3. I can't afford a Porsche therefore I drive a Volkswagen.
4. Shirley is one of my favourite people she can always cheer me up.
5. There will be ample opportunity to finish your homework but right now I need your help.
6. The flooring was all knotty pine yellowed with age the walls and furniture were of such design and colour as to blend with it.
7. Brock was killed early in the morning but the Americans were driven from Queenston Heights by nightfall.
8. Canada's history is not a very violent one however there were several rebellions of note.
9. John has gone away to become a teacher Martha now has twin baby girls Kevin is unemployed Julie is a lawyer or stockbroker (I forget which) and Paul is as usual drifting from job to job.
10. When the rain started they were trapped in the open nevertheless they stayed where they were until it let up and then watched the game with enjoyment despite being a little wet.

6

Correct the punctuation in these sentences[2] by changing commas to semicolons or colons where necessary.

1. They are taken from twelve collections I have published during this period, except for retouching lightly two or three poems, I have left them stand as they were.
2. To these I have added the following poems, "The Warm Afterdark," which I wrote in 1957, and "Divinity."
3. My father was an ineffectual visionary, he saw God's footprint in a cloud and lived only for his books and meditations.
4. Luckily for us, she was not, she was tougher than nails, shrewd and indomitable.
5. At this point, Byron's contempt for the poet becomes understandable, my mother's commonsensical expletives begin ringing in my ears.
6. Not who is winning the Cold War is the big issue confronting mankind, but this, will the Poet, as a type, join the Priest, the Warrior, the Hero, and the Saint as melancholy museum pieces?
7. They belong to a period of my life that is now behind me, a period of testing, confusion, ecstasy.
8. Unlike the scholar or literary historian who writes about life, the poet enjoys it, *lives* it.
9. If he has the true vocation, he will take risks, for him there can be no "dogmatic slumbers."
10. I, too, have seen the footprint in the cloud, though somewhat gorier than my father saw it.

7

Correct the punctuation in these sentences by using colons and semicolons where necessary.

1. Computers are marvellous tools, fast, efficient, accurate, but dumb. They remind me of a secretary I used to know, she's now my boss.
2. To put the matter in perspective, I'd like you to ask yourselves a question "What do I wish to accomplish?"
3. Taking a pad and pencil from the desk, he began to write, soon he was finished and showed us his creation, a limerick.
4. Push the concept of defeat from your mind, concentrate instead solely on victory.

[2] *Adapted from the Foreword to* A Red Carpet for the Sun, *by Irving Layton. Reprinted by permission of The Canadian Publishers, McClelland and Stewart Limited, Toronto.*

5. If I could push defeat from my mind, there would be only a vast emptiness left, victory is impossible when you play on this team.
6. Buying a house is a giant step towards maturity, which is why I shall live in an apartment until I'm at least 50.
7. If only jobs were as easy to get now as they were when our parents graduated from school, then we'd get the same chance they had to prove what we can do.
8. Noreen wants to be helpful, it's just that she is so clumsy that one of two things always happens, either she breaks something or she hurts herself.
9. I have tried weight-lifting, squash, jogging, and swimming, which is why I am tired, stiff, and bored.
10. Callous disregard for authority, an inability to apply patience to the solution of problems, and a fascination with the material, the trivial, and the impermanent, these are the legacies of the television age.

8

Correct these sentences wherever necessary.

1. We're unhappy about our teacher's evaluation procedures which are: irrational, arbitrary, unfair, and often malicious.
2. Cornering at a dangerous speed, the police car swerved into the oncoming lane, luckily, no one was coming.
3. One of the products of the computer age is increased leisure, and this, in turn, had led to a vastly increased interest in one of the enthusiasms of this generation; physical fitness.
4. A glance at the calendar will reveal that there are only 212 shopping days left until my birthday: that's just enough time for you to find the present I deserve.
5. Put the coffee on the table and the sandwiches by the window, I'll eat when I've finished this exercise.
6. The Four Horsemen of the Apocalypse are: Conquest, Slaughter, Famine, and Death.
7. They are another very good example of Biblical figures who have entered the language, others are: Samson and Delilah, David and Goliath, Solomon and Sheba.
8. After calling the meeting to order, the chairman voiced his chief concern, fund raising.
9. Public speaking has become one of my favourite activities, however, I'm still very shy when dealing with people individually.
10. The Canadian political scene has become much less interesting since the departure of Pierre Trudeau, whether you like him or not, he left his mark

on a generation of Canadians who were influenced by the phenomenon of: Trudeaumania.

9

Correct these sentences as necessary.

1. One thing always returned to his mind when he thought of his tour of Europe; the delicious beer.
2. While France had excellent wine, the more northern countries were famous for their breweries; a fact he came to appreciate.
3. My diary tells me that on this date last year; you gave me a dozen roses; I'm wondering if the romance is gone when I see that this year's gift is: a potted geranium.
4. There's nothing wrong with potted geraniums, I know lots of elderly people who positively adore them: it just happens that I'm seventeen, that's all.
5. A fear of heights is consistent with your other phobias; fear of falling, fear of failure, and fear of flying.
6. Reading spy novels is a waste of time, I admit, but it's better than sitting in front of the tube being sold products I don't need, and learning intimate details about the lives of people I don't care about.
7. Sing another of the old songs for us; we enjoy reliving those years with you: even though we weren't born then.
8. The Math Department is offering a seminar for English teachers, I understand it deals with addition and subtraction.
9. Tax forms become my big concern every April, the deadline always finds me in the same state: terrified.
10. We have reached the end at last, now there is only one thing left to do, check our answers before continuing.

10

This exercise will challenge your mastery of punctuation. There are many different ways to correct this paragraph, but use semicolons and colons wherever appropriate. (There are no answers provided for this exercise.)

It has been widely predicted by those who fear the future that we may be entering an age of sloth, as machines take more and more of the work and man is left more and more with leisure, the fearful suggest, man will cease to use his mind and his body he will become little more than a vegetable, leaving the challenging and creative work to his creations robots and computers one need only look at the recent past however to get a clue about the near future work has played a less important role in man's life for a generation or so now and it is instructive to see what this has brought about have the eight hour day and five day week made him less fit physically or less active mentally of course not indeed, the opposite is true the development of fitness centres, recreation clubs, and sports facilities has paralleled the decline in the physical demands of work similarly many new facilities have sprung up in the past several years to cater to man's intellectual health continuing education programs, adult education, learning clubs and creative associations.

---

chapter 20

Capital Letters and Punctuation Review

Capital Letters

Capital letters should be used in a few specific places and nowhere else. Some people seem to have "capitalitis": they put capital letters on words randomly, regardless of whether the words are nouns, adjectives, or verbs. Like "exclamatosis," "capitalitis" is a disease communicated by comic books, which capitalize every word.

Not very many people have this problem; if you are in the majority who generally use capitals properly, skip this chapter and go on to something else. If you are puzzled about capital letters, though, or have readers who are puzzled by your use of them, read on.

Capitalize the first letters of the following:

1. the first word of a sentence:

   Put out the garbage.

2. the names of specific persons:

   Grant Fuhr
   Mordecai Richler

   the names of specific places:

Alberta	Elm St.
Mars	Morocco
Oz	Regina

   and the names of specific things:

   St. Lawrence River
   British North America Act
   Hilltop Towers

3. the days of the week and the months of the year (but not the seasons):

Monday	July
Friday	summer
October	winter

4. the titles of specific people (but not the names of their positions), books, films, and courses (but not subject names, unless they're languages):

Governor General Ray Hnatyshyn	*but*	the position of governor general
Pope John Paul II	*but*	the position of pope
Mr. and Ms. O'Connor		
The Bare Essentials		
Citizen Kane		
Mathematics 101	*but*	the subject of mathematics
English 101; the English language		

5. the names of specific companies, businesses, organizations, and departments:

   Chateau Gai
   Arc Industries
   Winnipeg Rotary Club
   Conservative Party
   Personnel Department

Exercises

I

Correct the capitalization in these sentences. Answers are on p. 315.

1. henry smith wants to be a prince when he grows up.
2. the queen of england visited ontario last winter.
3. Confident of Victory, we marched on Paris, led by our Heroic Captain.
4. The Optimist Club of Canada sponsors a scholarship to the University of Alberta.
5. Laurie tries hard, but she'll never be as good at Typing as Frank.
6. *Silent Partner* was a Canadian-made film that featured International Stars but also many Young Canadian Actors.
7. Do you think fords are better than chevs in the middle price range?
8. We study English and mathematics, as well as our major subjects.
9. High School is a time of Growing and Development for Young People, a time for them to find a Direction for the rest of their Lives.

10. Office Supplies are in great demand, so, if you need pens or paper, you'd better see Ms Carlo in supplies right away.

2

Correct the capitalization.

1. Jamie sue rode down Dufferin street every day in the Fall to look at the leaves.
2. I went with my English Professor to the Calgary stampede.
3. Alan goes to the City on Weekends to see french films.
4. He told his parents he was at university and then went off to spend the winter in Mexico.
5. I want to grow up to be a Queen, or at least a Company President.
6. Jane studied Cooking, Art History, and French in Europe last Summer.
7. The Committee we had elected deprived us of our Human Rights.
8. He considers himself Liberal on matters such as the Dress Code.
9. Jim works for the Phone Company, which has an office on a Street near his home.
10. Are the doctor's rates too high?

3

1. Following my failure in science and math, I renewed my interest in english and spanish.
2. The governor general is the representative of Queen Elizabeth.
3. On our trip to alberta we were joined by winnifred in winnipeg, reginald

in regina, and henry in saskatoon; henry really didn't fit in with our group very well.

4. While we think of ourselves as Liberal-minded, we give our support to a Political Party that tends to attract the Conservative element: social credit.
5. In Quebec, the Premier is very influential not only in the policies of his Province, but in the politics of the whole Country.
6. All canadians should learn french and english to retain the historic cultural uniqueness of their Nation.
7. Our principal made the presentation, as had every principal before him as long as anyone in town could remember.
8. Few Teachers and even fewer Students really have a firm grasp of the Art of Poetry, though many think they can write Poems and judge the work of Others.
9. Among Canada's great historic waterways, the St. Lawrence river, the Mackenzie river, the Fraser river, and the Red river are, to me, the most interesting because of the great Historic Figures who are associated with each.
10. Putting partisan politics aside, we decided to follow the advice of governor general Ray Hnatyshyn and view the Candidates with an open mind and vote for the best person, rather than for the Party that promised the most.

4

Correct the capitalization in this paragraph. (No answers have been provided for this exercise.)

Never satisfied when things were quiet, Richard returned to france in the hopes of tracing his Father's family. In a small Village, just outside Lyons, he discovered an ancient family Bible that had been used to record the births and deaths of a branch of the family during the Seventeenth Century. Using this information, he was able to conclude that his Parternal Ancestors came from Switzerland. Accordingly, he moved on to Geneva, where his fluent french and english were both put to the test in getting access to the records he needed. Finally, he appealed to the mayor, and a Clerk from the Municipal Office came to help him with his quest. It was with the help of this Clerk that Richard finally discovered the Truth: the founder of his family was hanged in 1177 for stealing sheep! He was descended from a Thief.

Punctuation Review

The next five exercises will test your mastery of all punctuation studied in Unit Four. Go through them carefully, and check your answers before going on to the next set. If you make a mistake, go back to the chapter on that piece of punctuation and be sure you understand the rules that apply.

I

1. Enjoy the view we called out as they left for the mountaintop, we had wisely decided to wait for them in a meadow halfway up.
2. To be a millionaire by the time you are thirty, you will have to: take large risks, be lucky, and have creative ideas.
3. High School was indeed the best time of my life because I met the friends there that I would continue to see for many years and I learned the principles that were to guide me through later more difficult years.
4. The question of whether there is evolution doesn't worry most of the

people in my class, they're more concerned about whether there's a Dance on Friday.

5. Why won't he listen Marsha whispered tearfully.
6. With the crowd chanting Out Out the Referee had a hard time justifying his decision; a ten minute misconduct.
7. Typing as though his life depended on the completion of the assignment, Ted managed to get through the first chapter before supper, this left him with Chapter Two, The Next Day, to complete before bedtime.
8. The rain looked as though it would never let up so Gary and the two girls packed up to go home their vacation plans ruined.
9. Don't go, Angela fell to her knees and begged her friend to stay. Why must you leave now she asked, just when we're about to succeed.
10. You'll find he has just one fault my friend, he snores.

2

1. Jump. It's the only way out she cried.
2. Since there is so much time left why don't you go for a swim; or have a sauna.
3. If you keep this behaviour up, you'll certainly go a long way, all the way to jail.
4. Pushing past the horrified onlookers the Police Officer entered the building within minutes of the blast and encountered: chaos.
5. The Toronto Blue Jays like the Montreal Expos before them are winning friends among baseball fans in the United States.

6. Don't go near the water warned the twins' mother, however they were far too busy playing with the alligators to hear her.
7. My computer is a big improvement on the old typewriter I used to use, it still makes the same number of spelling errors though.
8. You'll never make it Stella we've got the whole building surrounded the detective yelled through his bullhorn, you might as well come out with your hands up.
9. Her lips curling into a sneer she replied you'll have to come in and get me copper.
10. The director his patience at an end screamed Cut. that scene is too long too boring and too bad. We'll have to take it again.

3

For having saved the Leprechaun's life Douglas was granted three wishes, the first he squandered on a mere one hundred dollars because he didn't believe the little man when he told Douglas that his wishes would come true. After more careful consideration Douglas wished again.

I want a bank account in a swiss bank he shouted and enough money so that I will never run out.

The leprechaun frowned and looked very disappointed in Douglas' wish but he screwed up his face went very red for a minute and then announced it's done but under his breath he muttered greedy young cub he needs a lesson.

Douglas was all ready with his next wish it was his greatest desire. He stared sternly at the leprechaun and in a loud voice said my last wish is the most important I want to live for one thousand years.

The tiny old man grinned then he screwed up his face and went very red for a minute. Finally he relaxed sighed a deep satisfied sigh and very pleased with himself walked twice around the young redwood tree that had just sprouted in front of him.

4

All too often it seems that the Canadian national pastime is complaining about the weather our hot summers are criticized because they're too hot while our springs are too wet our autumns too cool and our winters too long. If the climate is so bad here why does anyone live north of the U.S. border. Perhaps the problem is not that Canadians don't like living in Canada but rather that they love to complain.

The most popular sports teams in Canada were at one time those with the worst records; the Argonauts and the modern Maple Leafs. Could this popularity be due to the ample opportunity and scope they gave to their fans for complaint. Not only do we bemoan the losing record of such teams but when they do win we dwell with glee on the possibilities of disaster for next year.

The same syndrome might be seen in our attitude towards our Canadian heroes, it has often been said "that we are a nation without heroes" but I suspect that we have plenty of candidates: it's just that we enjoy complaining so much we try to find fault wherever we can and love pointing out the clay feet of our great figures. One cannot help but wonder how Canadians fare in heaven where everything is perfect, surely we must be desperately unhappy in such circumstances.

5

No answers have been provided for this last test of your punctuation skills.

1. I'd like to go with you John really I would but I've already promised Dennis that he'll be my escort at the dance, I guess we could meet afterwards at the restaurant though.
2. Movies such as Shivers Black Sunday and the Fog have not appealed to me since I saw Psycho as a teenager, I haven't been the same since.
3. The teacher cleared his throat to get their attention and then told them "to read chapter ten The Principle of Space Flight from their textbook The wonders of the Twentieth Century".
4. A warm bath and a cold drink are second only to one thing in my opinion, barbecued steak well done and covered in mushrooms onions steak-sauce and garlic.
5. Who was it who first said to succeed a woman must be twice as good as a man, fortunately that isn't difficult.
6. Drunk again, you'll have to learn to control your drinking my friend if you're going to live to see your fortieth birthday, it's only two years away.
7. Montreal St. John's Winnipeg and Medicine Hat all have a common theme in their history, the conflict between the native population and the European settler.

8. Running she said is thought to be bad for the joints, weight-lifting is just as bad. I think that all things considered I'd just as soon die in my bed with all my parts working as wear my body out bit by bit, wouldn't you.
9. Well it's time to pack up the homework put away the typewriter make some popcorn pull up the old easy chair and park myself in front of the TV set, the world series is on.
10. That my son is the way of the world, birth life death.

6

Write a paper of about two pages explaining how to do or make something or giving directions on how to get somewhere. Don't forget to check your spelling, sentence structure, and grammar. Pay particular attention to correct punctuation, and try to use an exclamation mark, a semicolon, and a colon at least once in the paper. Here are some topics you might choose from:

1. how to hitchhike
2. how to buy a used car
3. how to pick up girls/boys at a singles bar
4. how to win at Monopoly (poker, backgammon, bridge . . .)
5. how to prepare for a trip
6. how to choose a career (boss, husband/wife, college, apartment . . .)
7. how to cheat on a test
8. how to pour wine (stop a sneeze, throw a ball, pot a plant, go blonde . . .)
9. how to make someone happy
10. how to become unpopular

5

organizing your writing

chapter 21

Finding Something To Write About

Everybody knows that "content" is important in writing. Not so many seem to know that organization is just as important. In fact, you can't really separate the two: *what you say is how you say it.* Writing a paper (or an essay, or a report, or a letter, or anything else) is like doing a chemistry experiment: you need the right amount of the right ingredients, put together in the right proportions and in the right order. There are five steps to follow:[1]

1. choose a satisfactory subject;
2. choose the main points of your subject;
3. write a thesis statement

   OR

   write an outline;
4. write the paragraphs; and
5. revise the paper.

If you follow these steps faithfully, in order, we guarantee that you will write clear, organized papers.

Notice that when you get to step 3 you have a choice. You can choose to organize your paper either by means of a thesis statement or by means of an outline. The thesis-statement approach works well for very short papers — those no longer than about 400 words. An outline is necessary for longer papers and is often useful for organizing shorter papers, as well. (Ideally, you should learn to use both methods of organizing your writing; in fact, your teacher may insist that you do.)

Steps 1, 2, and 3 make up the preparation stage of the writing process. Be warned: these three steps will take you as long as — if not longer than — steps 4 and 5, which involve the actual writing. *The longer you spend on the preliminary steps, the less time your writing will take, and the better your paper will be.*

[1] *Some of the ideas presented in this unit are adapted from the approach developed by Sidney P. Moss in* Composition by Logic *(Belmont, Calif.: Wadsworth, 1966).*

Step 1: Choose a Subject

Unless you are assigned a specific subject by a teacher or by a superior at work, choosing your subject can be the most difficult part of writing a paper. Apply the following guidelines carefully, because no amount of instruction can make you write a good paper on something you don't know anything about or on something that is inappropriate for your purpose.

> A satisfactory subject is significant, single, specific, and supportable.

1. Your subject should be **significant**. As we have been suggesting all the way through this book, it is essential that you *keep your reader in mind*. Here, this means that you should write about something that someone would like to read about. Consider your audience and choose a subject that will be significant to that audience. This doesn't mean that you can't ever be humorous, but, unless you're another Stephen Leacock, an essay on "How I Deposit Money in My Bank" will probably be of little significance to your reader. The subject you choose must be worthy of the time and attention you expect your reader to give to your paper.

2. Your subject should be **single**. Don't try to do too much in your paper. A thorough discussion of one topic is much more satisfying to read than a skimpy, superficial treatment of several topics. A subject like "The Problems of League Expansion in Hockey and Other Sports" includes too much to be dealt with well in one paper. Limit yourself to a single topic, such as "The Problems of League Expansion in the NHL."

3. Your subject should be **specific**. This requirement is very closely tied to the "single" requirement. Given a choice between a broad, general topic and a narrow, specific one, you should choose the latter. In a short paper, you can't hope to say anything new or significant about a very large topic — "Employment Opportunities in Canada," for example. But you could write an interesting, detailed discussion on a more specific topic, such as "Employment Opportunities in Alberta's Hospitality Industry." You can narrow a broad subject by applying one more "limiting factors" to it. Try thinking of your subject in terms of a specific *kind*, or *time*, or *place*, or *number*, or *person* associated with it. To come up with the hospitality topic, for example, we limited the subject of employment opportunities in Canada in terms of both place and kind.

4. Your subject must be **supportable**. You must know something about the subject (preferably more than your reader knows about it), or you must be able to find out about it. Your discussion of your subject will be clear and convincing only if you can include examples, facts, quotations, descriptions, anecdotes, and other supporting details. Supporting evidence can be taken from your own experience or from the experience of other people. That is, your topic may or may not require you to do some research.

Exercises

1

Test the following subjects against the guidelines we've given. Can you tell what's wrong with them? Check your answers on p. 318.

1. rock and roll
2. the theory of evolution
3. the five senses
4. plucking your eyebrows
5. career possibilities in data processing and accounting
6. television is both good and bad
7. high school 100 years from now
8. my cat Fluffy
9. democracy is good
10. the dangers of skin diving and sky diving

2

Consider the following subjects in terms of the "4S" guidelines. Can you tell what's wrong with them?

1. air is necessary to life
2. some people are intelligent
3. the censorship of books and movies
4. money in other countries
5. famous Canadian women
6. how to use a pencil sharpener
7. predicting the future
8. today's teenagers have a hard time
9. taking out the garbage
10. the handicapped

3

List five subjects that you might choose to write about. Be sure each subject is significant, single, specific, and supportable.

Step 2: Choose the Main Points of Your Subject

Now that you have an appropriate subject for your paper, give some thought to the approach you're going to take to it. There are many possible ways of thinking and writing about a subject. In a short paper, you can deal effectively with only a few aspects of your topic. How do you decide what is the best approach to take? How do you decide which aspects of your subject to discuss, what **main points** to make and explain? One way is to make a list of everything you can think of that you might want to say about the subject. Some preliminary research may help, too; you may turn up some points about the subject that you hadn't thought of.

Another way — especially useful if you find you're stuck for ideas — is to ask yourself questions about your subject. Run your subject through this list of questions and see which one "fits" it best. (The symbol S stands for your subject.)

1. How is S made or done?
2. How does S work?
3. What are the main parts of S?
4. What are the main functions of S?
5. What are the important features or characteristics of S?
6. What are some significant examples of S?
7. What are the causes of S?
8. What are the effects or consequences of S?
9. What are the main kinds or types of S?
10. What are the similarities and/or differences between S and_____?
11. What are the main advantages (or disadvantages) of S?
12. What are the reasons for (or against) S?

These questions suggest some of the various ways of looking at or thinking about a subject. Most subjects will yield answers to more than one of these questions, but the question that produces the answers closest to what you want to say about your subject is the one that you should focus on. The answers to that question are the main points that you will discuss in your paper.

Here's how the procedure works. Assume you've been forced to accept as your subject "Writing Good Business Letters." Don't despair. Run down the list of questions until you find the one you can answer best. The process might go something like this:

1. How is a business letter written?
   No answer comes to mind. Scratch that question.
2. How does a business letter work?
   Silly question; it doesn't make sense.
3. What are the main parts of a business letter?
   Well, there are the inside address, the body, the salutation, and the complimentary close, but you don't know enough about these to write on them.
4. What are the main functions of the business letter?
   You can think of three: to request information, to place an order, and to complain about some product or service. This has possibilities, but you're not wildly enthusiastic about these aspects of your subject, so you go on.
5. What are the important characteristics of a good business letter?
   At last! Here's one you can answer satisfactorily. You know that a business letter should be clear, brief and to the point, and courteous. Assuming that you know (or can find out) a fair amount about these characteristics, you don't need to look any further. *Clarity, conciseness*, and *courtesy* are the main points of your subject that you will discuss in your paper. (Before you go any further, though, it's a good idea to apply the remaining

questions in the box to your subject, just to be sure there isn't another question that yields answers you like even better.)

Selecting the main points to write about isn't really a difficult process, but it can be time consuming. Don't rush. Take the necessary time; this is a crucial stage in the writing process.

Here are a few sample subjects, together with some main points that were discovered through this questioning procedure. Study this chart until you're sure you understand how to find suitable main points for any subject.

Subject	**Selected Question**	**Main Points**
a good teacher	5. What are the important characteristics of a good teacher?	— knowledge of one's field — ability to communicate this knowledge — respect for one's students
running for fitness	12. What are the reasons for people's interest in running?	— it improves one's physical condition — it improves one's mental condition — it is a low-cost approach to fitness
common-law relationships	11. What are the main disadvantages of common-law relationships?	— possible lack of commitment between partners — possible legal problems, should separation occur — possible lack of security for children born into such an arrangement
mental retardation	7. What are the causes of mental retardation?	— genetic defects — brain damage — early environmental deprivation
a successful party	1. How does one ensure a successful party?	— by inviting the right group of people — by planning the food and entertainment ahead of time — by providing a relaxed, friendly atmosphere
the accounting profession	9. What are the main kinds of accountants?	— Chartered Accountant — Registered Industrial Accountant — Certified General Accountant

As a general rule, you should try to identify *between two and five main ideas* for your subject. If you have only one main idea, you have a subject suitable for a paragraph, not an essay. If you have more than five, you have too much material for a short paper. Choose only the most important aspects of the subject, or else take another look at your subject to see whether it can be narrowed down somewhat.

Exercises

4

In this exercise, select a question from the box on p. 203 and come up with good main points for each subject.

Subject	**Selected Question**	**Main Points**
high school		
starting your own business		
my family's immigration to Canada		
living at home		
pop music		

5

For each of the five subjects you chose in exercise 3, list two to five main points. If suitable main points do not immediately leap to mind, apply the twelve questions in the box on p. 203 one at a time to your subject, until you find the one that fits best. The answers to that question are your main points.

Now take a close look at the main points you've chosen in exercise 5. It may be necessary to revise some of these before going any further. Are some points really too minor to bother with? Do any of the points overlap in meaning? Are there any points that are not really related to the subject?

To be completely satisfactory, the main points you have chosen must all be **significant** — worth writing a paragraph or more on. You shouldn't have any trivial ideas mixed in with the important ones.

Second, each of the main points you've chosen must be **different** from all the others: there must be no overlap in meaning. Check to be sure you haven't given two different labels to what is really only one aspect of the subject.

Third, the main points you have chosen must be clearly **related** to the subject. They must all be aspects of *that* subject, not some other subject. For example, if you're writing about the advantages of a subject, cross out any disadvantages that may have appeared on your list.

Exercises

6

Here is a list of subjects, each followed by some possible main points. Circle the unsatisfactory point(s) in each group.

Subject	Possible main points
1. reasons for teenage drug abuse	— peer pressure — school pressure — glue-sniffing — boredom
2. how home-made bread is made	— preparing dough — large bakeries — kneading dough — saving money — baking loaves
3. the advantages of being physically fit	— improved muscle tone — improved appearance — improved stamina — improved looks — improved social life
4. the main kinds of daytime television	— talk shows — *General Hospital* — quiz shows — soap operas — largely female audience — game shows
5. the functions of a travel counsellor	— planning a client's itinerary — booking the required arrangements — making travel plans — getting a passport — ensuring client has been satisfied
6. the most popular fad diets	— the Scarsdale diet — the Atkins diet — may be dangerous — the pineapple diet — weight is often gained back
7. characteristics of sharks	— tiny brains — white shark — tough and durable beasts — several sets of needle-sharp teeth

— hammerhead shark
— not all are dangerous to humans

---

8. the effects of the post-war baby boom

— overburdened schools in the 50s and 60s
— surge in birth of children from 1947–1965
— changing tastes in music due to large teenage population
— shortage of jobs for entry-level workers in 70s and 80s
— changing social norms brought about by large young population

---

7

Circle the unsatisfactory point(s) in each group.

1. why government lotteries are harmful

— they encourage compulsive gambling
— they are fun to play
— Lottario, Lotto 6/49
— they bilk money from people who have little
— they foster a "something-for-nothing" attitude

---

2. some differences between high school and college

— practical training is offered
— college students face more responsibilities
— college students are treated like adults
— college students can smoke in the halls

---

3. some benefits of biofeedback

— medical process by which a person learns to control autonomic body processes
— may relieve asthma and ulcers
— autonomic responses are involuntary, self-regulating processes
— may control blood pressure
— may relieve migraines and anxiety

4. the main points of comparison between football and rugby	— both games are team ball games — football requires helmets — both games are rough — both games are played on a large field — football is more of a spectator sport than rugby
5. ways to treat the hyperactive child	— drug therapy — intensely active — psychiatric counselling — cannot concentrate for long — change in family routines — change in diet
6. how to find a job	— watch job ads carefully — prepare a first-class résumé — send résumés and covering letters to possible employers — finding a job may take a while — prepare for interviews — buy a suit
7. different kinds of family structure	— nuclear family — in-laws — single-parent family — communal family — family breakdown — polygamous family
8. reasons for legalizing prostitution	— to save taxpayers money — to control spread of venereal disease — to eliminate juvenile prostitution — to ensure regular health checkups for prostitutes — to decriminalize prostitution

8

Study the main points you chose in exercise 5 (p. 205). Cross out any that aren't significant, different from all the others, and related to the subject. If necessary, add new main points, so that you end up with at least two main points for each subject.

Now that you've decided on a few good main points to discuss, put them in the **order** in which you want them to appear in your paper. There are four main ways to arrange your points; choose the way that is most appropriate for your particular subject.

1. **Chronological order** means in order of time, from first to last. Here's an example:

Subject	**Main points**
the process of dating	attraction meeting discovery intimacy disillusionment

2. **Climactic order** means saving your strongest or most important point for last. Generally you would present your strongest point last, your second-strongest point first, and the others in between, like this:

Subject	**Main Points**
disadvantages of cigarette smoking	danger to those around you disapproval of others expense danger to yourself

3. **Logically linked order** means that the main points are connected in such a way that one point must be explained before the next can be understood. Look at this example:

Subject	**Main Points**
main causes of juvenile delinquency	lack of opportunity for work lack of recreational facilities boredom

The logical link here is this: it's because of unemployment that recreational facilities are needed, and it's because of both unemployment and inadequate recreational facilities, that boredom becomes a problem. The first two points must be explained before the reader can fully understand the third.

4. **Random order** means the points can be explained in any order. A random arrangement of points is possible only if the main points are all equal in significance and not logically linked, as in this case:

Subject	**Main Points**
the garbage-disposal crisis	disposal sites are hard to find costs are high new technologies are not yet fully developed

Exercises

9

In this exercise, you are asked to arrange the main points of the subject according to the order proposed. Put the numbers in the blanks before the main points.

Topic	Order	Main Points
1. why pornography should be banned	chronological	_____it degrades the people involved in making it _____it brutalizes society as a whole _____it desensitizes the people who view it
2. differences between spoken and written language	climactic	_____speech is transitory; writing is permanent _____speech is direct and personal; writing isn't _____speech can't be revised; writing can
3. some causes of World War II	chronological	_____World Depression in early 1930s _____Hitler comes to power in 1933 _____heavy reparations demanded of Germany at end of World War I _____German aggression in Europe
4. effects of malnutrition	logical	_____malnutrition affects the productivity and prosperity of nations as a whole _____malnutrition impedes the mental and physical development of children _____undernourished children become sickly adults unable to

		participate fully in the economy of their society
5. how to start a gas lawnmower	chronological	____make sure there is enough gas in tank ____turn switch to start ____put lawnmower on flat ground ____when running, adjust to proper speed ____pull cord ____mow!
6. how colleges benefit society	logical	____they provide the individual with a higher level of general education ____society benefits from increased productivity and commitment of an educated populace ____they provide the individual with job skills
7. why pornography should not be banned	climactic	____organized crime benefits from illegal distribution ____censorship violates individual civil rights ____banning pornography would lead to censorship of legitimate art and literature
8. how to write a research paper	chronological	____read and take notes on selected research sources ____write the paper ____compile a working bibliography of research sources

__1__ narrow and define subject
_____ type and proofread paper
_____ prepare footnotes and bibliography
_____ revise the paper

For 9 and 10, choose your own main points and order them as you think best.

9. how to make a ______________

10. effects of alcohol abuse

10

Using the list of subjects and main points that you came up with in exercise 8, arrange the main points for each subject in the most appropriate order.

In this chapter you've learned how to choose a satisfactory subject and how to select (and order) the main points of that subject — the first two steps in the five-step process we outlined at the beginning of the chapter. Now it's time to decide whether you'll organize your paper by the thesis-statement method or by the outline method. Although we think the former generally works better for short papers and the latter for longer papers, this distinction isn't hard and fast. So, depending on your teacher's instructions, turn now to either chapter 22, "Writing the Thesis Statement," or chapter 23, "Writing the Outline."

chapter 22

Writing the Thesis Statement

Now that you've chosen your topic and selected some main points to discuss (see chapter 21), you're ready for the third step in organizing your writing. Remember that there are two ways of carrying out the third step: by writing a thesis statement and by writing an outline. If you're writing a very short paper (400 words or less), we recommend that you use the method presented in this chapter. If you're writing a longer paper, though, or if your teacher prefers the outline method, turn now to chapter 23, "Writing the Outline."

Step 3: Write a Thesis Statement

The key to clear organization of a very short paper is the **thesis statement** — a statement near the beginning of your paper that announces its subject and scope. The thesis statement is a tremendous help both to you and to your reader. It plans your paper for you, and it tells your reader exactly what he or she is going to read about. In fiction, letting readers know in advance what they're going to find would never do. But, for practical, everyday kinds of writing, this "advance notice" works very well. Term papers, technical reports, research papers, office memoranda, and business letters are no place for suspense or surprises. In these kinds of writing, you're more likely to get and keep your readers' interest if you indicate the subject and scope of your paper at the outset. The thesis statement acts like a table of contents, giving a clear indication of what is to follow. It's a kind of map of the territory covered in your paper; it keeps your reader (and you) on the right track.

Specifically, *a thesis statement is a sentence that clearly and concisely indicates the subject of your paper, the main points you will discuss, and the order in which you will discuss them.*

To write a thesis statement, you join the **subject** to the **main points**, which you have already chosen and arranged in order. To join the two parts of a thesis statement, you use a **link**. Your link can be a word or phrase, such as *are*, *include*, *consist of*, *because*, *since*, or it can be a colon.[1] Here is the simple formula for constructing a thesis statement:

[1] *Remember that a colon can be used only after an independent clause. See chapter 17 if you need a review.*

S	consists of	I, II (III, IV, V)
(subject)	(link)	(main points)

Here's an example:

S I
Three characteristics of a good business letter (are) conciseness,

II III
clarity, and courtesy.

Exercise

I

In each of the following thesis statements, underline the subject with a wavy line, circle the link, and underline the main points with a straight line. Answers are on p. 321.

1. There are three kinds of students whom teachers find difficult to teach: whiners, snoozers, and disrupters.
2. The most prolific producers of unnecessary jargon are politicians, sports writers, advertising-copy writers, and educators.
3. Pay television has faced challenges in Canada because of the relatively small market, the high monthly cost, and the stiff network competition.
4. Political violence has become ingrained in the social fabric of many Latin American countries including Nicaragua, El Salvador, Chile, and Argentina.
5. Dining in the cafeteria should be avoided if possible, for the food is high in cost, low in nutrition, and unappetizing in taste.
6. The Canadian national character was shaped by early conflicts such as the battle for Quebec, the rebellion of 1837, and the Riel rebellion.
7. Canada is little more than an American satellite, for the United States

influences our foreign policy, dominates our culture, and controls our economy.

8. Because they lack basic skills, study skills, or internal discipline, some students run the risk of failure in college.
9. The major improvements Western medical technology has made in impoverished parts of the world consist of widespread immunization, the availability of antibiotics, and improved sanitation.
10. Two cheers for democracy: one because it admits variety and two because it permits criticism. (E.M. Forster)

When you combine your subject with the main points into a thesis statement, there is one rule to remember:

The main points should be grammatically parallel.

This rules means that, if main point I is a word, then main points II and III and so on must be words, too. If point I is a phrase, then the rest must be phrases. If I is a dependent clause, then the rest must be dependent clauses. Study the model thesis statements you analyzed in exercise 1, noting that in each case the main points are in grammatically parallel form. For each of those thesis statements, decide whether words, phrases, or dependent clauses were used. If you feel your understanding of parallelism is a bit wobbly, review chapter 8 before doing the following exercises.

Exercises

2

Here is an exercise to help you remember the parallelism principle. In each set of words below, one word, phrase, or clause is not parallel to the others. Circle the letter of that item and rewrite it so that it is parallel.

1. I
   a. came
   b. saw
   c. conquered
   d. pack up and head for Rome

2. Your husband is
   a. strength
   b. intelligent
   c. good-looking
   d. well-heeled
3. Her wicked stepsisters were
   a. ill-tempered
   b. ungrateful
   c. ugliness
   d. self-centred
4. He completed the requirements
   a. skilfully
   b. with intelligence
   c. correctly
   d. quickly
5. We enjoy travelling
   a. by car
   b. sailing
   c. by air
   d. by train
6. A politician should be
   a. well-liked by his constituents
   b. respected by his colleagues
   c. esteemed by his party
   d. even the media trust him
7. We have all been
   a. watching our diet
   b. learning to exercise
   c. not to watch so much television
   d. thinking of fitness
8. Excessive use of marijuana can
   a. make you eat more
   b. diminish ambition
   c. induce lethargy
   d. cause psychological dependence
9. Her family has a
   a. mansion in Rosedale
   b. cottage in the Muskokas
   c. ski chalet in Aspen
   d. Swiss bank account that is unnumbered
10. To lower the crime rate we must ensure
    a. that citizens are involved in their communities

b. that jobs and adequate housing are available
c. enough fair-minded police visible
d. that courts work justly and speedily

3

Put a check before the sentences that are grammatically parallel.

1. _____His basement apartment was small, damp, cold, and lots of dirt.
2. _____To be a good marriage counsellor, a person must have insight, patient, compassion, and experience.
3. _____Told to include "Activities and Interests" on his résumé, Elmo described his as chomping potato chips, guzzling beer, and watching TV.
4. _____Too much coffee can give you nervous days, sleepless nights, and your heart may palpitate.
5. _____We require our employees to be honest, reliable, disciplined, and they have to know something.
6. _____Roderick is interested in the occult, so he spends his time reading about witches, warlocks, and wizards.
7. _____We knew we would be suffering from a severe case of jet lag when we got back, so we took a cab home, unpacked our bags, and went right to sleep.
8. _____Inflation is down, interest rates are up, and many people still don't have jobs.
9. _____Hobbies are important because they provide recreation, stimulation, and relaxation.
10. _____Writing acceptable college-level prose involves applying the principles of organization, sentence structure, spelling, and you have to punctuate, too.

4

Now correct the faulty parallelism in the sentences in exercise 3.

5

Correct the faulty parallelism in the following sentences.

1. Do you know the difference between polygamy, bigamy, and marrying only one person at a time?
2. Mr. Bumble had given up not only on the Liberals but also on the Conservatives and the New Democratic Party.

3. Elmo decided he'd rather be a plumber than to teach school.
4. A good coach must train and discipline the team, and he must provide motivation.
5. Two features of the semester system are flexibility and it's economical.
6. Going to college is good for broadening our social lives as well as to develop our career skills.
7. Compared to those of ten years ago, cars these day are smaller, more efficient, and they cost more.
8. We find it's more exciting to explore the tide pools at the seashore than lying in the sun all day.
9. Children who are brought up in the city have a very different outlook on life than the country.
10. Do the people of Canada want to be dominated by their neighbour to the south in economic and political terms and the culture?

6

Correct the faulty parallelism in the following sentences.

1. The four kinds of prose writing are narration, description, exposition, and persuasive.
2. College fraternities and sororities have become less popular in the past twenty years because of expense, they are time-consuming, and they discriminate against some students.
3. Freud's psychoanalytic theories, developed in the early years of this cen-

tury, not only have affected the course of psychology but also have had profound implications for education, artistic, and literary.

4. The *Star Wars* trilogy consists of three George Lucas films: the first is *Star Wars*, the second is *The Empire Strikes Back*, and three, *The Return of the Jedi*.
5. These movies have been enormously successful because of their action-filled plots, characters who engage us, and superb special effects.
6. Intramural sports offer three important things to college students: a way to get involved in the school, an opportunity to meet friends, and they can stay fit.
7. Medical scientists have studied the link between weather and such diseases as colds, arthritic ailments, and cancer.
8. Many English words have similar meanings, but they come from very different root languages: for example, *spectre* comes from the Latin *spectrum* (appearance); *phantom* comes from the Greek *phantasm* (image); and *ghost*, Anglo-Saxon *gast* — spirit.
9. Geologists are exploring several phenomena that may lead to an early-warning system for earthquakes: the variation of electrical resistance of rocks under pressure, releasing gas trapped in the crystal lattice of a rock, and the appearance of eerie lights, or luminous flares, in the sky before a quake.
10. It was the best times; it was the worst of times; it was the age of wisdom; it was the age of foolishness; it was the epoch of belief; it was the age of

incredulity; it was the season of Light; it was the season of Darkness; it was the spring of hope; and there was a lot of despair that winter, too. (With apologies to Charles Dickens, *A Tale of Two Cities*)

7

Find the subjects and main points you produced for exercise 10 in chapter 21. Combine each subject with its main points to make a thesis statement. Be sure the main points are in parallel form.

We said at the beginning of this chapter that the thesis statement plans your whole paper for you. Before we turn to the actual writing of the paper, it will be useful for you to have a general idea of what the finished product will look like. In a very short paper each main point can be explained in a single paragraph. The main points of your subject become the **topics** of the paragraph, as is shown in the model format for a paper with three main points.

Chapter 24 will tell you how to fill in the blanks. But, before you go on to that chapter, notice the proportions of the paragraphs in the model format. Since the main points are approximately equal in significance, the paragraphs of the body of the paper are approximately equal in length. (If your last main point is more important than the other points, however, the paragraph that explains it may be longer than the other paragraphs.)

Notice too, that the beginning and ending paragraphs are much shorter than the ones that explain the main points. Your introduction should not ramble on, and your conclusion should not trail off. Get to your main points as quickly as you can, and end with a bang, not a whimper.

Exercise

8

A paper that follows the model format exactly is Brian Green's "Writing a Good Business Letter," which appears in Appendix A. Read it and underline the thesis statements and topic sentences. Then turn to chapter 24.

Title ____________________

Paragraph 1: contains the introduction and the thesis statement

____
____
____
____
S consists of I, II and III.

Topic sentence introducing main point I.

Paragraph 2: contains your explanation of I

Topic sentence introducing main point II.

Paragraph 3: contains your explanation of II

Topic sentence introducing main point III.

Paragraph 4: contains your explanation of III

Paragraph 5: conclusion

[1] *Remember that a colon can be used only after an independent clause. See chapter 17 if you need a review.*

chapter 23

Writing the Outline

For longer compositions, business and technical reports, research papers and the like, the outline method often proves more successful than the thesis-statement approach. A good outline maps out your paper from beginning to end. It shows you — *before* you begin to write — what you have to say about each of your main points. Outlining spares you the agony of discovering too late that you have too much information about one point and little or nothing to say about another.

Step 3: Write an Outline

Once you've chosen a satisfactory subject and the main points you wish to discuss, the next step is to expand what you have into a point-form plan for your finished paper. To do this, you may need to do some further thinking or reading, gathering additional information and supporting facts. For ideas about what kinds of information you might use, see "Developing Your Paragraphs," p. 227. After you've assembled all the information you think you'll need, prepare the outline.

First, write down your main points in the order you've decided to discuss them. Leave lots of space under each main point. Using Roman numerals, number your main points I, II, III, etc. Now, under each point, indent and list the examples, facts, ideas, or other information you're going to use to explain it. Again, leave lots of space. Check to be sure these items are arranged in an order that will be clear to your reader.[1] Now label these A, B, C, etc.

If any of these pieces of information needs to be explained or developed, indent again and list the supporting materials, numbering them, 1, 2, 3, etc. Minor details, if there are any, are indented under the supporting materials to which they relate and are labelled a, b, c. Add the introduction and conclusion, and you're done. Your outline might look something like this:

Introduction[2]
    Attention-getter
    Thesis statement or statement of subject

[1] *The four kinds of order explained in chapter 21 can apply to the arrangement of ideas within a paragraph as well as to the arrangement of main points in a paper.*

[2] *Chapter 24 explains how to construct an introduction and conclusion.*

I. First main point
  A. item that develops first main point
  B. item that develops first main point
    1. supporting material that develops subheading B
    2. supporting material that develops subheading B
II. Second main point
  A. item that develops second main point
  B. item that develops second main point
  C. item that develops second main point
III. Third main point
  A. item that develops third main point
    1. supporting material that develops A
      a. detail
      b. detail
    2. supporting material that develops A
  B. item that develops third main point
Conclusion
  Summary
  Memorable statement

You'll probably find that before you can assign a number or a letter to a piece of information, you need to think carefully about where the item belongs in the structure of your paper. Questions about how to arrange your information under each main point and how much time to spend on any one point should be cleared up at the outline stage. If, for example, you find you have nine subheadings under main point I and only one under main point II, you need to do some rethinking to balance your paper. Main points should contain approximately equal amounts of information.

Preparing a satisfactory outline takes time. Be prepared to spend time adding, deleting, and rearranging your ideas and supporting materials until you're completely satisfied both with the arrangement and with the proportion of your outline.

Exercise

I

Below are the main points from a paper that explains, tongue-in-cheek, how to fail. Beneath these are eight statements that might have been used to support and develop these points. Read through the list of subordinate points and complete the outline by "plugging in" the support items under the appropriate main points. Discard any items that are not relevant to the main points. Turn to p. 323 to check your outline against ours.

Main Points:

I. Antagonize your teachers
II. Disdain your studies
III. Cheat on your work

Subordinate Points:

- don't buy the text for the course
- aim an occasional snort or snicker in the teacher's direction
- copy research assignments out of an appropriate library book
- wear your Walkman to class and turn up the volume whenever the teacher speaks
- sit at the back during exams and try to read your classmate's paper
- never take notes in class
- stop going to class
- tattoo your answers on your forearms

With your outline in hand, all you have to do now to write the paper is to make the supporting points into sentences and the main points into paragraph divisions. (Chapter 24 explains how.) Add an introductory paragraph and a concluding paragraph, edit carefully (see Chapter 25), and hand in a first-class essay.

To show you the relationship between an outline and the final product, we've recreated the outline that was used to write "Writing a Good Business Letter" (reprinted in Appendix A, p. 256).

I. Introduction
   Attention-getter: A good business letter is one that gets results.
   Thesis statement: a business letter should be concise, clear, and courteous

II. Concise
   A. The point should be made quickly
      1. assume your reader is busy
      2. assume your reader is not interested in trivia or personal messages
   B. Revision is necessary
      1. use precise language
      2. short letters have more impact than long
   C. There is still room for style and humour

III. Clear
   A. Organization is important
      1. know what you want to say
      2. construct the paragraphs to guide the reader through to the conclusion
   B. Acceptable letter format should be used
   C. Rereading will aid clarity
      1. take the point of view of your reader
      2. ensure accuracy of facts, figures, explanations

IV. Courteous
  A. Tone is important
    1. sarcasm and insults don't work
    2. be polite
  B. Writing and typing must be done with care
    1. correct grammar and spelling are part of courtesy
    2. mistakes will make the reader think less of you

V. Conclusion
  Summary: "The business letter can pay big dividends on the time you invest in giving it a concise message, a clear structure, and a courteous tone."

Once you've mapped out your plan in an outline, the task of writing the essay itself is greatly simplified. You can see where you're going, and how to get there. Remember, *the more time you spend planning, the less time you spend writing — and the better your writing will be.*

Exercises

2

Read "Writing a Good Business Letter" in Appendix A. Find the paragraphs that correspond to the various headings and subheadings in the outline above. Label the paragraphs to show where they fit into the outline: I, A, B, 1, 2, etc.

3

Read Nell Waldman's "Flunking with Style" in Appendix A and write an outline for it. When you've finished, turn to p. 259 to compare your outline with ours.

4

Turn to the subjects and main points you developed for exercise 10 in chapter 21 and create an outline for a paper on one of those subjects.

---

chapter 24

Writing the Paragraphs

You are now at step 4 in the writing process. Armed with either your thesis statement or your outline, you are ready to turn your main points into paragraphs. Sounds like a magician's trick? It isn't. The "sleight-of-pen" involved requires only that you know what a paragraph looks like and how to put one together.

A paragraph looks like this:

	A sentence that introduces the **topic** (or main idea) of the paragraph goes here.
Three or more sentences that specifically support or explain the topic go in here.	______________________
	A sentence that concludes your explanation of the topic goes here.

Sometimes a main point can be explained satisfactorily in a single paragraph. Sometimes, if it's a complicated main point requiring lots of support, several paragraphs are needed. Nevertheless, whether it is explaining a main point of a paper or an item supporting a main point, every paragraph contains two things: *a statement of the topic* (usually the first sentence in the paragraph) and *development of the topic*.

As the blueprint above shows you, beginning with a sentence that states clearly your main idea (or *topic*) is a good way to start a paragraph. The next three, four, five, or even more sentences will develop the topic. The key to making the paragraph *unified* (an important quality of English paragraphs) is to make sure that each of your supporting sentences relates directly to the topic introduced in the first sentence.

Exercise

I

Read Bertrand Russell's "What I Have Lived For" (Appendix A). Study the second, third, and fourth paragraphs and find in each the three basic components of a paragraph: the introduction of the topic, the supporting sentences, and the conclusion of the topic. Answers are on p. 324.

Developing Your Paragraphs

How do you put a paragraph together? First, write your **topic sentence**, telling your reader what point or idea you're going to discuss in the paragraph. Next, develop your point. An adequately developed paragraph gives enough supporting information to make the topic completely clear to the reader. An average paragraph runs between 75 and 150 words (except for introductions and conclusions, which are shorter), so you can see you will need lots of supporting information for each point.

Now, unless you are writing from a very detailed outline and have all the supporting material you need listed in front of you, you need to do a little more thinking at this point. Put yourself in your reader's place. What does the reader need to know in order to understand your point clearly? If you ask yourself the six questions listed below, you'll be able to decide what **kind of development** to use to support a particular topic sentence. The choice of development is up to you. Decide on the basis of your topic and what the reader needs to know about it.

1. Is a *definition* necessary? If you're using a term that may be unfamiliar to your reader, you should define it. Use *your own words* in the definition. Your reader needs to know what *you* mean by the term — and, besides, quoting from the dictionary is a very boring way to develop a paragraph. Below, in an essay on Kanata, Ontario, and its high technology industries, John Robert Colombo defines "backplane" by explaining both what it is and what it does:

> Digital is a world leader in computer manufacturing, and at Kanata it produces a component essential to most computers, the backplane. A backplane is a vertical plane with sockets on both faces into which are inserted, on one side, the printed circuit cards which make up the computer's CPU and, on the other side, the cable attachments for peripheral devices such as terminals, printers, and disk drives. The backplane permits internal communication within the CPU and functions as an interface between the computer's logic, memory, and input/output modules.

You should include a definition, too, if you're using a familiar term in a specific or unusual way. Here, Alan Simpson defines what he means by "a little about everything" in an essay on the ideal education:

> The "little about everything" is best interpreted these days by those who have given most thought to the sort of general education an informed individual ought to have. More is required than a sampling of the introductory courses which specialists offer in their own disciplines. Courses are needed in each of the major divisions of knowledge — the humanities, the natural sciences, and social sciences — which are organized with the breadth of view and the imaginative power of competent

staffs who understand the needs of interested amateurs. But, over and above this exciting smattering of knowledge, students should bite deeply into at least one subject and taste its full flavour. It is not enough to be dilettantes in everything without striving also to be craftsmen in something. ("The Marks of an Educated Man," *Context* I, No. 1 (Spring 1961), pp. 4–7.)

Exercise 2

Write a definition paragraph of six to ten sentences based on the following topic:

Few people seem to understand what is meant by the term "courtesy."

2. Would *examples* help clarify the point? Listing a number of examples is probably the most common method of developing a topic. Readers become confused or even suspicious when they read unsupported generalizations or statements of opinion. One of the most effective ways of communicating your idea is by providing clear, relevant examples. In paragraph 4 of "What I Have Lived For," Bertrand Russell provides three examples to clarify his point:

> Love and knowledge, so far as they were possible, led upward toward the heavens. But always pity brought me back to earth. Echoes of cries of pain reverberate in my heart. Children in famine, victims tortured by oppressors, helpless old people a hated burden to their sons, and the whole world of loneliness, poverty, and pain make a mockery of what human life should be. I long to alleviate the evil, but I cannot, and I too suffer.

Below, in her essay "Surviving Your Daughter's Adolescence" (Appendix A), Janet Read uses examples to develop her paragraph:

> Finally we come to the hardest rule for a parent to follow: don't, under any circumstances, argue. Females between the ages of thirteen and eighteen are world-class debaters. They can argue black is white, rain is snow, or bitter is sweet. The most hazardous time is the period when your baby of a few short years ago is learning to drive. She will become, after only two driving lessons, an authority on rules of the road. We have all coped with back-seat drivers, but nothing will have prepared you for this experience. The teenager feels a learner's permit is a licence to tell her parents how to drive. There are a few useful phrases you can employ to reduce the risk of argument: "Yes, dear." "Is that right?" "How astute of you to notice that!" These simple phrases can forestall an argument that would entertain your entire neighbourhood.

Exercise 3

Write a six-to-ten-sentence paragraph based on the topic sentence below, using the example method of paragraph development.

College is a great place to meet people.

---

3. Is a *series of steps* or *stages* involved? Sometimes the most effective way to develop the main idea of your paragraph is by explaining how to do it — that is, by relating the process or series of steps involved. Make sure you break the process down into its component parts and detail the steps logically and precisely. Below, Brian Green explains the process of writing a good business letter:

> The business letter must be clear. You should have a very firm idea of what you want to say, and you should let the reader know it. Use the structure of the letter — the paragraphs, topic sentences, introduction, and conclusion — to guide the reader point by point from your thesis, through your reasoning, to your conclusion. Paragraph often, to break up the page and to lend an air of organization to the letter. Use an accepted business-letter format: there are several, and they can be found in any book of business English. Reread what you have written from the point of view of someone who is seeing it for the first time, and be sure that all explanations are adequate, all information provided (including reference numbers, dates, and other identification). A clear message, clearly delivered, is the essence of business communication.

Exercise 4

Write a six-to-ten-sentence paragraph developed as a series of steps telling your reader how to make or do something.

---

4. Would *specific details* be useful? Providing your reader with concrete, specific, descriptive details can be a very effective way of developing your main point. In some paragraphs, numerical facts or statistics can be used to support your point — just be sure your facts are correct and your statistics up-to-date! Pick out the specific details John Robert Colombo uses to develop this paragraph:

> There are no tall buildings in Kanata. There is no busy downtown core; instead, there is an integration of living and working areas. Respect is paid to urban design and to the topography. If you were to drive through it today, you could count nearly 6,000 single detached dwellings, modest homes set on wide lawns, with well-maintained shopping plazas

and pleasantly landscaped parks. There are libraries in Kanata but no concert halls, art galleries, or museums. Presumably one goes to Ottawa for cultural experiences. The population is well educated — there are probably more Ph.D.s per capita in Kanata than anywhere else in Canada — and well paid. Kanata is not a poor community.

Exercise

5

Write a six-to-ten-sentence paragraph describing the most unusual-looking person you know. Be sure to include a topic sentence at the beginning.

5. Would a *comparison* or *contrast* help clarify your point? A *comparison* points out similarities between objects, people, or ideas; it shows how two different things are alike. A *contrast* points out dissimilarities between things; it shows how two objects, people, or ideas are different. A *comparison and contrast* identifies both similarities and differences. In the paragraph below, the writer contrasts machines and human workers:

> We know that the trend to automation cannot be stopped or reversed. Wherever they can, industry and business will continue to install computers and robots to replace human workers in order to remain competitive. Machines don't require salaries, fringe benefits, coffee breaks, pregnancy leave, or vacations. They never miss a weld, make a spelling error, forget to tighten a bolt, or miscalculate. We also know that if one industry or one country stops automating, its competitors will quickly drive it from the marketplace.

In the paragraph below, notice how Alan Simpson develops his point by first comparing two kinds of people and then contrasting them with another kind of person:

> To be able to listen to a phony argument and to see its dishonesty is surely one of the marks of an educated man. We may not need to be educated to possess some of this quality. A shrewd peasant was always well enough protected against impostors in the market place, and we have all sorts of businessmen who have made themselves excellent judges of phoniness without the benefit of a high-school diploma; but this kind of shrewdness goes along with a great deal of credulity. Outside the limited field within which experience has taught the peasant or the illiterate businessman his lessons, he is often hopelessly gullible. The educated man, by contrast, has tried to develop a critical faculty for general use, and he likes to think that he is fortified against imposture in all its forms. ("The Marks of an Educated Man")

Exercise

6

Write a six- to ten-sentence paragraph comparing and/or contrasting two performers (or teachers or employers). Be sure to include a topic sentence at the beginning of your paragraph.

6. Would a *quotation* or *paraphrase* be appropriate? Occasionally you will find that someone else — an expert in a particular field, a well-known author, or a respected public figure — has said what you want to say better than you could ever hope to say it. In these cases, quotations — as long as they are kept short and not used too frequently — are useful in developing your topic. Alan Simpson quotes Ralph Waldo Emerson to introduce the point of this paragraph:

> The first [test of an educated mind] is a matter of sophistication. Emerson put it nicely when he talked about getting rid of "the nonsense of our wigwams." The wigwam may be an uncultivated home, a suburban conformity, a crass patriotism, or a cramped dogma. Some of this nonsense withers in the classroom. More of it rubs off by simply mixing with people, provided they are drawn from a wide range of backgrounds and exposed within a good college to a civilized tradition. An educated man can be judged by the quality of his prejudices. ("The Marks of an Educated Man")

A paraphrase is a summary — in your own words — of someone else's idea. In this paragraph below, Simpson provides a long quotation as an example of jargon, then paraphrases or rewords it in plain English:

> There is the monstrous proliferation of gobbledy-gook in government, business, and the professions. Take this horrible example of verbal smog.
>
> It is inherent to motivational phenomena that there is a drive for more gratification than is realistically possible, on any level or in any type of personality organization. Likewise it is inherent to the world of objects that not all potentially desirable opportunities can be realized within a human life span. Therefore, any personality must involve an organization that allocates opportunities for gratifications, that systematizes precedence relative to the limited possibilities. The possibilities of gratification, simultaneously or sequentially, of all need-dispositions are severely limited by the structure of the object system and by the intra-systemic incompatibility of the consequences of gratifying them all.
>
> What this smothered soul is trying to say is simply, "We must pick and choose, because we cannot have everything we want." ("The Marks of an Educated Man")

In writing your own paragraphs, you will often find that you need to use more than one method of development to explain your points. The six methods outlined above can be used in any combination you choose.

Exercises

7

Name the kinds of development used in the following paragraphs. Then turn to p. 325 to check your answers.

1. "Writing a Good Business Letter," paragraph 1.
2. "Flunking with Style," paragraph 2.
3. "Surviving Your Daughter's Adolescence," paragraph 2.
4. "Flunking with Style," paragraph 4.
5. "What I Have Lived For," paragraph 3.
6. "Flunking with Style," paragraph 3.
7. "What I Have Lived For," paragraph 2.

8

Choose one of the following topic sentences or make up one of your own. Write a paragraph of about 100 words, using at least two different methods of paragraph development.

1. Some rock stars have bizarre personal lives.
2. Communicating clearly isn't easy.
3. A home usually reflects the owner's personality.
4. All my life I have wanted to be_____.
5. _____is the most intriguing person I know.

Writing Introductions and Conclusions

Two paragraphs in your paper are *not* developed in the way we've just outlined: the introduction and conclusion. All too often, these paragraphs are dull or clumsy and detract from a paper's effectiveness. But they needn't. Here's how to write good ones.

The introduction is worth special attention because that's where your reader either sits up and takes notice of your paper or sighs and pitches it into the wastebasket. Occasionally, for a *very* short paper, you can begin simply with your thesis statement or statement of subject. More usually, though, an **attention-getter** comes before the statement of subject. An attention-getter is a sentence or two (or sometimes a paragraph) designed to get the reader interested in what you have to say.

There are several kinds of attention-getter to choose from:

1. interesting incident or anecdote related to your subject
2. statement of opinion you intend to challenge (see "Flunking with Style," paragraph 1)
3. definition (see "Writing a Good Business Letter," paragraph 1)
4. quotation
5. little-known or striking fact

Add your thesis statement to the attention-getter and your introduction is complete.

The closing paragraph, too, usually has two parts: a summary of the main points of your paper (phrased differently, please — *not* a word-for-word repetition of your thesis statement or your topic sentences) and a **memorable statement**. Your memorable statement may take several forms:

1. show the value or significance of your subject (see "Surviving Your Daughter's Adolescence," paragraph 5)
2. refer back to the content of your opening paragraph (see "Writing a Good Business Letter," paragraph 5; also "What I Have Lived For," paragraph 5)
3. relevant or thought-provoking quotation, statement, or question
4. suggestion for change
5. challenge to the reader to get involved (see "Flunking With Style," paragraph 5)

Keeping Your Reader With You

As you are writing your paragraphs, keep in mind that you want to make it as easy as possible for your reader to follow you through your paper. Clear **transitions** and an appropriate **tone** can make the difference between a paper that confuses or annoys the reader and one that enlightens and pleases him.

Transitions are those words or phrases that show the relationship between one point and the next, causing a paragraph or a paper to hang together and read smoothly. They are like turn signals on a car: they tell the person following you where you're going. Here are some common transitions that you can use to keep your reader on track:

1. *to show a time relation*: first, second, third, next, before, during, after, now, then, finally, last
2. *to add an idea or example*: in addition, also, another, furthermore, similarly, for example, for instance
3. *to show contrast*: although, but, however, instead, nevertheless, on the other hand, in contrast, on the contrary
4. *to show a cause-effect relation*: as a result, consequently, because, since, therefore, thus

Here is a paragraph that has adequate development but no transitions:

> There are many reasons why you should not smoke. Smoking is harmful to your lungs and heart. It is annoying and dangerous to those around you who do not smoke. It is an unattractive and dirty habit. It is difficult to quit smoking. Most worthwhile things in life are hard to achieve.

Not very easy to read, is it? The reader is jerked abruptly from point to point until, battered and bruised, he reaches the end. This kind of writing is unfair to a reader. It makes him do too much of the work. The ideas may all be there, but the reader has to figure out for himself how they fit together. After a couple of paragraphs like this one, even a patient reader can become annoyed.

Now read the same paragraph with the transition added:

> There are many reasons why you should not smoke; among them, three stand out as the most persuasive. First, smoking is harmful to your lungs and heart. Second, it is both annoying and dangerous to those around you who do not smoke. In addition to these compelling facts, smoking is an unattractive and dirty habit. On the other hand, once you begin, it's awfully difficult to quit; but then, most worthwhile things in life are hard to achieve.

Here the reader is gently guided from one point to the next. By the time he reaches the conclusion, he knows not only what ideas the writer had in mind but also how they fit together. The transitions make the reader's job easy and rewarding.

One final point. As you write the paragraphs of your paper, try to be conscious of your **tone**. *Tone* is a word used to describe a writer's attitude towards the subject and the reader. The words you use, the examples, quotations, and other supporting materials you choose to help explain your main points — all these contribute to your tone. When you are trying to explain something to someone — particularly if it's something you feel strongly about — you may be tempted to be highly emotional in your discussion. If you allow yourself to "get emotional," chances are you won't be convincing. What will be communicated is the strength of your feelings, not the depth of your understanding or the validity of your opinion. To be clear and credible, you need to restrain your enthusiasm (or your anger) and present your points in a calm, reasonable way.

We have two suggestions that may help you find and maintain the right tone. First, never insult your reader, even unintentionally. Avoid phrases like "any idiot can see," "no sane person could believe," and "it is obvious that. . . ." Remember that what is obvious to you isn't necessarily obvious to someone who has a limited understanding of your subject or who disagrees with your opinion. Don't "talk down" to your reader, as though he were a child or a simpleton. Don't use sarcasm. And avoid profanity.

Second, don't apologize for your interpretation of your subject. Have confidence in yourself: you've thought long and hard about your subject, you've found good supporting material to help explain it, and you believe in its significance. Present your subject in a *positive* manner. If you hang back, using phrases like "I may be wrong, but . . ." or "I tend to feel . . . ," your reader won't be inclined to give your points the consideration they deserve. Keep your reader in mind as you write, and your writing will be both clear and convincing.

Exercises

9

Rewrite the following paragraph, adding transitions where necessary and correcting any lapses in tone. Compare your revision to ours on p. 325.

> I'm new to college life. I hardly know anything about it. Don't consider me an expert. There are three ways to achieve academic success. I want to do well. A person doesn't have to go to class, which is nice. Going to class helps you learn more. Teachers don't bug you to do the work. It's easy to miss assignments or notes if they don't. The workload gets heavy all of a sudden in midterm. It sure is tough to keep up. I may be wrong but it seems to me that the key to academic success is self-discipline and responsibility for one's studies as a college student.

___

___

___

___

___

___

___

___

___

10

Write a response to the prescription for academic success outlined in exercise 9 above. Remember to keep your tone consistent, and don't forget transitions.

11

Do either A or B:

A. Using one of the thesis statements you prepared in chapter 22, exercise 7, write a paper of approximately 400 words.

B. Using the outline you prepared in chapter 23, exercise 4, write a paper of approximately 600 words.

---

chapter 25

Revising the Paper

It is difficult to overemphasize the importance of revision in good writing. Students should devote to revision approximately one-third of the total time they spend producing a paper. In fact, many professional writers estimate that 80 percent of their writing time is spent in revising.

If you're like most writers, amateur or professional, you think revision is torture. By the time you've finished the first draft, you've had it! You've said what you had to say; all you want is to send the thing on its way and let the reader cope. The temptation to skip revising is difficult to resist, but the rewards definitely make it worthwhile. The rule below is essential to good writing:

Never submit your work without rereading and revising.

There are three steps to this part of the writing process. Each step requires that you read through your entire essay, painful though this may be. Your first reading should concentrate on **audience**; your second reading should emphasize **structure**; and your third should focus on **correctness**. Let's look at these steps one at a time.

1. Audience. Let as much time as possible pass before your first reading of the draft. Two weeks is ideal. Ten minutes, or even half a day, is *not enough*. The danger in rereading too soon is that you're likely to "read" what you *think* you've written — what exists only in your head, not on the paper.

A cooling off period affords you a clearer, more accurate perception of what you have written. It's helpful to approach the paper as if it had been written by someone else and you were serving as editor. This first time through, concentrate on how the paper will affect the person who is going to read it.

Introduction
- Will it catch the reader's attention, make him or her want to read on?
- Is the thesis statement clear and easy to follow?
- Is the tone appropriate (friendly, authoritative, personal, or persuasive, depending on content)?

Body
- Is the organization (as previewed in the thesis statement) maintained?
- Is the tone consistent?

	• Is the arrangement of the main points effective, or would another order be more appropriate? • Is the desired effect achieved? (That is, will the reader be convinced, informed, entertained, or moved?)
Conclusion	• Does the summary clearly draw together the main points that have been presented? • Does the last statement effectively clinch the argument? Does the paper come to a satisfying conclusion (or does it simply stop)?

2. Structure. Again, it is advisable (although we recognize it is not always possible) to put your work aside for a while before coming to the second step in the revision process. As you read your paper through this second time, look critically at your paragraphs.

- Does each paragraph have an identifiable topic sentence?
- Are transitions between paragraphs clear and effective?
- Does each paragraph focus on *one* topic or main point?
- Is the topic in each paragraph adequately developed?

3. Correctness. Finally, reread your paper a third time to make a final check on grammar, sentence structure, spelling, and punctuation. If you turn to the inside back cover of this book, you will find a Revision Guide. As you read over your paper, keep this guide beside you as a reminder of all the things you should be watching for. Naturally, there will be some errors that give you more difficulty than others. Highlight these troublesome points on your Guide and pay special attention to them as you reread your essay for the last time.

If spelling is a particular problem for you, it is a good idea to read your paper backwards, beginning with the last word. Reading from back to front forces you to look at each word in isolation and helps you spot words that look suspicious. Whenever you're in doubt about the spelling of a word, look it up! If you find this step too much to bear, ask a good speller to read over your paper for you and identify any errors.

Now you're ready to submit your paper, confident that it says what you want it to say — both about its subject and about you, the writer.

Exercise

Using the Revision Guide, reread and revise the paper you wrote for exercise 11 in chapter 24.

beyond the bare essentials

Introduction

We have now covered all the essentials for clear, correct, well organized, and easily understood writing. In this short unit we will go beyond those essentials to some of the pitfalls you may encounter when applying all you've learned up to now. We'll discuss levels of usage; how to avoid clichés, jargon, and slang; the problem of wordiness; and what we call *abusages* — misused phrases and words that creep into writing and reveal ignorance of the language.

Many of the errors we will describe in this unit are not grammatical errors; however, they do interfere with your ability to communicate with your reader. A reader may simply not understand what you're talking about if you use jargon or slang; he or she may think very poorly of you (and your message) if your level of usage is inappropriate or if you use clichés or abusages. Your message will be communicated if your writing is clear and correct (the bare essentials); your message will be more easily and favourably received if your writing is appropriate to the message and to the reader (beyond the bare essentials).

Although these chapters do not concern the essential nuts and bolts of writing, they do contain information that may improve your writing as much as anything else you've learned in this book. Now that you're writing longer papers and having less trouble with the essentials, you are ready to consider the points in this unit in your reading and revision. The result will be writing that is not only technically correct but also stylistically appropriate.

chapter 26

Levels of Usage

All communication involves three factors: a sender, a message, and a receiver. This book is designed to help the sender — the person who has something to say — to communicate clearly and correctly. What the sender has to say is, of course, the message. Messages should always be adjusted to suit the receiver. This adjustment is the responsibility of the sender. There is no point in sending a message, whether it's a love letter or a spoken instruction, in Spanish if the receiver understands only English. Likewise, there is little to be gained from sending a message in colloquial English (such as you would use when speaking with your close friends) when the receiver is a prospective employer whom you have just met.

There are many **levels of usage** in spoken English. They range from almost unintelligible mutters and groans, through colloquial slang and professional jargon, right up to the formal, correct English used in the law courts, in the Speech from the Throne, and on other formal occasions. The same range is possible in written English: from graffiti up to the formal essay. The subject matter often helps determine the level.

The key to finding the proper level for your message is to consider not only the subject but also the receiver. Sometimes compromises must be made, as when you send one message to a wide variety of receivers. In general, you aim at the higher levels of receiver and trust that the others will understand. Thus, wedding invitations, even those to the bridegroom's buddies, are usually stylized and formal.

No one has to tell you what level of language to use when you communicate with your friends at lunch or after school; that level has been clearly established over many years. Sometimes, however, it's not clear what level you should be using, and at such times a careful consideration of the needs and preferences of your receiver is necessary. If your sociology teacher wants you to write papers in a formal style, and you want to get good marks, you will have to write formally. Likewise, because employers in general favour formal letters of application over casual ones, if you want to get a job you will have to write your letter in a formal style. A more relaxed and personal style may be appropriate for a talk given to your class. Letters to friends and conversations with parents are still less formal, although they probably retain a degree of correctness not found in your conversations with your friends (or enemies).

There are no hard and fast divisions of language into levels; nevertheless, to help you choose the style most appropriate to the message and the receiver you are considering, we have outlined the basic characteristics of colloquial, general, and formal language.

	Colloquial	General	Formal
Vocabulary	casual, everyday; usually concrete; some slang, colloquial expressions, contractions	the language of educated persons; nonspecialized; balance of abstract and concrete; readily understood	often abstract; technical; specialized; no contractions or colloquialisms
Sentence and Paragraph Structure	sentences short, simple; some sentence fragments; paragraphs short	complete sentences of varying length; paragraphs vary, but often short	all sentences complete; sentences usually long, complex; paragraphs fully developed, often at length
Tone	conversational, casual; sounds like ordinary speech	varies to suit message and purpose of writer	impersonal, serious, often instructional
Uses	personal letters, some fiction, some newspapers, much advertising	most of what we read: newspapers, magazines, novels, business correspondence	legal documents, some textbooks, academic writing, scientific reports

No level is "better" than another. Each has its place and function. Your message, your receiver, and your purpose in writing are the factors that determine which level of usage is appropriate.

Exercises

1

Write three paragraphs explaining why you were late for an important meeting — one for an employment interviewer, one for your father, and one for your teammates.

2

In the books, magazines, notes, and so on that you have with you now, try to find a piece of writing that is clearly colloquial, one that is general, and one that is formal. Then list briefly the characteristics of the typical person for whom each piece of writing is intended. Include physical features in your description, as well as education, hobbies, and anything else that you can speculate on.

chapter 27

Clichés, Jargon, and Slang

Clichés

A **cliché** is a group of words that was put together, quite creatively, long ago and that has been used and overused ever since. To write in clichés all the time is to write boringly or, even worse, to have your serious meaning found funny.

Elmo was determined to follow in his father's footsteps.

"To follow in [someone's] footsteps" is a cliché. Clichés do have meaning for your reader, but they're tired, worn-out ways of expressing that meaning. It is difficult, if not impossible, to eliminate clichés from your writing, but you can be aware of them and try to use them infrequently. Don't write automatically. Spend some time thinking about what you want to say; then say it in your own words, not someone else's.

Exercise

I

Rewrite these sentences, expressing the ideas in your own words.

1. For Constanza, work was a rat race, but she hung in until the third time her boss asked her to work overtime. That was the last straw. She hit the street and made tracks, feeling free as a bird and light as a feather.
2. Life in the fast lane agreed with her for a while, but it goes without saying that she soon went broke and, sadder but wiser, began to look for another job.
3. Although they came out swinging early in the season, the Dinosaurs had to work like dogs to keep up with the rest of the league. By mid-season, the coach was getting hot under the collar and the team was in the dog

house. Better late than never, they began winning again with only three games left; however, their loss on the last day of the season was the straw that broke the camel's back.

4. You're taking a big chance when you go out on a limb to buy a new set of wheels from someone you don't know. Here's a word to the wise: for peace of mind, you can't go wrong buying from an established dealer who will be there in your hour of need when something goes wrong. The extra money you might pay is a drop in the bucket compared to what the car could cost you in the long run.
5. Last but not least, I would like to introduce my better half, the little woman who has stuck by me through thick and thin. It's a crying shame that my pride and joy can't be here as well, but she's safe and sound at home watching her dear old dad accept this award on TV.
6. Lewis tried to break the ice by doing his flamingo imitation; however, Samantha was not impressed and chewed him out for acting like a fool. The rest of the people at the party were pleased as punch that their relationship seemed to be on the rocks, because no one had a good word to say about Samantha and most felt that Lewis was rotten to the core.
7. While variety is the spice of life, too much change can be a pain in the neck. Many of my friends are stressed out because of the day in, day out pressure of climbing the ladder of success. I like to take one day at a time and go with the flow; my husband says I'm just bone lazy.
8. After staying out until the wee small hours of the morning, Vince was

white as a sheet and sick as a dog when we shook him awake at the crack of dawn. His blushing bride dissolved in tears when she saw his condition, but instead of getting down in the dumps, she took drastic action and by the time they tied the knot, he was bright-eyed and bushy-tailed. Needless to say, they lived happily ever after.

9. In an attempt to keep abreast of the times, our college took a quantum leap into the 1990s by hiring a budding genius to manage its budget. In the long run, I'm sure she'll be worth her weight in gold, but in her first few days on the job she has seemed bored out of her mind.
10. Like a bolt from the blue, Cecilia arrived on the scene, dressed to the nines and high as a kite. Roger was swept off his feet in an instant, making me green with envy since I was head over heels in love with him. To Roger, Cecilia was a breath of fresh air, but I thought she was full of hot air.

Broadcasting is one of the chief refuges of the cliché. It's a rare newcast that doesn't include the expression "informed sources" or "claimed the life" or "skyrocketing inflation." Listening carefully for such overworked phrases on the radio and television will make you more aware of them in your own writing and perhaps less likely to use them.

Exercises

2

List ten clichés that you hear every day from teachers, friends, and parents.

3

List ten clichés that you might hear on tonight's news and sports broadcast.

Jargon

Jargon is a special breed of cliché. It is made up of the technical words or phrases used in connection with a particular trade or profession. Often such "trade language" enters the everyday language we use outside our jobs. Like other types of cliché, jargon is a poor substitute for creative, original expression. The sports world has a highly developed jargon: "third and six," "at the post," "slapshot," "uppercut," "on deck." Many of these expressions find their way into everyday conversation. Although jargon may be useful or even necessary in the context of the job, it is clumsy and inappropriate in most writing.

The chief fault in using jargon is that it limits your audience to those who have the same vocabulary as you. To the rest of the world, your writing becomes difficult to understand, or even meaningless. You can't expect to communicate in your English essays with sentences like this: "The professor replied with a logical uppercut that caught George right between the eyes and laid him out for the count." This may be a colourful way to describe the winning of an argument, but it will be effective only with readers who are boxing fans.

At its worst, jargon is the imitation of a specialized vocabulary. With its abstract words and long, complicated sentences, such jargon becomes sound without meaning, as the following sentence illustrates.

> Thus the meaningful verbalization of conceptual improvisation at the interpersonal interface is contra-indicated by frustrations arising from idiosyncratic linguistic actualization, vocabulary-wise, so that the verbalized formulations of the initiating consciousness actuate the latent rejection mechanisms.

The cure for this kind of jargon is consideration for your reader. If you really want your reader to understand you, write in a simple, straightforward style.

Exercise

4

Write as many examples of jargon as you can for each of the following professions. If you treat this as a class exercise, you'll quickly see just how many examples there are.

1. fashion merchandising: sleeper, runner, holiday line, . . .
2. engineering: R factor, chairman, slump, . . .
3. advertising: story board, paste-up, rate card, . . .
4. accounting: profit margin, grossed up, T4, . . .
5. computer programming: interface, input, address, software, . . .

Slang

Slang is street talk, inappropriate for the written language. There are innumerable examples of slang, from *A-OK* to *zowie*, and even dictionaries don't attempt to keep all the terms straight. Unless you're quoting someone who uses slang, avoid it and find words or expressions appropriate to written English. If you're in doubt, check your dictionary. The notation *sl.* or *slang* will appear after the word if it is slang, or after the meaning of the word that is a slang meaning. (Some words, such as *chick* and *neat*, have both a general meaning and a slang meaning.)

Like jargon, slang can limit, or even block, your communication with a reader. Slang is the most quickly dated type of language: what is appropriate now may well be laughed at in a few months. ("Right on, man. What a groovy scene! Far out!") Also, like jargon, slang is understood only by a limited group of people. You may exclude many readers if you use slang familiar only to a small group.

Exercises

5

For one day, keep a list of the slang expressions you hear or read.

6

List some slang terms applied to family members e.g., wife — little woman, old lady, better half.

---

chapter 28

Wordiness

Wordiness is a problem that may develop if you try too hard to impress a reader with your use of words. Keep in mind that no reader wants to read "fill" or "padding." All writing should be as concise as it can be and still convey the message clearly. Even authors like Dickens and Michener, who have written huge quantities, choose their language carefully and don't waste their readers' time with unnecessary words.

Here's an example of what can happen when, in trying to impress, you lose sight of the need to communicate. Do you recognize anything of your style in this?

> In my own opinion, I feel very strongly indeed that the government of this Dominion of Canada is basically in need of an additional amount of meaningful input from its electors, the people of this country, at this point in time, frankly speaking. For too long a period of time, the leaders of this nation in Ottawa have, rightly or wrongly, gone heedlessly off on their own particular course of action without the benefit of consultation or dialogue with the people, who, it stands to reason, are most willing and able to provide, clearly and without doubt, a distinct and clear path to follow into the future world of tomorrow.

By eliminating wordiness, you can make this into a clear statement. Try it!

The following are some of the worst offenders we have discovered in student writing. In some cases, many words are used when one or two would do. In other cases, the wording is redundant (says the same thing twice).

Wordy	**Acceptable**
"absolutely complete"	complete
"absolutely nothing"	nothing
"at that point in time"	then
"basic fundamentals"	fundamentals
"circled around"	circled
"collect together"	collect
"completely free"	free
"continue on"	continue
"dead bodies"	corpses *or* bodies
"disappear from view"	disappear

"entirely eliminated"	eliminated
"equally as good"	as good
"exactly identical"	identical
"final conclusion"	conclusion
"green in colour"	green
"having the same thing in common"	having in common
"I personally feel"	I feel
"in my opinion, I think"	in my opinion
"in this day and age"	now
"new innovation"	innovation
"personal friend"	friend
"proceed ahead"	proceed
"real, genuine leather"	genuine leather
"repeat again"	repeat
"repeat the same"	repeat
"small in size"	small
"such as, for example"	such as
"surrounded on all sides"	surround
"true fact"	fact
"very (most, quite, rather) unique"	unique

Exercises

I

Revise these sentences, making them more concise and understandable. Suggested answers are on p. 325.

1. Basically, I myself prefer the real, genuine article to a phony imitation.
2. Although small in size and an ugly yellow in colour, the car was, in point of fact, exactly identical to his last one.
3. The final conclusion wasn't known until he was completely free to announce himself successfully elected.
4. I will repeat again, for those of you who disappeared from view, that at this point in time we are completely free.
5. They circled around behind the enemy and, at 04:00 in the morning on July 12, surrounded them on all sides and entirely eliminated the threat of an invasion.

6. There was absolutely nothing they could do except keep on repeating the true facts.
7. In my opinion, it is my belief that this particular new innovation will never live to see the light of day.
8. There comes a certain point in time when the last final reckoning is done, and you reach a final conclusion.
9. Although his ideas seem to be fairly unique, we must be absolutely and completely positive that we don't repeat the same mistake again.
10. I personally think she is faking her illness and pretending to be sick so she can stay at home and not have to go to work.

2

Tell a well-known fairy tale or story in one paragraph, using as much padding and wordiness as you can. Exchange paragraphs with another student and simplify each other's horrible prose.

---

chapter 29

Abusages

Some words and terms that appear in writing are simply incorrect or used incorrectly. We've named these misspelled, misused, or made-up words **abusages**. The presence of abusages in writing makes the writer appear ignorant in the eyes of anyone who knows anything about the English language. The list of abusages that follows is a partial one, but it does include some of the worst offenders. You should add to it the abusages that your teacher hates most.

"alot"	There is no such word. Use *many* or *much*.
"anyways"	Also, "anywheres" and "a long ways." There is no *s* on these words.
"could of"	Also, "would of," "might of," "should of," and so on. The helping verb is *have*: *could have, would have,* etc.
"didn't do nothing"	This, along with all other double negatives ("couldn't get nowhere," "wouldn't talk to nobody," and so on), is wrong. Write *didn't do anything* or *did nothing.*
"irregardless"	There is no such word. Use *regardless*.
"irrevelant"	This is a misspelling. Spell the word *irrelevant*.
"media" used as a singular word	The word *media* is plural. The singular is *medium*. Write *Television is a mass medium. Print and radio are also examples of mass media.*
"off of"	Use *off* alone: *I fell off the wagon.*
"prejudice" used as an adjective	It is wrong to write "She is prejudice against men." Use *prejudiced*.
"prejudism"	There is no such word. Use *prejudice*: *He should show no prejudice to either side.*
"real" used as an adverb	"Real sad," "real swell," and "real nice" are wrong. Use *really* or *very*.
"reason is because"	Use "the reason is that": *The reason is that I don't use a deodorant.*
"suppose to"	Also, "use to." Use *supposed to* and *used to.*

"themself" Also, "theirself," "ourselfs," "yourselfs," and "themselfs." The plural of *self* is *selves*: *themselves, ourselves* and so on. Don't use "theirselves," though; there's no such word.

"youse" There is no such word. *You* is used for both singular and plural. When waiting on tables, don't say "May I help youse?" to a group of English instructors, if you want a tip.

Exercise

I

Correct the following sentences where necessary. Answers are on p. 325.

1. I could of done alot of things, but I chose to become rich and powerful real quickly.
2. Irregardless of what you say, I think the media is generally reliable.
3. The reason Dennis came home was because he couldn't do nothing more to help at the hospital.
4. They teach us alot of irrevelant things at this school.
5. Debbie's father is not prejudiced; he hates all her boyfriends, regardless of their background.
6. Mark was suppose to be in the race, but he fell off of his bike during practice.
7. I should of stayed home, but I went anyways.
8. The reason youse are failing is because you don't do no homework.
9. The police department was accused of prejudism against minority groups.
10. Steve did nothing to keep her from doing what she was supposed to do.

A whole category of abusages is created by misuse of pronouns.

Him and I had a fight.

Bob and her are the best spellers.
It came down to a choice between she and me.

There are two groups of pronouns: those used for subjects and those not used for subjects. In chapter 3 you reviewed how to find the subject of a sentence. When that subject is, or is referred to by, a pronoun, the pronoun should be one of these:

I	we
you	you
he, she	they

When the pronoun is *not* the subject of the sentence, you should use one of these:

me	us
you	you
him, her	them

He and *I* had a fight. (The pronouns are the subject of the sentence.)
Bob and *she* are the best spellers. (The pronoun is part of the multiple subject "Bob and she.")
It came down to a choice between *her* and *me*. (The pronouns are not the subject of the sentence.)
The girls in the blue uniforms are *they*. (The pronoun stands for the subject of the sentence, *girls*.)
He is more honest than *she*. (The verb *is* is understood at the end of the sentence, and *she* is the subject of that verb.)

Exercise

2

Correct the pronouns in these sentences as necessary.

1. We went camping, and they went with us.
2. Her and Craig tried to build the fire themself.
3. "Those are them," we said when we found the canoes.
4. Everyone went swimming but she and I.
5. Us and them heated beans on a Coleman stove.
6. Her and me took a flashlight and went looking for bears.
7. I think she was more scared than me.
8. Back at camp, they waited; she was more worried than him.

9. Two porcupines chased she and I through the woods.

10. "These are they," we told our friends.

3

Eliminate all of the abusages from this dreadful paragraph.

My friend Tim did real good in his last year of high school so his parents gave him a trip to Europe for two months before college. Two friends and him got themselfs on a cheap flight to Amsterdam and rented a car off of a guy who gave them a real good deal. They drove south to the French Riviera where there was suppose to be alot of other young travellers, but it rained most of the time they were there. Irregardless of the rain and the cold temperatures, they would of gone swimming anyways, but when they discovered the beach was not sand but rocks, they got real discouraged and decided to go to Paris. There, they should of been more careful because late one night they almost got into a fight even though they didn't do nothing to cause it. The prices were real high as well. Tim thought the Parisians were displaying prejudism against tourists by charging nine dollars for a beer, but anyways they couldn't do nothing about it because they couldn't speak the language too good. They were real glad to get themselfs off of the plane in Vancouver. While they all felt it could of been worse, Europe wasn't nothing like they expected from what their friends had told them. Anyways, they decided it just wasn't like it use to be.

appendices

Readings

Writing a Good Business Letter

Brian Green

1 A good business letter is one that gets results. The best way to get results is to develop a letter that, in its appearance, style, and content, conveys information efficiently. To perform this function, a business letter should be concise, clear, and courteous.

2 The business letter must be concise. Little introduction or preliminary chat is necessary. Get to the point, make the point, and leave it. It is safe to assume that your letter is being read by a very busy person with all kinds of paper to deal with. Such a person does not want to spend very much time with a newsy letter about your ski trip or medical problem. Hone and refine your message until the words and sentences you have used are precise. This takes time for revision and rereading but is a necessary part of writing a good letter. A short business letter that makes its point quickly has much more impact on a reader than a long-winded, rambling exercise in creative writing. This does not mean that there is no place for style or even, on occasion, humour in the business letter. While it conveys a message in its contents, the letter also provides the reader with an impression of you, its author: the medium is part of the message.

3 The business letter must be clear. You should have a very firm idea of what you want to say, and you should let the reader know it. Use the structure of the letter — the paragraphs, topic sentences, introduction, and conclusion — to guide the reader point by point from your introduction, through your reasoning, to your conclusion. Paragraph often, to break up the page and to lend an air of organization to the letter. Use an accepted business-letter format: there are several, and they can be found in any book of business English. Reread what you have written from the point of view of someone who is seeing it for the first time, and be sure that all explanations are adequate, all information provided (including reference numbers, dates, and other identification). A clear message, clearly delivered, is the essence of business communication.

4 The business letter must be courteous. Sarcasm and insults are ineffective and can often work against you. If you are sure you are right, point that out as politely as possible, explain why you are right, and outline what the reader is expected to do about it. Always put yourself in the place of the person to whom you are writing. What sort of letter would you respond to? How effective

would sarcasm and threats be in making you fulfill a request? Another form of courtesy is taking care in your writing and typing of the business letter. Grammatical and spelling errors (even if you call them typing errors) tell a reader that you don't think enough of him or her to be careful. Such mistakes can lower the reader's opinion of you faster than anything you say, no matter how idiotic. There are excuses for ignorance; there are no excuses for sloppiness.

5 The business letter is your custom-made representative. It speaks for you and is a permanent record of your message. It can pay big dividends on the time you invest in giving it a concise message, a clear structure, and a courteous tone.

What I Have Lived For[1]

Bertrand Russell

1 Three passions, simple but overwhelmingly strong, have governed my life: the longing for love, the search for knowledge, and unbearable pity for the suffering of mankind. These passions, like great winds, have blown me hither and thither, in a wayward course, over a deep ocean of anguish, reaching to the very verge of despair.

2 I have sought love, first, because it brings ecstasy — ecstasy so great that I would often have sacrificed all the rest of life for a few hours of this joy. I have sought it, next, because it relieves loneliness — that terrible loneliness in which one shivering consciousness looks over the rim of the world into the cold unfathomable lifeless abyss. I have sought it, finally, because in the union of love I have seen, in a mystic miniature, the prefiguring vision of the heaven that saints and poets have imagined. This is what I sought, and though it might seem too good for human life, this is what — at last — I have found.

3 With equal passion I have sought knowledge. I have wished to understand the hearts of men. I have wished to know why the stars shine. And I have tried to apprehend the Pythagorean power by which number holds sway above the flux. A little of this, but not much, I have achieved.

4 Love and knowledge, so far as they were possible, led upward toward the heavens. But always pity brought me back to earth. Echoes of cries of pain reverberate in my heart. Children in famine, victims tortured by oppressors, helpless old people a hated burden to their sons, and the whole world of loneliness, poverty, and pain make a mockery of what human life should be. I long to alleviate the evil, but I cannot, and I too suffer.

5 This has been my life. I have found it worth living, and would gladly live it again if the chance were offered me.

[1] *From* The Autobiography of Bertrand Russell. *Copyright The Bertrand Russell House. Reprinted by permission of the publisher, George Allen and Unwin, Ltd.*

Flunking with Style[1]

Nell Waldman

1 People often remark that succeeding in school takes plenty of hard work. The remark implies that failure is a product of general idleness and zero motivation. This is an opinion I'd like to challenge. My long and checkered past in numerous educational institutions has taught me that to fail grandly, to fail extravagantly, to go down in truly blazing splendour, requires effort and imagination. To fail your year in the grand style, you must antagonize your teachers, disdain your studies, and cheat on your work. Keep the following guidelines in mind.

2 The first step, antagonizing your teachers, isn't difficult if you keep in mind what it is that teachers like: intelligent, interested, even enthusiastic faces in front row centre. Show that you're bored before the class begins by slouching in a desk at the back of the room. Wear your Walkman, and don't forget to turn up the volume when the teacher starts to talk. Carry on running conversations with your seatmates. Aim an occasional snort or snicker in the teacher's direction when she's putting a complex point on the board. Above all, never volunteer an answer and respond sullenly with an "I dunno" if the teacher has the nerve to ask you a question. Before long, you'll have that teacher bouncing chalk stubs off your head. Once you've earned the loathing of all your instructors, you'll be well on your way to a truly memorable failure.

3 The second step, disdaining your studies, is easy to master; they're probably B-O-R-I-N-G anyway. First, don't buy your books until close to midterm and keep them in their original condition; don't open, read, or note anything in them. Better yet, don't buy your texts at all. Second, never attempt to take notes in class. Third, stop going to class completely, but have lots of creative excuses for missed assignments: "My friend's aunt died;" "My gerbil's in a coma;" "My boyfriend was in another car wreck;" "My dog ate the lab report;" "I've got mono." You can bet your teachers will be really amused by these old standbys. By now you are well on your way to disaster.

4 The third step, cheating, will deliver the *coup de grâce* to your academic career. Should an instructor be so sadistic as to assign a research paper, just copy something out of a book that the librarian will be happy to find for you. Your instructor will be astonished at the difference between the book's polished professional prose and your usual halting scrawls; you're guaranteed a zero. During your exams, sit at the back and crane your neck to read your classmate's paper. Roll up your shirtsleeves to reveal the answers you've tattooed all over your forearms. Ask to be excused three or four times during the test so you can consult the notes you've stashed in the hall or the washroom. Be bold! Dig out your old wood-burning kit and emblazon cheat notes on the desk. If you want to ensure not just failure but actual expulsion, send in a ringer — a look-alike to write the exam for you!

5 If you follow these guidelines, you will be guaranteed to flunk your year. Actively courting failure with verve, with flair, and with a sense of drama will

[1] From Sarah Norton and Nell Waldman, eds., *Canadian Content* (Toronto: Holt, 1988).

not only ensure your status as an academic washout but will also immortalize you in the memories of teachers and classmates alike. The challenge is yours! Become a legend — pick up the torch and fall with it!

Surviving Your Daughter's Adolescence[1]

Janet Read

1 Living with a teenage daughter can cause friction in an otherwise peaceful home. To survive the years of turbulence, you may find it helpful to observe three basic rules: never criticize, never say "No," and never argue. Observing these rules does not mean the teen will always get her own way, but the right words in the right place can turn a potential confrontation into a calm discussion.

2 For a loving mother, the first rule can be extremely difficult. When your beautiful daughter appears at the breakfast table looking as if she were going into combat instead of into class, it will not be easy for you to offer a compliment. Take a deep breath, count to three, and tell her in a convincing tone how much you like her sporty new outfit. A compliment may make her wonder if battle gear is really the look she wants to achieve. After all, if Mom likes it, how can her friends be expected to approve? Don't be surprised if she leaves for school looking almost presentable. In any event, you can be sure that three-quarters of the student population looks just like your child. If all else fails, remember your class picture of 1966.

3 When you are trying to keep peace, the next rule is never to give a negative reply. This simply means that you never say an outright "No." Her request may seem preposterous to you, but not to a fourteen-year-old. During this period in your child's life, peer pressure is the most difficult thing for her to deal with. Often the request — to go to the dance club, for instance — is coming indirectly from her friends. Instead of immediately blurting out the "N-word," try to find out her reasons for feeling her life will be over if she can't attend this one event. The strategy may turn your basement into a substitute Palace Pier for an evening, but it will give you peace of mind.

4 Finally we come to the hardest rule for a parent to follow: don't, under any circumstances, argue. Females between the ages of thirteen and eighteen are world-class debaters. They can argue black is white, rain is snow, or bitter is sweet. The most hazardous time is the period when your baby of a few short years ago is learning to drive. She will become, after only two driving lessons, an authority on rules of the road. We have all coped with back-seat drivers, but nothing will have prepared you for this experience. The teenager feels a learner's permit is a licence to tell her parents how to drive. There are a few useful phrases you can employ to reduce the risk of argument: "Yes, dear." "Is that right?" "How astute of you to notice that!" These simple phrases can forestall an argument that would entertain your entire neighbourhood.

5 I am not trying to give the impression that faithful observance of these three rules will mean your daughter's teenage years will be clear sailing all the time. They can however, make the waters of adolescence a lot calmer.

[1] *This essay was written in class by a student in her first term of college.*

A Flock of Freshmen[1]

Marty J. Chan

1 Chirping inept or incisive questions, preening themselves or chattering with each other unaware of the scrutiny of a hawk-eyed professor, freshman students, hunting for wisdom, a degree and a high-paid job, perch on their seats like birds on the tree of knowledge, seeking attention and answers or falling prey to a professor's swooping wrath. Most freshmen thrive in their new habitat — the university — to which they have migrated from the north, south, east, and west. Careful examination of the species reveals five varieties: the true blue intellectual, the mimicking intellectual, the buzzing planner, the idle sleeper, and the modest intellectual.

2 Beware the buzzing planner and the mimicking intellectual: these two types will disrupt a class unless restrained. If spotted early, however, the buzzing planner can be controlled and the mimicking intellectual tamed. Unfortunately, an inexperienced lecturer cannot immediately distinguish one type from another. Only when he has become familiar with their habits can he identify these types. But by that time it may be too late. Thanks to ill-bred planners and mimicking intellectuals, the class may have flown into chaos. Help is at hand, however: a catalogue of freshman student types will enable instructors to spot troublesome students and avert disorder in the classroom.

3 Because of the typical plumage of freshmen, the five types remain indistinguishable during the first few classes. First-year students, no matter what their type, wear clothes ranging from ragged jeans and leather jackets to neatly pressed dresses and sharp-looking business suits. Punctuality is not a distinguishing characteristic, either: all students arrive for class anywhere from ten minutes early to fifteen minutes late.

4 True blue intellectuals and mimicking intellectuals (commonly known as "mimickers") are the hardest types to identify. They compete with each other for a claw-hold on their professor's attention. Mimickers, as their name suggests, copy the habits of true blues: the true blue relies on natural intelligence while the mimicker steals words and ideas from his wise cousin.

5 To differentiate between these two types, the novice instructor must learn to separate the true blues from the mimickers. For example, if a student behaves familiarly with the professor in the first two classes, or if he rewords what has just been said — either by the professor or by another student — he is a mimicker. After years of classroom experience, a professor learns to rely on the more direct means of identifying a true blue: listening for keen comments. The true blue intellectual is distinguishable from the mimicker because she is well-read, perceptive, and confident of her abilities. When she speaks, she is courteous to the lecturer and respectful of her peers. In addition, her comments reflect the subject matter of the class and often provide new insights. Mimicking intellectuals, in contrast, are often boorish. They often interrupt lectures with remarks they believe to be relevant but which in reality are either a paraphrase of what the lecturer has said five minutes earlier or

[1] *This paper was submitted as an assignment in an advanced level writing course at the University of Alberta.*

a parroting of a true blue's comment. The mimicker often cuts off his classmates' questions to say something banal. Not only is he unaware of his rudeness, but also he is oblivious to the irrelevance of his asides.

6 Experienced professors tame these creatures through brutal honesty. Telling the mimicker that he is nothing more than a parrot clips his wings and makes him docile. An inexperienced lecturer, however, may encounter difficulty in clipping wings and hence find himself confronted by a flock of ruffled and angry mimickers.

7 The lecturer who has a room full of squawking mimickers has less to fear, however, than the one with a buzzing planner in his teaching sanctuary. The buzzing planner is most talkative before and during class and most vain afterwards. Her interests are meeting new friends, preening herself, and planning her weekend, and she explores these interests noisily while suffering the inconvenience of attending a lecture. Marked by a high rate of absenteeism, a buzzing planner is a terror when present and a relief when missing. A flock of planners will frequently disrupt a lecture with their whispered conversations which can reach a chaotic crescendo if they perceive the lecture to be boring.

8 Of the five freshman types, the buzzing planner can be the most dangerous to an untested instructor, which is why she belongs in a class by herself. If left to her own vices, the buzzing planner will actively undermine the instructor. She achieves her ends by asking trivial or untimely questions, forcing the instructor to backtrack and delay the lecture. A wise professor can silence the planner by backing away from her question and diving into the next topic. Unfortunately, those still inexperienced in classroom management often find themselves off course after having been turned around by a buzzing planner.

9 On one occasion in my English course, for example, two buzzing planners led a new lecturer astray with their questions. While he was desperately trying to regain his composure, they chirped on about a topic completely unrelated to the lecture. In the end, the lecturer exploded and shouted the planners into silence. An experienced professor would have asked them to leave, a suggestion any buzzing planner will fly at delightedly. My English lecturer never did regain control of the class, for the students had lost respect for him and his untamed fury. True blue intellectuals dropped his course, leaving behind the mimickers and buzzing planners. By the end of the school year, the instructor had left the university carrying a shotgun of hostility for his students. Buzzing planners destroyed his career.

10 The idle sleeper, on the other hand, is both easily identified and relatively harmless. He is the one who sits at the back of class, rests his head on his books before the lecturer begins, and begins snoring ten minutes into the period. The sleeper contributes nothing to the class other than to flip through the pages of a textbook, pretending to look studious, if the professor asks a question. Last to arrive and first to leave, the idle sleeper is an irritating but innocuous addition to the class. Though seasoned professors occasionally prey on this species in order to pluck them out of the class, new lecturers would do well to let the idle sleepers lie.

11 An inexperienced lecturer can easily mistake a modest intellectual for an idle sleeper, an error which results in ruffled feathers and egg on the instructor's face. These two types are quite distinct, though they appear alike on the surface. The sleeper is silent because three-quarters of the time he is coma-

tose. The modest intellectual is quiet because she is too shy to offer her insights, though her thoughts are often as perceptive as those of the true blue intellectual. The modest intellectual's shyness stems from a lack of confidence in her abilities, which is why she rarely volunteers her knowledge. When asked to comment, however, she may provide keen perceptions.

12 The experienced professional eye can spot these creatures without difficulty. A seasoned lecturer knows how to ask direct questions of her students to coax the modest intellectual out from among the covey of sleepers, while the novice lecturer snares all types within his net without an inkling of how to sort his flock.

13 Knowing the five types of freshmen is helpful, but knowledge alone is not enough to control them. The ability to classify cannot help a fledgling professor cope with a classroom full of first-year students. Only a seasoned professor knows the tricks to use to quiet the planners, rouse the sleepers, inspire the mimickers, and encourage the true blue and the modest intellectuals. The inexperienced lecturer must endure their cries and pecks, earn a few grey hairs, and teach hundreds of these creatures before he learns how to tame a flock and groom his students into scholars.

Answers

Chapter 1: Three Suggestions for Quick Improvement

1

1. surely
2. liking
3. believable
4. arrangement
5. moving
6. barely
7. radiator
8. experiencing
9. absolutely
10. using

2

1. safely
2. arguing
3. sizable
4. accelerating
5. extremely
6. improvement
7. reducing
8. usable
9. immediately
10. requiring

3

1. sincerely
2. coherence
3. valuable
4. guidance
5. discouraging
6. icy
7. completely
8. purchasing
9. collapsible
10. encouragement

4

1. boring
2. movement
3. scarcely
4. unusable
5. careful
6. advertisement
7. excusable
8. providing
9. sensible
10. improvement

5

1. safety
2. ranging
3. reducible
4. balancing
5. entirely
6. insurance
7. definitely
8. careless
9. responsible
10. distancing

7

1. planning
2. stopping
3. admitted
4. nailing
5. stirred
6. commissioner
7. putting
8. writing
9. mapping
10. interrupted

8

1. shipper
2. beginning
3. dropped
4. training
5. forgetting
6. appearance
7. planned
8. happening
9. stopper
10. insisted

9

1. suffering
2. quizzed
3. permitting
4. stripped
5. meeting
6. compelling
7. cropped
8. tipping
9. allotting
10. quartered

10

1. preferring
2. omitted
3. transferring
4. developing
5. controller
6. occurred
7. equipping
8. forgotten
9. biting
10. preferred

11

1. bidding
2. comforting
3. forgetful
4. admitting
5. available
6. regretting
7. regrettable
8. controllable
9. disappearance
10. deferred

12

1. overlapped
2. expelling
3. quizzed
4. acquitted
5. focusing
6. excelling
7. developed
8. transferred
9. paralleled
10. rebelling

13

1. occurrence
2. existence
3. coherence
4. concurring
5. interference
6. subsistence
7. difference
8. dependence
9. recurrence
10. insistence

15

1. brief
2. cashier
3. receive
4. pierce
5. relief
6. retrieve
7. ceiling
8. believe
9. deceitful
10. hygiene

16

1. thief
2. piece
3. grief
4. conceive
5. priest
6. frontier
7. achieve
8. conceit
9. beige
10. Fahrenheit

17

1. wiener, weighed
2. freight, surveillance
3. receipt, eight
4. relief, conceit
5. reigns, heir

18

1. chow mein, stein
2. Neither, Geiger counter
3. neighbour, niece
4. reins, sleigh
5. conceivable, either

19

1. grieved, vein
2. their, belief, protein
3. species, height
4. seized, receivers, foreign

20

1. heroes
2. histories
3. criteria
4. ghettos
5. personnel
6. crises
7. data
8. phenomena
9. nuclei (or nucleuses)
10. appendixes (or appendices)

21

1. loneliness
2. copied
3. craziness
4. easier
5. prettiest
6. replies
7. replying
8. thirtieth
9. unnecessarily
10. trafficking

22

1. em—ploy—er
2. con—sists
3. suc—cess
4. man—age—ment
5. pro—cess
6. ship—ping
7. ac—count—ing
8. through (Words of one syllable cannot be divided.)
9. dis—tri—bu—tion
10. busi—ness

Chapter 2: Sound-Alikes, Look-Alikes, and Spoilers

1

1. effect, courses
2. Our, accepted
3. dessert, than
4. you're, losing
5. quiet, hear
6. whose, conscience
7. fourth, than
8. it's, its
9. advise, choose
10. Does, dining

2

1. principle, principal
2. fourth, chose
3. except, dessert
4. You're, conscience
5. quiet, hear
6. except, minor
7. lose, too, morale
8. conscience, your
9. stationary, its
10. Does, woman

3

1. hear, here
2. stationery, two
3. lose, it's
4. your, minors
5. conscience, choosing, course
6. accept, Council
7. coarse, effect
8. peace, quiet
9. Who's, women's
10. piece, forth

4

1. many, deserts
2. Where, quiet
3. two, latter
4. consul, principle
5. Many, lose
6. You're, your, dose
7. principle, then
8. It's, later
9. later, except
10. quite, woman

5

1. allot, dining
2. peace, our
3. than, morals
4. Where, we're
5. stationary, forth
6. hear, you're, chose, course
7. are, conscious, their
8. affected, personal
9. whose, advice
10. principal, peace, minor

6

1. affects, morale
2. compliment, than
3. advice, personal
4. miner, does
5. their, moral
6. hear, you're
7. Who's, personal, stationery
8. choose, latter, course
9. dessert, quite
10. Too, where

7

1. then, excepted
2. loose, accept
3. it's, principle
4. advise, personal
5. accepted, compliments
6. minors, they're
7. chose, dining
8. hear, your
9. than, our
10. too, coarse, to

8

1. its, too, to
2. choose, whose
3. Personnel, then, counsel
4. conscious, effect
5. does, affect
6. Council, its, later
7. personal, women
8. compliment, conscious
9. Many, personnel, morale
10. Whose, complement

9

1. coarse, desert
2. then, your
3. advice, counsel, accepted
4. There, lose
5. woman, stationery
6. minor, effect
7. too, too, to
8. conscious, effects
9. its, does
10. council, whose, advise

10

There once was a sailor who, *losing* his job to a steam engine, set out to become a successful business man. His first venture was as encyclopedia salesman, but he found that he didn't have the necessary *personal* touch to win *acceptance* from his customers. Indeed, he was fortunate to escape one encounter with his life, after calling his prospective customer "Matey" throughout *their* negotiations.

He next sought the relative *peace* and *quiet* of the skilled trades, turning his hand to carpentry. The *effect* of that decision was even more unhappy, for he no sooner set *forth* on the venture *than* he lost *two* fingers while attempting to cut a board with a dull saw. *Later*, after he regained *consciousness*, he swore (rather *coarsely*) that he would never again try a job that required him to handle sharp implements.

The sailor then became a *miner*, but concluded that his fellow *miners* were *too* unfriendly, and so he *deserted*. He tried his hand (or what remained of it) at selling *stationery*, working in a tire repair shop, and bartending. It was on this last job that he *received* the *advice* that would lead to his success. A *woman* who relieved him at 8:00 every night recommended that he forget his *principles* and turn to politics. Her advice was sound.

From local *council* to provincial politics, and on to Parliament, our sailor leapt from success to success. He found that his previous jobs had prepared him well for his new career. His *morale* soared. In campaign speeches he was able to say, "As *your* MP, I shall guide the ship of state, while nailing down new reforms, and toiling beneath the surface to draft legislation. I shall go door to door to ask for *your* support and when I get it, I shall serve you tirelessly!" He was irresistible. Election after election, his constituency *chose* him as their representative.

Chapter 3: Cracking the Sentence Code

1

1. Algy met
2. bear met
3. bear was
4. bulge was
5. Grizzlies are
6. Meeting is
7. bears run
8. (you) believe. They do
9. Females are known
10. How to defend oneself presents

2

1. Canada is
2. word means
3. Newfoundland is
4. Are you
5. drivers are jailed
6. exceptions are made
7. is CN Tower
8. Crime is
9. playing is
10. lay keys

3

1. Money does
2. are steps
3. Flin Flon is named
4. idea was
5. (you) drive
6. Study makes
7. (you) turn
8. city is
9. Love comes
10. is concept understood

4

1. Doing is
2. friend is
3. Were they
4. were children
5. Are you
6. Stampede is held
7. Replacing is
8. (you) stop
9. address is
10. Peace, order, and good government are

5

1. He is sleeping
2. you should have been paying
3. Should we write
4. fall comes
5. did you get
6. We do want
7. are we meeting
8. men will think
9. coach has begun
10. swam shark

6

1. country is covered
2. would anyone want
3. Canadians are becoming
4. will I agree
5. person may forgive
6. have been players ones
7. You can become
8. did you stay
9. Have you been
10. has coach become interested

7

1. gasoline will be
2. network will have been completed
3. are records known
4. man will take
5. provinces were railroaded
6. I am studying
7. Could government have managed
8. Have you been caught
9. little is known
10. Are you

8

1. A bird ~~in the hand~~ is worth two ~~in the bush~~.
2. Only a few ~~of us~~ have done our homework.
3. Some ~~of your answers~~ are entertaining but wrong.
4. More than a dozen brands ~~of video recorder~~ are now ~~on the market~~.
5. (You) meet me ~~at six at the corner of Bathurst and Dupont~~.
6. A couple ~~of hamburgers~~ should be enough ~~for each of us~~.
7. Do you know anything ~~about the latest rumours of scandal in the government~~?
8. There is a show ~~about laser technology on television~~ tonight.
9. ~~After eight hours of classes~~, the thought ~~of collapsing in front of the TV set~~ is very appealing.
10. One episode ~~of *All My Children*~~ was more than enough.

9

1. The verb ~~in this sentence~~ is "is."
2. ~~For many students~~, lack ~~of money~~ is probably the most serious problem.
3. ~~In the middle of May~~, ~~after the end of term~~, the Intercollegiate Arm-Wrestling Championships will be held.
4. One strand ~~of fibre optics~~ can carry both telephone and television signals.
5. ~~During the second week of term~~, the class will be taken ~~on a tour of the resource centre~~.
6. ~~Contrary to your expectations~~, and ~~despite the rumours~~, your instructor does not bite.
7. ~~On Callisto~~, one ~~of Jupiter's thirteen moons~~, snow may "fall" up, not down.
8. ~~On the shore of Vancouver Island~~, you can find both oysters and clams.
9. One ~~of the most entertaining comedies of the 1980s~~ was *A Fish Called Wanda*.
10. ~~In similar circumstances~~, most ~~of us~~ would probably have taken his money.

10

1. ~~By this time~~, you must be tired ~~of the pointless game shows on TV~~.
2. The happiness ~~of every country~~ depends ~~upon the character of its people~~.
3. ~~Above my desk~~ hangs someone else's diploma.
4. ~~During the course of the discussion~~, several ~~of us~~ lost our tempers.
5. ~~In the evenings~~ and ~~on weekends~~, he works ~~on his 1958 Chevy~~.
6. The "short side" ~~of a goalie~~ is the side closer ~~to the post~~.
7. New steps should be taken to encourage the flow ~~of capital into small businesses~~.
8. ~~After waiting for more than an hour~~, we finally left ~~without you~~.

9. So far only two ~~of your answers~~ ~~to the questions~~ have been incorrect.
10. One ~~of the country's most distinguished reporters~~ will speak ~~on the responsibilities~~ ~~of the press~~.

11

1. The average height ~~of Canadian women~~, ~~excluding those~~ ~~in Quebec~~, is 165 cm.
2. ~~By waiting on tables~~, ~~(by) babysitting~~, and ~~(by) doing other jobs~~, I manage to make ends meet.
3. The pile ~~of books and papers~~ ~~on your desk~~ is about as neat as a tossed salad.
4. Only a few ~~of the news reporters~~ ~~on television~~ are responsible for researching and writing in addition to reading the news.
5. ~~Except for me~~, everyone understands prepositions.
6. No book ~~of Canadian humour~~ would be complete ~~without a couple of "Newfie" jokes~~.
7. Our teacher's uncertainty ~~about the date~~ ~~of the War of 1812~~ made us less than confident ~~about his knowledge~~ ~~of Canadian history~~.
8. A daily intake ~~of more than 600 mg~~ ~~of caffeine~~ can result ~~in headaches~~, ~~(in) insomnia~~, and ~~(in) heart palpitations~~.
9. Six to ten cups ~~of coffee~~ will contain 600 mg ~~of caffeine~~.
10. ~~Despite its strong taste~~, espresso contains no more caffeine than regular coffee.

12

1. The current trend ~~in electronics~~ is to put telephones ~~in our pockets~~ and televisions ~~in our telephones~~.
2. ~~Along with many other Canadian expressions~~, the term *bluenose*, meaning a Nova Scotian, is ~~of uncertain origin~~.
3. ~~Within a week~~, please give me your report ~~on the pyrazine anion project~~. (The subject is you.)
4. ~~In the spring~~, parked ~~in front~~ ~~of his TV set~~, Barry trains ~~for the Stanley Cup playoffs~~.
5. Government programs ~~to encourage training~~ ~~in basic skills~~ have been cut back steadily ~~over the past few years~~.
6. ~~In the Arctic wastes~~ ~~of Ungava~~, there is a mysterious stone structure ~~in the shape of a giant hammer~~ standing ~~on end~~.
7. There is no obvious explanation ~~for its presence~~ ~~in this isolated place~~.
8. ~~According to archeologist Thomas E. Lee~~, it may be a monument left ~~by Vikings~~ ~~in their travels west~~ ~~from Greenland~~.
9. Here, ~~on an island~~ called Pamiok, are the ruins of ~~what may have been a Viking longhouse~~.
10. If so, then centuries ~~before Colombus' "discovery"~~ ~~of America~~, the Vikings were ~~in what is now northern Quebec~~.

14

1. Jack, Jill went
2. Georgie Porgie kissed, made
3. Jack, Jill went, fetched
4. Maple sugar, wild rice are
5. I tried, tried, did succeed
6. Jim, Brian will go

7. canoeists, dog were missing
8. Timothy Findley farms, writes. lectures
9. (you) wait, phone
10. Shooting, scoring are

15.

1. Misspellings can create, (can) cause
2. *Durham County Review* printed
3. soldier was praised, was described
4. soldier called, demanded
5. writer, editor soothed, promised
6. paper apologized, explained
7. (you) drive, see; (you) drive, see
8. drivers obey, lose
9. (you) drink, you want, (you) drive, you do
10. Come-by-Chance, Blow-me-Down, Run-by-Guess, Jerry's Nose are

16

1. (you) take, (you) leave
2. Jan, I studied, failed
3. were goldfish, ball, couple
4. He worked, saved, died
5. Everybody went, spent
6. are Camembert, Fontina, Quark
7. companies, publishers, manufacturers are profiting
8. We took, went
9. politicians attempt, try
10. government will provide, (will) eliminate, (will) find, (will) land, (will) win

Chapter 4: Still More about Verbs

1

1. became
2. brought
3. had
4. sang
5. flung
6. froze
7. got (gotten)
8. lent
9. swung
10. laid

2

1. led
2. lost
3. said
4. slept
5. swum
6. told
7. threw
8. stolen
9. rode
10. written

3

1. wore, worn
2. built, built
3. slid, slid
4. blew, blown
5. bore, borne
6. hit, hit
7. ridden, rode
8. spent, spent
9. won, won
10. told, told

4

1. wound, wound
2. tore, torn
3. lay, lain
4. bit, bitten
5. grew, grown
6. had, had
7. burst, burst
8. ran, run
9. made, made
10. brought, brought

5

1. bid, bid
2. rung, rang
3. saw, seen
4. broken, broke
5. fought, fought
6. kept, kept
7. put, put
8. wrote, written
9. threw, thrown
10. taken, took

6

1. thought, thought
2. begun, began
3. felt, felt
4. bought, bought
5. done, did
6. gave, given
7. paid, paid
8. lent, lent
9. gone, went
10. hurt, hurt

7

1. came, come
2. rose, risen
3. left, left
4. sped, sped
5. taught, taught
6. fell, fallen
7. chose, chosen
8. heard, heard
9. flew, flown
10. struck, struck

8

1. held, held
2. stole, stolen
3. swung, swung
4. hid, hidden
5. said, said
6. drew, drawn
7. met, met
8. swore, sworn
9. forgave, forgiven
10. laid, laid

9

1. driven, drove
2. meant, meant
3. hung, hung
4. dealt, dealt
5. found, found
6. led, led
7. known, knew
8. forgot, forgotten (forgot)
9. sold, sold
10. spoke, spoken

10

1. hanged, hanged
2. stood, stood
3. lost, lost
4. got, got (gotten)
5. slept, slept
6. froze, frozen
7. shaken, shook
8. set, set
9. swum, dived; swam, dived (dove)
10. ate, drank; eaten, drunk

Chapter 5: Solving Sentence-Fragment Problems

We have made the sentence fragments into complete sentences only for the first set and only to give you an idea of how the sentences might be formed. Many different sentences can be made out of the fragments given; just be sure each of your sentences has a subject and a verb.

1

1. F This chapter is about sentence fragments.
2. F We have to go to the wall.
3. F I'll be glad to do it for you.
4. F She keeps falling asleep in class, after working all night.
5. F The pinochle players are meeting in the upper lounge.
6. S
7. F Watching television is a cheap form of entertainment.
8. F I am hoping to hear from you soon.
9. F I have saved for just such an emergency.
10. S

2

1. F
2. F
3. F
4. F
5. F
6. F
7. S
8. F
9. F
10. S

3

1. S
2. S
3. F
4. F
5. F
6. F
7. F
7. F
9. F
10. F

4

1. F
2. S
3. F
4. F
5. F
6. F
7. S
8. S
9. F
10. S

5

1. F
2. F
3. S
4. F
5. F
6. F
7. F
8. F
9. F
10. F

6

1. F Although
2. F Before
3. F Since
4. F Whose
5. F Until
6. F As
7. F If
8. S
9. F Before
10. S

7

1. F After
2. F Whatever
3. F Even if
4. F As long as
5. F When
6. F Unless
7. F who
8. S
9. F When
10. F although

8

1. F In order that
2. F Though
3. F Since
4. F If
5. F Provided that
6. F Even if
7. S
8. F Whenever
9. S
10. F so that

9

1. F who
2. F that
3. S
4. S
5. F Where
6. F when
7. F Whether
8. F whichever
9. F until
10. F that

10

1. S
2. F Though, who
3. F that
4. S
5. S
6. S
7. F If
8. F Because, that
9. F Until, as long as, whichever
10. F When, where

12

Although spring is my favourite season, and I look forward eagerly to its arrival after the long winter, there are some things about the season that I could do without. When the warm weather begins, I am always tempted to buy new, fashionable shoes which are ruined in the wet muck that is everywhere. Unless I act quickly, my dog also becomes a problem in the spring.

She delights in tracking mud from the back yard into the house. After she creates a mess that Mr. Clean would need steroids to tackle, she will go back outside and find something sticky and smelly to roll in. Until the warm weather dries up the mud and my dog loses the annual urge to coat herself with disgusting substances, my joy at the arrival of spring is always a little restrained.

13

Fads in popular music come and go with astonishing speed. After the movie *Urban Cowboy*, country and western music became popular among people who had never dreamed of wearing pointed boots with high heels. Though the C and W fad was short-lived, it did produce a host of new fans. Most of these quickly moved on to other musical trends while those of us who had always loved C and W settled down to being cultural outcasts again after our brief time in the limelight. As soon as John Travolta gave up his Stetson for dancing shoes, the western theme bars and restaurants threw out the barn board and cactuses and began redecorating. Most recently, however, since people like k.d. lang have brought a mainstream following back to country music, sophisticated urban listeners are once again buying Conway Twitty and Ian Tyson. Even though musical tastes change quickly, there are die-hard C and W fans who can always be identified by their collection of Tommy Hunter records.

14

Since my marks at the end of high school were anything but impressive, I thought the chances of my acceptance at college or university were not very good. Secretly, however, I wasn't at all sure that college or university was where I wanted to go. I had also applied to the Armed Forces program that pays for your education if you agree to serve for four years after graduation, provided that you meet certain conditions. On the same day that the official transcript of my dismal marks appeared in the mail, two schools I had applied to sent their rejections, as did the Armed Forces, calling me "an academic risk." Until the next day, when a fourth letter arrived, I hid the marks and the rejection letters from my parents and suffered, as I have never suffered before or since. Fortunately, since the fourth letter was an acceptance from an unusually enlightened (or desperate) school, I was able to enjoy the summer. Eventually I graduated with a respectable average and became a writer. Last year, I got my revenge on the Armed Forces for their lack of faith in my academic potential when they bought three thousand copies of my text book – in order to teach their recruits how to write.

Chapter 6: Solving Run-On Problems

1

1. Kevin is lazy; Allan is no better. Or: Kevin is lazy. Allan is no better.
2. Stop me if you've heard this one. There was this bus driver on his first day at work.

3. correct
4. Ronnie says he likes hiking, but he never goes very far. Maybe that's why he's still overweight.
5. correct
6. It bothers me to see her playing cards all the time; she could easily fail her semester.
7. Dennis was transformed; overnight he had turned from a plain-looking student into a fashion plate.
8. Fall is my favourite time of year; the colours are beautiful.
9. A fine mess this is. I'll never forgive you for getting me into this situation.
10. correct

2

1. I want to play the banjo; the only thing stopping me is a complete lack of musical talent.
2. correct
3. There are many good films made in Hollywood; I wish I could tell which they were before paying my admission to the cinema.
4. correct
5. This is an excellent book; the authors must be very intelligent.
6. In the early days in Canada, the Americans were seen as a constant threat; even Ottawa was not considered safe.
7. Let him come on his knees and beg for it; that's the only way he'll ever get the money from me!
8. correct
9. More people are heating their homes with woodstoves these days; the result is "ecologists' smog."
10. The fog is closing in; we'll be lucky to get home before dawn unless the weather changes.

3

1. Give careful thought to your answer; a great deal depends on what you decide.
2. correct
3. correct
4. My chiropractor has given me several exercises he says will make my back stronger; in time I'm sure he will be proven right.
5. Karen was given the choice of joining her father's firm as a general labourer or continuing at school; she's sure to take the job if I know Karen!
6. correct
7. When our hockey team travels to Moncton, we always stay at the same motel; it's not expensive but is close to the arena and appears to be well maintained.
8. Go to the door and see who's there; I'm too busy with my homework right now.
9. correct
10. correct

4

1. I don't know whose those shoes are; they were left here after our last party. Probably they belong to one of your friends. (. . . are. They. . . .) (. . . are, but they. . . .)
2. With her huge, brown, adoring eyes and obedient disposition, my dog runs my life; I know I'll never find a woman who can compare. (. . . life. I. . . .)
3. Cats are the most wonderful of creatures; they are often more human than humans, as any true cat lover can tell you. (. . . creatures. They. . . .) (. . . creatures, for they. . . .)
4. In comparing cars, there are many factors to consider; the most important of these is probably price. (. . . consider. The. . . .) (. . . consider, but the. . . .)
5. Let's go the other way; to get there as quickly as possible is our most important task at the moment. (. . . way. To. . . .) (. . . way, for to. . . .)
6. correct
7. Fast food is generally less nutritious than home-cooked meals; though I know of some home cooking that rates below cardboard in nutritional value, I still prefer it as a rule. (. . . meals. Though. . . .)
8. Appraising his progress is difficult; when you realize that he has completed none of the assignments, written none of the tests, and attended only three of the classes, you can see why I despair. (. . . difficult. When. . . .) (. . . difficult, for when. . . .)
9. This day has held quite enough excitement. I'm going to bed, so I get a good rest. Please try to keep the noise to a minimum and don't turn on the light. (. . . rest; please. . . .)
10. There's something very comforting about a fireplace, but a chimney fire is no joke; make sure your chimney is cleaned twice a year. (. . . joke. Make. . . .) (. . . joke, so make. . . .)

5

Last term we had an exchange student from the south of France. Her name was Sophie and she came to Canada to learn the language and to experience something of our culture. She was amazed by our fondness for fast food; she found it inedible. Another cultural difference Sophie observed was the emphasis Canadian girls place on dress and cosmetics. They often applied fresh makeup between classes and they dressed as if they were going to a fashionable restaurant instead of school. Sophie loved to dress up, too; she delighted in the dramatic designs that the French are famous for. She wore them only on special occasions, however. The multicultural aspects of Canadian society, the newness of all the towns and cities, and the vast size of the country all impressed her during her visit. The huge expanses of untouched wilderness she found a little intimidating. Though she was homesick, especially at first, Sophie enjoyed her year in Canada. When she was packing to return to her home near Cannes, she was already planning her next visit — a canoeing holiday in Algonquin Park.

7

1. *Field of Dreams* is one of my favourite films because it seems so true to life. I'm thinking of reading the short story, which is titled *Shoeless Joe Jackson Comes to Iowa*.

2. People tend to forget that a complete education involves the body as well as the mind. In most high schools, physical education isn't taken seriously, and at college there is almost no emphasis at all on athletics except for support of a few varsity teams. All this would change if the Ministry of Education changed its policy; however, that doesn't seem likely.
3. When the Travelling Wilburys split up, my favourite group became Tom Petty and the Heartbreakers. Since rap has become popular, I like Run DMC. I don't listen to music much any more, though, because my stereo's broken. I lost my part-time job, so I can't afford to have it fixed.
4. Bruce hates alarm clocks and refuses to keep one in his apartment. He's the guy who used to go out with my sister; she dropped him because he was always late.
5. It's always best to tell the truth, because one lie leads to another, and eventually you'll get caught.
6. They took up sailing last year; we haven't seen them since.
7. I'm tired, and I guess you must be, too. Let's just finish this last one and then turn in. We can get an early start tomorrow and polish off the rest before noon so we can have the rest of the day to ourselves.
8. Foolish people are those who, through ignorance or stupidity, refuse to believe there's anything they don't know. When a situation comes along they aren't familiar with, and they don't know how to act, they just plough ahead without a care. Usually they end up making the situation worse and adding to their richly deserved reputation as fools.
9. I think there are many components of a sense of humour; one is the ability to see the absurd in normal situations, and another is the very rare gift of being able to see oneself as an object of fun or ridicule. Almost no one has the latter ability to any degree.
10. Canadian politics are really very straightforward and simple, if you think about it. We have several levels of government, each with its own powers and jurisdictions and each responsible to its constituents. Difficulties arise, though, when jurisdictions overlap or aren't clearly defined.

8

Having decided on a canoe trip to La Verendrye Park, north-east of Ottawa, Jean-Pierre and Bernard began to make plans. It did not take them long to discover that they really didn't know all that much about each other, and that, while Bernard was an experienced canoe tripper, Jean-Pierre had a great many fears and misconceptions. Jean-Pierre, for example, could not imagine what two people could eat for two whole weeks in the wilderness. Bernard took charge of the planning and used his knowledge and experience to organize a list of supplies and equipment. The trip north to the park was their opportunity to become better acquainted. They found they had a great deal in common, including a love of music. Jean-Pierre could actually play an instrument: he was quite proficient with the banjo he had brought along. They rented a canoe near the park, registered with the park officials, and set about final preparations. However carefree they appeared on the surface, each had concerns about the trip: Pierre about what they would eat, and Bernard about his companion's canoeing ability.

They survived the first day, despite a constant drizzle and a 500-metre portage that wound its way through swampy terrain, getting them soaked up to the knees and dampening their spirits. The first camp was a huge success. Jean-Pierre proved to have a real talent for fishing, so they ate fresh-caught trout. The weather cleared, so they could sit around the fire and watch the moon come up. Eventually the mosquitoes became a nuisance, forcing them into the protection of the tent. The two weeks flew by. Back home, when they reflected on the trip, they agreed that their fears had been needless. Jean-Pierre had put on three kilograms, and Bernard confessed that he had never canoed with a better bow-man. In fact, they had had such a good time, they decided to make it an annual event.

9

American gun laws continue to be a mystery to most Canadians, who look at the annual death toll south of the border and compare it to our own more modest statistics. It seems obvious to us that our restrictive regulations are responsible for our relatively few gun incidents, and we wonder at the blind prejudice of Americans that they cannot see as clearly as we do that open access to firearms leads to more gunshot deaths. In fact, one statistic clearly proves our point of view: for every intruder killed by a privately owned handgun in the United States, two hundred innocent people are killed in domestic disputes or accidents.

In using such figures to question the wisdom of our southern neighbours, we overlook the reason for their insistence on free access to guns. Their country was born out of a revolution against what they saw as a despotic king. The only thing that made the revolution possible (and ultimately successful) was that every household had at least one gun and at least one person who knew how to use it. In truth, armed civilians were responsible for the founding of America. This fact led directly to the provision in their constitution that every citizen has the right to bear arms (though I know of more than one person who assumes this means that every American citizen has the constitutional right to wear short sleeves). To argue against the right to bear arms is, in many minds, to be un-American. It is of little significance to such minds that the right to own a gun to protect America from her enemies is an outmoded concept in the age of Star Wars and missile-firing submarines.

10

Dire Straits is a band that transcends all the labels and loyalties associated with rock groups. There seems to be consensus that this is a group that defies categories and yet picks up devoted fans from practically every branch of rock's broad range. At their most recent concert at a stadium within driving distance of our community, there was a great deal of excitement and enthusiasm. The amazing thing was that such a variety of people were determined to get tickets and arrange transportation. One friend of mine, a teacher in his mid-forties who snarls at little children and claims to like only kittens and puppies . . . as long as they're well done, behaved like a schoolboy in his eagerness to get good seats. Having got them, he boasted openly about his success. Another friend, a serious rock musician, who confesses to be an admirer of Dire Straits for their professionalism and for the fact that they are what he calls "a working band" rather than studio musicians, claims the lyrics of Mark Knopfler, the band's leader, are unsurpassed in contemporary music; moreover, Knopfler's guitar playing is among the best in the business. At the other end of the scale, my neighbour's two teenage daughters squealed with delight and phoned practically every other fourteen-year-old in the county, when they were presented with tickets for a graduation gift. In short, everyone — young, old, and in-between — had a great time at the concert. Dire Straits proved their incomparable talent once again.

Chapter 7: Solving Modifier Problems

1

1. Some people never go to movies unless they're French or Italian.
2. Elmo bought a Dustbuster that cost $29.95 for his girlfriend.
3. They decided to pay me nearly $350 a week.
4. correct
5. We laughed at the antics of the clown wearing two left shoes and a funny little flowered hat.
6. I hate parties where food is served on little paper plates to the guests.
7. Ferdinand has insulted almost everyone he's gone out with.
8. In a rage, the angry hippo chased me towards the zookeeper.
9. My brother could only hope to win the jackpot.
10. On Thursday the boss told me I would be fired.

2

1. In Minoan Crete there are wall paintings of boys with no clothes on jumping over bulls.
2. Only two suitable jobs were advertised.
3. This course can be completed in six weeks by anyone who has learned English grammar.
4. For a small fee, the obituary column lists the names of people who have died recently.
5. Walking through Wonderland, Alice discovered a mushroom.
6. She ate only one bite and found herself growing larger.
7. They told me to come back every week and check the notice board.
   Or: They told me to come back and check the notice board every week.
8. For their own satisfaction, parents want to know what their children are doing in school.
9. The cause of the accident was a little guy with a big mouth in a small car.
10. With his binoculars, Ferdinand spotted a dwarf hippo.

3

1. People who shoplift get caught frequently.
2. He watched television almost all night.
3. Tammy Faye eagerly tried to convince the members of her fan club to wear two or three sets of false eyelashes.
4. With the wooden spoon, stir the flour into the butter in the saucepan.

5. correct
6. No one except petrochemical company executives is allowed to throw any pollutants into the river.
7. With only an old black-powder rifle, he took a stand against a tree while waiting for the bear.
8. Walking to school, I passed the security guard and two workmen.
9. Here in Petawawa, I am pleased to meet student representatives of our twenty-two colleges.
10. Perhaps you're on your own in Vancouver, with a sparkling city to explore and a couple of tickets in your pocket to an event at the new covered stadium.

5

1. As a college English teacher, I am annoyed by dangling modifiers.
2. Having rotted in storage, the grain could not be sold by the farmers for the profit they were counting on.
3. Before turning in for the night, you should place your hairpiece on the plastic head.
4. Driving through the Arizona desert, we felt our mouths become drier and drier.
5. Turning to the appendix, you will find in the third paragraph the example I quoted.
6. Before applying the varnish, sand the surface smooth.
7. Upon entering, I saw the store was completely empty.
8. Attempting to hotwire an '88 Trans Am, a suspect was arrested by the police.
9. Looking over his shoulder, the man slowly backed up the car.
10. In very cold weather, you should warm up the engine thoroughly before attempting to drive.

6

1. After changing the tire, you should release the jack.
2. Having decided on pizza, we should decide next whether to order beer or wine.
3. After waiting for you for an hour, I knew the evening was ruined.
4. Jogging through Stanley Park, I saw a bronze horse.
5. After spending nine dollars on them, I have lost most of the spare keys.
6. Having set the microwave on automatic, I quickly cooked the turkey to perfection.
7. Having completed the beginning, we will turn to the ending, the next most important part of the essay.
8. Convicted of aggravated assault, she was sentenced to two years in Kingston.
9. After having been in prison for so long, the convict found the world to be spinning at a hectic pace.
10. After shovelling the walks, the driveway, and the sidewalk, I was annoyed when it snowed another 10 cm.

7

1. Since I am a college English teacher, dangling modifiers annoy me.
2. Because the grain rotted in storage, the farmers could not sell it for the profit they were counting on.
3. Before you turn in for the night, place your hairpiece on the plastic head.
4. As we drove through the Arizona desert, our mouths became drier and drier.
5. If you turn to the appendix, the example I quoted is in the third paragraph.
6. The surface must be sanded smooth before you apply the varnish.
7. When I entered, the store was completely empty.
8. While he attempted to hotwire an '88 Trans Am, a suspect was arrested by the police.
9. As the driver looked over his shoulder, he slowly backed the car up.
10. In very cold weather, the engine should be thoroughly warmed up before you attempt to drive.

8

1. After you change the tire, release the jack.
2. The next question is whether to order beer or wine, now that we have decided on pizza.
3. After I had waited for you for an hour, the evening was ruined.
4. As I jogged through Stanley Park, a bronze horse came into view.
5. Most of the spare keys, after I spent nine dollars on them, have been lost.
6. After I set the microwave on automatic, the turkey quickly cooked to perfection.
7. After you have completed the beginning, the ending is the next most important part of the essay.
8. When she was convicted of aggravated assault, the judge sentenced her to two years in Kingston.
9. After the convict had been in prison for so long, the world seemed to be spinning at a hectic pace.
10. After I had shovelled the walks, the driveway, and the sidewalk, it snowed another 10 cm.

9

1. Because the glasses are made of very thin crystal, the dishwasher breaks them as fast as I can buy them.
2. As we were driving through Yellowstone, a buffalo blocked the road.
3. As a college student constantly faced with stress, I find the pressure intolerable.
4. His socks, which were long and red, were full of holes.
5. My guests loved the coq au vin, which had been braised in wine.
6. After deciding whether the wine should be blended, add the sugar.
7. We were impressed as she rode by in a bikini on a horse.
8. The sign in the restaurant window read: "Our Establishment Serves Tea in a Bag Just Like Mother." (Or, more grammatical, "Just Like Mother, Our Establishment Serves Tea in a Bag.")
9. As I peered out of my office window, the Goodyear Blimp sailed past.
10. Having broken its wings, the seagull was taken to the SPCA.

10

1. Although he lives 50 km away, he manages to come to nearly every class.
2. The sign said that only students are admitted to the pub.
3. The lion was recaptured by the trainer before anyone was mauled or bitten.
4. While asleep, he kicked the blankets off the bed.
5. Through a plate-glass window, I saw the Queen and her entourage arrive.
6. Having ruled out the other two Japanese imports, we'll choose the Mazda.
7. Swimming isn't a good idea if the water is cold or polluted.
8. The man wore a hideous hat on his head.
9. In last week's letter, I learned about Joan's having a baby.
10. The counsellor, who recently put his foot in his mouth, has alienated the students.

11

1. After completing the study of staffing requirements, we will hire an assistant to the personnel manager.
2. Joe found his dog gnawing avidly on a bone.
3. He said we would have a test on Tuesday. *Or*: on Tuesday he said we would have a test.
4. Our guests didn't find the meal, which was left over from last week's party, very appetizing.
5. Employees who are frequently late are dismissed without notice. *Or*: Employees who are late are frequently dismissed without notice.
6. Since Jim forgot twice this week to pick me up, I'm quitting his car pool.
7. Maria turned the green and mushy avocados into great guacamole.
8. Before they could dispose of much of the loot, the thieves were caught by the police.
9. Though they drink it daily, many people don't trust Lake Ontario water.
10. It is a tradition to pay one's respects in a funeral parlour to friends and relatives after they have died.

Chapter 8: The Parallelism Principle

I

1. The three main kinds of speech are demonstrative, informative, and persuasive.
2. . . . Two of the most difficult are supporting her household and being sole parent to her child.
3. He advised me to take two aspirins and call him in the morning.
4. Books provide us with information, education, and entertainment.
5. To make your court appearance as painless as possible, prepare your case thoroughly, and maintain a pleasant, positive attitude.
6. The apostrophe is used for two purposes: contraction and possession.
7. Swiftly and skilfully the woman gutted and scaled the fish.
8. I am overworked and underpaid.

9. You need to develop skill, strategy, and agility to be a good tennis player.
10. The two main responsibilities of a corrections officer are security and control.

2

1. A part-time job can develop your decision-making skills, your sense of responsibility, your self-confidence, and your independence.
2. The three keys to improving your marks are study, hard work, and bribery.
3. I couldn't decide whether I should become a chef or a data processor.
4. . . . : the widespread lack of strong religious beliefs and the absence of strict moral codes.
5. A course in logical reasoning will help us evaluate what we read and make sound decisions.
6. When you're buying a new car, you should look at more than just the size, style, and cost. The warranty, operating cost, and trade-in value should also be taken into consideration.
7. Mrs. Hunter assigns two hours of homework every night and an essay each week.
8. The two most important characteristics of a personal work space are how neat and well organized it looks and how private it is.
9. Playing with small construction toys is beneficial to young children because it develops their fine motor skills, encourages concentration and patience, and stimulates their creative imagination.
10. My supervisor told me that my performance was generally satisfactory but that my writing must improve.

3

1. The role of the health instructor is to teach preventive medicine, care of the sick, and rehabilitation of the injured.
2. The most common causes of snowmobile accidents are mechanical failure, poor weather conditions, and driver carelessness.
3. The portable classrooms are ill-equipped, poorly lighted, and inadequately heated.
4. The advantages of a thesis statement are that it limits your topic, clarifies the contents of your paper, and shows how your paper will be organized.
5. Unemployment deprives the individual of purchasing power and reduces the country's national output.
6. A good nurse is energetic, tolerant, sympathetic, and reliable.
7. The money spent on space exploration should be used to provide aid to underdeveloped countries and funding for medical research.
8. The best house cats are quiet, clean, affectionate, and elsewhere.
9. . . . : a new appreciation for the beauty of nature and a new admiration for members of the opposite sex.
10. You can conclude a paper with a summary of main points, a question, or a quotation.

4

1. Our winter has not been very pleasant with vicious ice storms, heavy snowfalls, and dangerous freezing rain.

2. Baseball is a game that requires a high level of skill and natural talent.
3. Many foreigners see Canadians as conservative, patriotic, and orderly.
4. Patience and dexterity will make you a good model builder, pianist, or meat cutter.
5. Being a dutiful son, a loyal husband, and an affectionate father made Jason so stressed that he took up boxing as an outlet for his aggression.
6. I shall prove to you that rock music is neither dangerous nor addictive.
7. Selena has three passions in her life: dancing with her boyfriend, listening to Ian Tyson's music, and driving fast cars.
8. After this year at school, I intend to go into nursing or teaching.
9. After nine years of making up incorrect sentences for students to fix, Brian can no longer write properly or express himself correctly.
10. Both managers and workers must make compromises if this committee is to succeed.

5

1. mechanically manually
2. being a nurse being a pilot
3. achieve her goals find true happiness
4. sense of humour wealth intelligence
5. daily exercise wholesome food regular checkups
6. a good cigar a glass of brandy conversation with friends
7. speed comfort good cornering
8. look for bargains choose quality shop for value
9. security value safety
10. tanned golden brown clothed in a skimpy bathing suit accompanied by a big boyfriend

Chapter 9: Refining by Combining

1

1. The picketers left the streets when the police arrived.
2. The angry bystanders knocked down the assassin, tearing him limb from limb.
3. She was forty-one years old, but she looked about twenty.
4. He always quits just when you need him.
5. Roy Rogers, who was known as Leonard Sly, made much money in cowboy movies.
6. Even though football is violent, North Americans love it.
7. Politicians charge that newspapers distort facts.
8. Many people are not aware that television manipulates feelings.
9. Although Walter hates zucchini, he planted some anyway.
10. Whereas scientists in the ancient world looked to the stars for guidance, modern scientists may travel to the stars.

2

1. If I don't get there by noon, come looking for me because I may be in trouble.

2. When the moon was full, we sat huddled in our very warm, down-filled sleeping bags for a long time before it was time to turn in for the night.
3. Crying out for mercy, the student who had been caught distributing anti-government propaganda threw herself at the soldier's feet.
4. Lonely, disillusioned and bitter, Jill stumbled into the rest room, her shoulders bowed and her shopping bags heavy in her hand.
5. Sensing danger, the moose lifted its head, ears stiff and straight, body tense, ready to explode into action at the slightest sound.
6. Key glanced at first base, went into his windup and then threw a hanging curve up in the strike zone that Wade Boggs, anticipating, unloaded over the right field wall.
7. The old train station, which was once the hub of the city, is now the dilapidated refuge of rats.
   Or: The old train station, which is now the dilapidated refuge of rats, was once the hub of the city.
8. Gasping for air, Matthew stumbled down the stairs, horrified by the sight of Geoffrey and his friends wrestling in the living room.
9. The rich, dark, unbelievably sweet chocolate sauce melted over my Death by Chocolate dessert.
10. Thinking it is a tough course, few students register for philosophy, but Philosophy 101 is Monica's favourite course.

3

1. The City of Toronto boasts about the CN Tower because it has a record as the world's tallest free-standing structure: 555 metres high.
2. Completed in 32 months on a downtown site, the Toronto SkyDome has the world's first fully retractable stadium roof, which weighs 6 345 tonnes — equivalent to the weight of 2,376 family sedans. Though the SkyDome spans eight acres and can hold about 70,000 people, it has only 575 parking spaces on its site. Toronto is the eleventh North American city operating a domed stadium.
3. On May 13, 1989, in Beijing, China, 3,000 students began a hunger strike in Tiananmen Square. During this largely peaceful demonstration lasting for four weeks, the students erected a home-made, 10-metre-high replica of the Statue of Liberty, calling it the "Goddess of Democracy." Soon, thousands of armed troops descended on the square, first firing off tracer bullets and tear gas. After loudspeakers urged students to leave, the soldiers opened fire directly on the crowds and charged them with bayonets, killing and wounding hundreds of demonstrators. By Sunday morning, June 4, 1989, there had been a massacre.
4. For most, citizenship is an abstract term meaning loyalty, obedience, and conformity; for a few, it means thinking for themselves, acting independently, and taking control of their own lives. It is often used as a passive term meaning playing one's part in the existing scheme of things, no questions asked.
5. Citizenship is an active term when it has been acquired as the result of struggle. It means enjoying the rights that have been won: the right to vote, to organize, and to equality before the law. Now citizenship means participation and involvement at all levels of society.

6. Lawyers, doctors, and business men are professionals who constitute fewer than ten percent of the Canadian workforce, occupy almost three-quarters of the seats in the House of Commons, and occupy two-thirds of the offices in local party organizations.
7. Blue-collar workers comprise nearly fifty percent of the population, but they hold fewer than ten percent of the positions either in local parties or in Parliament. Moreover, women, native people, and minorities are under-represented in Canada's political and economic institutions, a fact that calls into question our nation's commitment to democracy.
8. Nursing is a discipline concerned with the promotion of the well-being of the individual in society. A nurse respects the dignity, autonomy, and individuality of each human being.
9. Professional nurses provide preventive, educational, restorative, and supportive services, assisting individuals, families, and groups.
10. The RN performs acts requiring substantial specialized knowledge, skill, and judgement. In addition, the RN assesses health needs, and plans, implements, and evaluates nursing care.

Chapter 10: Subject-Verb Agreement

1

1. *Rocket*
2. numbers
3. Elmo and his girlfriend
4. invoices
5. you
6. print media
7. *Superman*
8. reasons
9. anyone
10. pressures

2

1. They think they will begin an investment course . . .
2. Those policy changes affect the entire program.
3. Their jobs have been . . .
4. The women are here because their husbands wanted to emigrate.
5. He does his best work when he is unsupervised.
6. She insists on having her way.
7. Both of Cinderella's sisters were horrid in their own way.
8. Those men's attitudes aren't doing them any good.
9. Toronto sports fans are delighted to . . .
10. All those who care about their appearance should have monthly facials.

3

1. Elvis Presley artifacts and memorabilia are Elmo's consuming passion in life.
2. Clothes are what he spends most of his money on.
3. The one luxury I allow myself is cigarettes.
4. The cause of my obesity was huge meals and constant snacking.
5. Strong leadership and more jobs are what Canada needs now.
6. Too many absences from class were the reason for his failure.

7. The cause of strikes is often disputes over wages and benefits.
8. What she finds fascinating is the differences between the Chinese and the Canadian attitudes towards the elderly.
9. Discussions about politics are something he always enjoys.
10. The only known antidote to a vampire attack is garlic, a cross, and a stake through the heart.

4

1. seems
2. is
3. is
4. are
5. are
6. is
7. were
8. cause

5

1. is
2. writes
3. is
4. is
5. remains
6. wants
7. is
8. is

6

1. was
2. was
3. believes
4. is
5. seems
6. is
7. is
8. dares

7

1. works
2. is
3. interests
4. hopes
5. is
6. is
7. was
8. is

8

1. is
2. seems
3. prides
4. fight
5. Has
6. was
7. gives
8. find

9

1. seems
2. seems
3. seems
4. is
5. is
6. was
7. is
8. is

10

1. A group of unbiased men and women is . . .
2. Anybody who really wants to . . .
3. correct
4. Every one of the contestants thinks . . .

5. The amount of money generated by touring rock stars is . . .
6. If there are . . .
7. Neither Peter nor I am . . .
8. The lack of things to write about causes . . .
9. Michael Jackson, along with his brothers, parents, pets, and retinue, has . . .
10. correct

11

1. The source of all the problems was . . .
2. correct
3. Neither university nor the community colleges appeal . . .
4. Only the first ten minutes of his lecture was . . .
5. Nothing except junk foods appeals . . .
6. correct
7. Every one of the applicants looks . . .
8. This afternoon the class is . . .
9. Absolutely everyone . . . has advised me . . .
10. I'll bet neither you nor he is . . .

12

There are many good reasons for staying fit. The loss of strength, flexibility, and endurance that results from lack of exercise is a very compelling factor, but everyone who joins the many health clubs in this city has individual reasons as well. The people I talked with say appearance or weight loss is their big motivation for working out. No one among the two hundred patrons of a local health club was there for the social aspects of the place, according to my poll. Either daily aerobics or weightlifting was what they wanted from their club, and the intensity of the workouts was clear evidence that they were serious. The manager of the club, along with all the members of his staff, was very careful to point out that supervised exercise is essential for best results, but neither he nor his workers were in favour of fad diets or sweat programs.

13

1. singular
2. singular
3. plural
4. singular
5. singular
6. singular
7. singular
8. plural
9. singular
10. singular

14

1. could be singular or plural
2. singular
3. singular
4. plural
5. singular
6. singular
7. singular
8. plural
9. singular
10. singular

16

The rewards of obtaining a good summer or part-time job go well beyond the money you earn from your labour. Contacts that may be valuable in the future and experience in the working world are very important parts of school-time employment. Even if the jobs you end up getting while attending school are not in the field of your future ambitions, there are many benefits that will show up later. For example, when scanning your résumé an employer always likes to see that you know what working for other people is all about: arriving at the work site on time, getting along with fellow workers, taking instructions. Neither instinct nor instruction takes the place of experience in teaching the basic facts of working life. These important considerations, in addition to the money that is the immediate reward, are what give work its real value to those students who seek summer jobs or part-time employment. Everyone who has ever gone to school and worked during vacations is able to confirm these observations.

Chapter 11: Pronoun-Antecedent Agreement

1

1. Is this the dog that bit the mail carrier who carries a squirt gun?
2. The path that I took led me past the home of a hermit, who lived all alone in the forest that surrounded our town.
3. The goal that came in 15:45 of the third period was scored by a player (whom) I used to know at high school.
4. That can't be Janice O'Toole, the little girl (whom) I used to bounce on my knee!
5. The building that we entered next was owned by the company that employed my father.
6. He is the man (whom) I turn to whenever I feel depressed because of something my sister has said or done.
7. correct
8. The four tests that we wrote today would have defeated anyone who wasn't prepared for them.
9. The wind whistled around the cabin, against which they had propped their skis while waiting to see whether the skiers (whom) they had passed earlier could catch up.
10. . . . It also allows you to spot people (whom) you'd like to meet.

2

1. his
2. herself
3. his
4. her
5. their, their
6. they, his
7. his
8. itself
9. himself, he, he
10. they, them

3

1. Max is good at skating, which he practises daily.
2. Because he was wearing earplugs, he didn't hear her cry for help.
3. It never occurred to Mr. Cohen that he would be Stephen's teacher.
4. It seemed that the donkey brayed every time he looked at it.
5. Management's refusal to allow a cost-of-living clause caused the union to walk out.
6. "You'll soon get a job," he told his brother.
7. Whenever Ann and Carol met, Ann acted in a very friendly way so that no one would suspect that she hated Carol.
8. Joe told Henry that Henry was losing his hair.
9. Matthew dented his calculator by throwing it on the floor.
10. This letter is in response to your ad for a waitress and bartender, male or female. Being both a waitress and a bartender, I wish to apply for the position.

4

1. Anyone who has finished all his homework by now can't have done it properly.
2. correct
3. Everybody I know is going, even if she can't get a date.
4. Each of my roommates finally left to find an apartment of his own.
5. I'd like to meet someone who is tall, dark, handsome, and rich; in fact, he doesn't even have to be tall, dark, or handsome.
6. Here everybody is allowed to find her own path to success, according to what she considers success to be.
7. The book tries to prove that nobody can rise above his own level of ability without the help of friends.
8. Constant nagging would make anyone lose her mind unless she learned to ignore it.
9. Somebody who has many friends will have to go; he will need friends if he hopes to return.
10. Everyone likes to think that he is unique, but each of us is his own idea of perfect, so in fact we are all the same.

5

1. Each of the cars has its own faults, but nobody else wants this one, so I'll take it.
2. Every child is a product of her environment as well as her parentage.
3. correct
4. The men who made up the team agreed that everybody would have to complete his assignment.
5. Writing articles is what she does best, although she hasn't been able to complete one lately.
6. She'll put her baby to bed now because the infant is short-tempered.
7. Everyone must get in his place for the game to begin.
8. Anybody who is without a partner will have to be sure he finds one who is about his height.

9. Neither the jacket nor the pants fit the way they should.
10. He said that Dave wasn't trying hard enough and that anyone who said he was would get a punch on his nose.

6

1. Golf is a game that is good for those who want to enjoy competition in the outdoors without getting their bodies sweaty or hurt.
2. Each person who wants to come on our annual ski trip to the Gatineau Hills must pay the money well in advance.
3. We have tried to convince all students to see their teachers regarding their evaluations.
4. Everyone seems to think that age will never affect him but at about thirty, everyone starts to realize that time is, indeed, passing.
5. Is there anyone who is so sure of victory he never contemplates an excuse for defeat?
6. We are trying to find a comfortable, well-padded chair with curved legs for an elderly lady.
7. They'll try to find accommodations for the tourists, even though they don't really know what the travellers want.
8. We'll try to choose someone whose intelligence and creativity are so outstanding that she won't need any supervision.
9. I remember the old days when anyone who had a computer wore horn-rimmed glasses, understood calculus, and didn't know if her shoes were tied.
10. Deborah told Dorothy that Dorothy had an excellent chance of making the team if she just did everything Deborah told her to do when speaking to the coach.

7

Anyone who has competed in a triathlon (a three-part race consisting of swimming, cycling, and running) knows that proper training is an absolute necessity, not only to success, but also to survival. Swimming is one of the toughest contests, because it demands cardiovascular fitness as well as strength, and it makes demands on the whole body. While each of the three segments has its own challenges, the cycling part of the triathlon is the event that separates serious athletes from part-time fitness buffs. Here, the latter will find they can't summon enough energy after their swim to stay close to their opponents if their opponents have trained harder than they. Serious athletes will begin to assert their dominance now, and by the end of the bike ride, those who have achieved a high level of physical efficiency through their training will still have a chance of a high placing. For the competitor in a triathlon, survival is often the primary goal. The body's reserves are called upon, now, and only the dedicated, well-trained athlete will be able to survive. For most, reaching the finish line is a personal test, and the only competition is with one's previous finish times. Those who still have winning on their minds after the swim, the cycle race, and the run have physical and mental reserves beyond the ordinary.

Chapter 12: Tense Agreement

1

1. He goes home and *tells* her what happened.
2. She was so tired that she *went* right to sleep.
3. The plane was chartered, the bags were packed, and the champagne *was* on ice.
4. The referee stands there, blinking, unable to believe what he *is* seeing.
5. correct
6. correct
7. First you will fry the onion; then you *will* brown the meat.
8. As soon as you rub the lamp, a genie *appears*.
9. "Safety colours" are bright and *attract* immediate attention.
10. When Bon Jovi came on stage, the crowd *went* crazy.

2

1. First, comb your hair into spikes; then *coat* your head with glue.
2. correct
3. The Peter Principle states that every person *rises* to his or her level of incompetence.
4. The couple next door had a boa constrictor that *kept* getting loose.
5. He began by asking a rhetorical question that he *proceeded* to answer.
6. She didn't say anything; she just *stormed* out of class.
7. While our team suffered one defeat after another, the Russians *rejoiced*.
8. correct
9. The new employee was too inexperienced to do the job in the time she *was* given.
10. If you'll be still for a minute, *I'll* explain everything.

3

1. Prejudice is learned and *is* hard to outgrow.
2. He used to get into trouble when he *drank*.
3. If you will just keep your eyes and ears open, you *will* learn something new every day.
4. After I had already put the car away, I *realized* Ann *was* still waiting for me at school.
5. The guard didn't say anything. He just *stood* there and *stared* at us.
6. correct
7. In the movie, King Kong climbs the Empire State Building and *gets* buzzed by small planes.
8. Her argument became silly when she *went* on to suggest that watching television weakened the genes.
9. We were embarrassed when Elmo *got* up and *said* . . . *were* eunuchs.
10. In the dead of night, while coyotes howled in the distance, someone — or some *thing* — *was* prowling in the dark recesses of the cave.

4

1. In 1897, Bram Stoker published his novel *Dracula* and gave the world one of its most enduring horror stories.

2. The story is based on numerous legends of the undead who remain immortal because they prey on the blood of the living.
3. The Count himself is modelled on Prince Vlad V of Wallachia (1431–1476) who had a penchant for impaling his enemies on spikes.
4. There is no historical evidence, however, to suggest that this Vlad the Impaler drank their blood after he skewered them.
5. Stoker's novel depicts a loathsome but powerful count who leaves Transylvania for England, where red-blooded victims abound.
6. He takes pleasure in sucking the life from pure young maidens who become, in their undead state, craven creatures who use a kind of lurid sexuality to seduce their own victims.
7. Like the Count, these creatures lie in their coffins during the day, gorged with blood, and roam during the night to satiate their blood lust.
8. correct
9. Told in epistolary fashion (that is, in letters, diaries, and journals supposedly pieced together), *Dracula* is, of course, a grotesquely sensational tale that is wildly improbable.
10. Nonetheless, that the story is rooted in archetypal fears and retains a powerful hold on our collective imagination is attested to by the fact that Stoker's novel has never been out of print.

5

The winters of my childhood were long, long seasons. We lived in three places — the school, the church and the skating-rink — but our real life was on the skating-rink. Real battles were won on the skating-rink. Real strength appeared on the skating-rink. The real leaders showed themselves on the skating-rink.

School was a sort of punishment. Parents always want to punish children and school is their most natural way of punishing us. However, school was also a quiet place where we could prepare for the next hockey game, lay out our strategies. As for church, we found there the tranquillity of God: there we forgot school and dreamed about the next hockey game. Through our daydreams it might happen that we would recite a prayer: we would ask God to help us play as well as Maurice Richard.

We all wore the same uniform as he, the red, white and blue uniform of the Montreal Canadiens, the best hockey team in the world; we all combed our hair in the same style as Maurice Richard, and to keep it in place we used a sort of glue — a great deal of glue. We laced our skates like Maurice Richard; we taped our sticks like Maurice Richard. We cut all his pictures out of the papers. Truly, we knew everything about him.

6

On the ice, when the referee blew his whistle the two teams would rush at the puck; we were five Maurice Richards taking it away from five other Maurice Richards; we were ten players, all of us wearing with the same blazing enthusiasm the uniform of the Montreal Canadiens. On our backs, we all wore the famous number 9.

One day, my Montreal Canadiens sweater became too small; then it got torn and had holes in it. My mother said, "If you wear that old sweater people are going to think we're poor!" Then she did what she did whenever we needed new clothes. She started to leaf through the catalogue the Eaton company sent us in the mail every year. My mother was proud. She didn't want to buy our clothes at the general store; the only things that were good enough for us were the latest styles from Eaton's catalogue. My mother didn't like the order forms included with the catalogue; they were written in English and she didn't understand a word of it. To order my hockey sweater, she did as she usually did; she took out her writing paper and wrote. . . .

7

Monsieur Eaton was quick to answer my mother's letter. Two weeks later we received the sweater. That day I had one of the greatest disappointments of my life! I would even say that on that day I experienced a very great sorrow. Instead of the red, white and blue Montreal Canadiens sweater, Monsieur Eaton sent us a blue and white sweater with a maple leaf on the front — the sweater of the Toronto Maple Leafs. I always wore the red, white and blue Montreal Canadiens sweater, all my friends wore the red, white and blue sweater; never had anyone in my village ever worn the Toronto sweater; never had we even seen a Toronto Maple Leafs sweater. Besides, the Toronto team was regularly trounced by the triumphant Canadiens. With tears in my eyes, I found the strength to say:

"I'll never wear that uniform."

Chapter 13: Person Agreement

1

1. he
2. he
3. she
4. you
5. one
6. his
7. she, she
8. it
9. we
10. you

2

1. You mustn't upset the instructor if you wish to leave class on time.
2. Anyone going to the class party can pick up his tickets now.
3. Men who don't think women are their equals may have to get used to living on their own.
4. Canadians don't seem to realize that the situation may get out of hand if they don't vote wisely.
5. You must try to control your temper when you feel frustrated or angry.
6. correct
7. Everyone is going to get what he deserves.
8. If one is convicted on that charge, a fine is the least of one's worries.
9. After we had driven about 300 km, we could feel the sleepiness begin to weight our eyelids.
10. correct

3

1. A great way to develop your skills is to push yourself to the limit.
2. Everyone who wants more from life must stand up and shout his name as loudly as he can.
3. Canadians who travel abroad should remember they're representing their country.
4. Following one's hunch can lead to disaster — or to an easy solution to one's problem.
5. Once you have been elected to Parliament, you should always remember that you are in the public eye.
6. In this country, you receive more acclaim as a hockey player than you do as a symphony conductor.
7. Anyone who drives one of those things should be aware of the risk he's taking.
8. correct
9. Can one really be happy if he doesn't own an electric pencil sharpener?
10. Why must people always want something they don't have, even when they have more than they'll ever need?

4

1. I enjoy living in the country, because there I don't have to deal with traffic or pollution, and I can always get to the city if I want to.
2. You never really know whether she's joking or not, do you?
3. I collect art because I can always get my money back on the investment, and I can sometimes make a killing.
4. No one can help him, because if one tries one is quickly and rudely rebuffed.
5. Americans who vacation in Canada should take the opportunity to add to their collection of china at bargain prices.
6. A graduate from high school who can't construct a proper sentence ought to be ashamed of himself.
7. You can't go around picking up after your sloppy relatives all day, can you?
8. When we left the hotel's air-conditioned comfort, the heat knocked us over.
9. correct
10. An expert wine taster will find this a very acceptable vintage, and even one who knows little about wine will enjoy himself with a bottle or two.

5

1. When you're bright, talented, and rich, you don't really have to try very hard to impress your elders, especially if you are also handsome.
2. . . . We were amazed by the beauty of the country, especially the spectacular mountains. We learned quickly why the Group of Seven painted many of their most famous pictures there.
3. You can't beat a charcoal grill for preparing great hamburgs in the summertime. You get so tired of pan-fried meat patties all winter long.

4. . . . We really didn't get out as much as we should have when it was cold, but we are going to make up for that now.
5. . . . How can you understand the game unless you know what's going on?
6. You mustn't push him too far, because he will either lose his temper or become hysterical, and that isn't what you want.
7. . . . We get good service, which we don't find very often, and we find the bill tolerable as well.
8. . . . suddenly we all got the idea. We couldn't wait to get our hands in the air to tell the others what we had discovered.
9. . . . Years of hard work and sacrifice had left us tired and somewhat bitter, but the feeling of accomplishment at that moment made us feel it was all worth it.
10. . . . Often I got so tired that I wanted to give up.

6

People who get married while they're still in college may have an especially hard time completing their studies. If both spouses are in school, they may not have enough money for an apartment, and they may have to live with their parents for a while. Students whose spouses work may find themselves studying on weekends while their spouses rest or socialize. The wife who supports a student husband, along with the husband who supports a student wife, may find that the responsibility weighs heavily on her. Anyone in such a situation would be likely to feel at the end of his wits sometimes, so students whose marriages are shaky may find that they are having a very hard time of it and that their schoolwork is suffering. On the other hand, these various demands may strengthen a marriage, and a student who marries may find that his or her motivation to succeed at school has increased. Some married students may even find themselves studying more, using the time they would otherwise have spent dating.

7

A woman who enjoys baseball may have difficulty explaining her passion to those who find the game a bore. Each February, the die-hard fan begins to sharpen her listening and watching skills by tuning in to spring training games. If you have ever seen one of these fanatics watch a baseball game, you can't help but notice the alertness and intensity with which she follows the play. It is this single-minded dedication that the non-fan finds himself unable to comprehend. How can one be so interested in something that one must watch for three hours to see almost nothing take place? How can one get excited by a no-hitter, which, by definition, means that nothing has happened during the game? Baseball fans maintain that the game to which they are addicted has many more pleasures than mere action. They cite fielding plays and the strategy of pitcher versus hitter matchups in defence of the game that they would rather watch than any other. Those for whom these pleasures hold little appeal might enjoy watching golf or lawn-bowling.

Chapter 14: The Apostrophe

1

1. there's
2. didn't
3. they'll
4. it's
5. don't
6. it'll
7. it's
8. we're
9. you're
10. he's

2

1. she'll
2. we've
3. I'm
4. won't
5. who's
6. shouldn't
7. they're
8. who's
9. you'll
10. hasn't

3

1. can't
2. you're
3. they'll
4. wouldn't
5. who's
6. won't
7. it'll
8. they're
9. we've
10. you've

4

1. They'll have to stay home because they're still sick.
2. It's been a long time since they've had a good holiday.
3. We're many kilometres from where we were then.
4. You're not going to try your luck again, are you?
5. It's been so long since someone who'll stand up for what is right has run for office.
6. You're going to class because it's good for you; you'll never get far unless you've got your education.
7. Let's see if they're up to the standards we've set.
8. We'll have to do better if we're to succeed.
9. They've finally done what she's suggested.
10. Since you've been in Europe, we've adopted the metric system in Canada.

5

1. Who's, I've
2. There's, we've
3. It's, you've
4. I've, they're, there's
5. you'll, isn't
6. couldn't, I'm
7. won't, he's
8. I've, you're
9. You'll, he's
10. We're, we'll, he's, haven't, doesn't

6

1. wagon's
2. sea's
3. everybody's
4. love's
5. Alice's
6. horse's
7. men's
8. Ross' (or Ross's)
9. congress' (or congress's)
10. agents'

7

1. saleswoman's
2. nurses'
3. its
4. candy's
5. someone's
6. Joneses'
7. Niagara Falls' (or Falls's)
8. women's
9. stewardesses'
10. lady's

8

1. hers
2. Bess' or Bess's
3. their, theirs
4. your yours
5. babies'
6. history's
7. one's
8. actress' (or actress's)
9. chairperson's
10. ladies'

9

1. month's, their
2. children's, yours
3. dog's, its
4. George's, wife's
5. its, jeweller's
6. Phyllis' (or Phyllis's), Dickens' (or Dickens's)
7. Fishermen's, their
8. spray's, trees'
9. authors', school's
10. moment's, week's

10

1. Hikers' equipment is on special during the week's sale at Brown's Sporting Goods.
2. Women's liberation is a touchy topic for Gail's sister, who's lost a job to a man.
3. The waitress'(s) tip ended up in the busboy's pocket.
4. correct
5. The men's room is down the hall, but its door isn't marked.
6. Gordie Howe's records may eventually fall, but his career's achievements will never be surpassed.
7. America's wealth has some Canadians wondering whether our country's independence is worth maintaining.
8. Its coat shone like gold in the sun's dying rays.
9. Scholars' aims and athletes' goals can both be achieved at college.
10. Men's and women's traditional roles are being questioned as this generation's leaders refuse to take any of yesterday's values for granted.

11

1. It's, its, it's, week's
2. They're, it's

3. You're, police's, your
4. Betty's, Children's
5. Who's, anybody's
6. Their, their, they're
7. It's, your, son's
8. Today's, melodies, its
9. you're, it's, their
10. boys, cheater's, Gord's, father's

12

1. Philip's best friend, who's a Junior A goaltender, came out to coach their team's goalie.
2. Blondie's the name of my dog's first puppy. We're going to keep her when the rest of the litter's old enough to sell.
3. Everybody's favourite men's store is Peebles', where, in a week's time, you'll be able to save hundreds in their fall sale.
4. While Nan's boyfriend's car was being repaired, Kevin rented a car and invited her to his school's formal. It's been a long time since she's been out in anyone else's company.
5. We should've had your spaghetti sauce; it's bound to be better than theirs. We'll know better next time we're invited to Gord's parents' place.
6. Didn't you see the U.S. Navy's commercial on television? It's intended to make your parents want a sailor's uniform on you.
7. Apostrophes don't seem very significant until you've lost fifty percent of your paper's value for leaving them out.
8. Joanne's dreams concern her longings for life's better things: fast cars, boys' admiration, parents' approval, glamorous homes, and large bank accounts.
9. The party's over. It's time to call it a day. We're finished with our night's fun and dreading tomorrow's dawn.
10. The lady's going to mend her ways and try to find out if it's true that virtue's reward is a long life. Unfortunately, Las Vegas' call is very strong and there's some doubt about her ability to resist its summons back to the fast lane.

13

1. boys'
2. knife's
3. audience's
4. its
5. secretaries'
6. they're
7. who's
8. you're
9. it's
10. couldn't

14

1. gentlemen's
2. typist's
3. anyone's
4. enemy's
5. enemies'
6. won't
7. it's
8. there's
9. hasn't
10. shouldn't

Chapter 15: Question and Exclamation Marks

1

1. incorrect
2. incorrect
3. correct
4. correct
5. correct
6. incorrect
7. incorrect
8. correct
9. correct
10. correct

2

1. correct
2. correct
3. incorrect
4. incorrect
5. correct
6. correct
7. incorrect
8. incorrect
9. incorrect
10. incorrect

3

1. period
2. period
3. question mark
4. period
5. question mark
6. period
7. period
8. question mark
9. question mark
10. period

4

1. Take that, you monster!
2. Why, you've been hit!
3. Stifle it, Edith!
4. Oh, Henry, it's beautiful!
5. Does this mean we're engaged?
6. Heavens above! Who was that masked man?
7. We have the winning number!
8. All right, I quit!
9. What do you care, you heartless creature?
10. Overtime! Are you serious?

5

1. question mark
2. exclamation mark
3. exclamation mark
4. question mark
5. exclamation mark or period
6. question mark
7. period
8. exclamation mark or period
9. question mark
10. exclamation mark

6

1. question mark
2. exclamation mark
3. exclamation mark, question mark
4. period
5. question mark, exclamation mark
6. exclamation mark
7. period
8. question mark, exclamation mark
9. exclamation mark, exclamation mark
10. question mark, question mark

7

1. She isn't sure whether or not there's a game tonight.
2. Why can't she do the right thing and tell him how she feels about him?
3. "Slide!" The whole team was screaming in unison.
4. Is there life after high school's long days of boring classes and nights consumed by homework?
5. What good will it do if I continue to be pleasant to those who take such delight in making me look foolish?
6. We wondered how to behave after the boss had burst into tears and gone home.
7. The team questions the meaning of life as it relates to curling.
8. Despite the head-first slide into third, the umpire bellowed, "Out!"
9. Oh joy! You've bought me a pair of Bermuda shorts! Be still, my beating heart!
10. Why can't the sports fans who yell so loudly about the mistakes of their heroes try to put themselves in the same position as those they criticize and try to be a little more forgiving?

8

When Tony Fernandez, the leadoff hitter, came to the plate, I was ready. My first pitch, a slow curve, caught the outside corner. "Strike one!" howled the umpire. Why was I pitching to Tony Fernandez? What was an English teacher doing on the mound in the SkyDome? Who was that rag-tag collection of players surrounding me? The answers make one of the strangest chapters in baseball history. Undefeated in our recreation league, we had challenged the semi-pro team in our community, defeated it, and gone on to beat three other professional teams from nearby cities. Then *Sports Illustrated* printed a story about our exploits. It was unbelievable! The magazine article attracted international attention. We were stars! It was inevitable that the Blue Jays would want to take advantage of the publicity we were getting, so they invited us to play at the Dome and paid our transportation to Toronto.

I struck out Fernandez with my slider, took care of McGriff on three pitches, and got Gruber with an overpowering fastball. Hey! This was easy. The second and third innings were repeats of the first: all nine batters striking out! My teammates were getting restless, so in the fourth and fifth, I allowed a couple of easy ground balls and gave the outfielders their turn with a couple of easy fly balls in the sixth. Then I went back to work and struck out the side in the seventh, eighth and ninth. Meanwhile, I had driven in the only run with a hard-hit double down the first-base line. The crowd went berserk. "Sar-ah!" they chanted over and over. After the game, the Blue Jay management asked me to sign up as a free agent, but I said, "Thanks, but grammar is my game."

9

Why, you little sneak! I'll pull your ears off! Can't you even do as you're told when you know you'll be found out if you cheat? Haven't you the decency to admit your guilt? You should be expelled! If I have my way, you'll wonder what hit you! When the principal is finished with you, some of that confidence will be gone, believe me! If I ever hear of a repetition of this behaviour, it'll be the end of your career at this obedience school! Now, I'll give you one more chance to do it right. Fetch, Rover!

Chapter 16: Quotation Marks

1

1. "Who was the lady I saw you with last night?" asked the straight man.
2. Groucho replied, "That was no lady; that was my wife!"
3. "That's a really good price," said Georgia as she eyed the floor-length mink.
4. correct
5. "Put that gun down," yelled the officer, "or I'll shoot!"
6. The coach asked his best player, "Why don't you wear a face mask?"
7. "The time has come," the Walrus said, "to speak of many things."
8. "Leave me alone, Sandra," Sarah pleaded.
9. correct
10. "I'd like to help," said David, "but I'm far too busy just now."

2

1. Trying desperately to catch up, Paul gasped, "Wait for me!"
2. Referring to the chapter called "Punctuation," Nell said, "This book is really helpful in improving my writing."
3. correct
4. "Put yourself in my place and you'll understand why I feel hurt," Stephen said.
5. "I cannot believe," exclaimed Debbie, "that you really did it!"
6. "Is there hope?" asked Judy. "Can we still get back?"
7. correct
8. Brian finally asked, "When do we eat?"
9. The reply was, "When you cook some food."
10. In frustration and anger, Sheila told the entire company she was quitting. "I've had enough!" she yelled.

3

1. "Considering your record," intoned the principal, "I'm inclined to suspend you for a month."
2. "Go ahead," replied Percy. "I'm not afraid to stand up for something I believe in," he added.
3. "Television is a vast wasteland," Newton Minnow said, and many have added that it is also potentially dangerous.
4. "Lights! Camera! Action!" These three words, so often said by Hollywood directors, have entered the language as a synonym for an exciting beginning.
5. Carefully and deliberately, John turned to his tormentor and spoke. "I don't want to play this game any more."
6. "Say you love me," he pleaded. "OK," she replied, "You love me."
7. "I challenge you, sir, to a duel," François cried. "You have the choice of weapons."
8. correct
9. "Ridiculous!" Brigit snorted nervously. "I've never seen him before in my life."
10. "Put that out," said the waitress, pointing to a sign that said No Smoking.

4

1. "This," cried the carnival salesman, "is genuine simulated leather."
2. "I suggest that the victim then tried to defend himself with this feather," cried the prosecuting attorney dramatically.
3. There was an uproar in the courtroom. "How could he defend himself against a 12-gauge shotgun with a feather?" was the most common question.
4. "Well," suggested the prosecutor, "since he couldn't reach the banana in time, the feather was the best he could do."
5. At this, the defendant leaped to his feet and admitted that he was, indeed, guilty. "How did you know about the banana?" he muttered as he was led away.
6. "Elementary, my dear Winston," laughed the lawyer, misquoting the great Sherlock Holmes, who had said much the same thing.
7. "Draw! Slap leather!" yelled the gunfighter. With great calm, the sheriff replied, "Huh?"
8. correct
9. "Can you find the relevant passage?" asked the teacher as she leafed through Leacock's short story, "My Banking Career."
10. "Oh!" said Miss Manitoba. "This is such a thrill and honour that I don't know what to say or anything."

Chapter 17: The Colon

1

1. correct
2. incorrect
3. correct
4. incorrect
5. correct
6. incorrect
7. correct
8. incorrect
9. incorrect
10. incorrect

2

1. incorrect
2. incorrect
3. incorrect
4. correct
5. correct
6. incorrect
7. correct
8. incorrect
9. correct
10. correct

3

1. correct
2. They finally realized there was only one course open to them: obedience.
3. Gary had trouble with his canoe: it tipped over and then sank.
4. There is someone who can save us, though: Captain Canuck!
5. He tossed and turned all night and found the same images recurring in his dreams: a river and a wolf.
6. His body was beyond the point of exhaustion, but he tried to force himself on by thinking of one thing: victory.

7. correct
8. I have a very large garden, but it grows only two things: tomatoes and weeds.
9. She has one goal that she is determined to achieve: the world record.
10. Two issues remained to be settled: wages and benefits.

4

2. Only one thing was needed: a boat.
4. On the list we must include chips, mix, ice, and peanuts.
6. Three qualities of a good quarterback are leadership, intelligence, and physical strength.
8. The pond is deep and cold.
9. Dogs have many qualities that make them superior to cats: loyalty, intelligence, working ability, and friendliness.
10. Let me give you an example: Louis Riel.

5

1. I'd like to help, but I can't.
2. I'll take the following volunteers: John, Susan, David, and Colin.
3. We'll have to go back to get tent poles, matches, and paddles.
6. No one wants to go with him, for two very good reasons: money and time.
8. My boss is so mean she must be bitter or crazy.

Chapter 18: The Comma

1

1. Careful investment of money and time can lead to wealth, fame, and happiness.
2. correct
3. Does anyone remember John, Paul, George, and Ringo?
4. correct
5. Cutting the lawn, washing the dishes, and doing the shopping are my least favourite activities.
6. MacDonald, Laurier, Borden, and Pearson are four dissimilar men who have at least one thing in common.
7. He is an all-round athlete who enjoys many sports: skating, skiing, cycling, riding, and hunting.
8. She has strong ambition, a cool head, good health, and an inquiring mind; everyone hates her.
9. correct
10. Many people see Canada as a land where only French is spoken, ice and snow are year-round hazards, and violent hockey is the only pastime.

2

1. He is, you know, one of our best teachers.
2. Sandy Wilson, a B.C. film-maker, made *My American Boyfriend*.

3. You'll have to do better than that, Steve, if you want to join us.
4. Despite her reputation, she is, we have found out, fairly bright.
5. correct
6. One of my favourite performers is Gordon Lightfoot, the former Presley imitator from Orillia.
7. Where will you go now, Heather?
8. Hockey seats, despite the huge increase in prices, are still always sold out in Toronto and Montreal.
9. The bride, in a departure from tradition, wore a yellow pant suit.
10. We tried, all of us, to be of some help.

3

1. He and I are good friends, yet we sometimes argue.
2. Now we'll have to try bribery, or we can resort to force.
3. We can't win this game, nor can we afford to lose it.
4. The car swerved wildly, but it narrowly missed the crossing guard.
5. She tried and tried, and soon her efforts paid off.
6. I'd like to buy a house as an investment, but I can't afford the down payment right now.
7. My part-time job isn't very rewarding, so I'm coming back to school next fall.
8. There are not many dangers, so we must conquer our fear of failure.
9. This is her last semester, so she's concentrating on school for a change.
10. Clutching his wounded shoulder, he fell through the air, but he managed to land on his feet.

4

1. In the end, quality will win.
2. John, if you don't quiet down, you'll have to leave.
3. If there were any justice, I'd have been rewarded for what I did.
4. Well, I don't believe it!
5. When the sun came up in a clear blue sky, we all sighed with relief.
6. Adorned with blue bows, her shoes clashed with her green outfit.
7. Moved beyond words, he was able only to gesture his thanks.
8. Carefully placing one foot in front of the other, she managed to walk along the white line for several metres.
9. Falling, staggering to his feet, then falling again, he stumbled painfully towards the finish line.
10. Where a huge hardwood forest had stood, now there was only blackened ground.

5

1. The job interview isn't so bad if you're prepared, relaxed, and confident.
2. With a shout of glee, the boys ran to the heavily laden Christmas tree.
3. There is something wrong here, but I haven't yet determined what it is.
4. In the end, they'll be caught, so all we have to do is wait.
5. George Washington, the first president of the United States, was an officer in the British army before the American Revolution.

6. Charlottetown, Quebec, and Kingston were the sites of conferences that eventually led to Confederation in 1867.
7. Well, Mrs. O'Hara, if that's the best you can do, it's out of my hands.
8. correct
9. A good dictionary, used properly, can be an important tool for developing a mature vocabulary.
10. If there were any point in complaining, I would have protested long ago, but I don't think anything can change their course of action now.

6

1. My world is made up of handsome men, fast cars, loud music, expensive clothes, and other dreams.
2. The movie, despite some excellent action sequences, was a failure because of the terrible script.
3. If starvation and lack of recognition made great artists, Canada would be a land of Picassos.
4. The letter of application is the most important document you will ever write, yet you have spent only an hour composing it.
5. Wrapping the watch in a handkerchief, he produced a mallet and smashed the expensive timepiece to smithereens, or so it appeared.
6. The retirement of Bobby Orr from hockey was the end of an era for the game, but those who saw him play will never forget it.
7. In the 1960s, blue jeans became a uniform for the young, but now they are popular only as very casual attire, and a much more fashionable look has emerged.
8. Despite some early problems, the National Gallery in Ottawa has become one of the most interesting and exciting exhibits in North America, don't you think?
9. There, you've gone and broken it again!
10. correct

7

1. Your fall order, which we received last week, has been filled.
2. An excellent pool is available for those who like to swim, and, for those who play golf, there is a beautiful eighteen-hole course.
3. John, realizing his position, resigned.
4. Inside, the piano was going at full blast.
5. What you hear, what you read, and what you think all help to form your intellectual background.
6. Quickly, girls, or we'll be late.
7. Ever since, I have been a regular theatre goer.
8. A few days after they sailed, the boat sprang a leak.
9. A fine fellow, a member of the yacht club, was drowned.
10. Antonio's grandmother was very short, black haired, and extremely thin.

8

1. When you enter the store, go to the counter on your left, ask for Ms Bertrand, and tell her that you want to see the latest prints.
2. These cold, wet, grey days are not good for the crops.

3. The thick syrup boiled over and spilled on the stove, on the table, and on the floor.
4. correct
5. Conflicts have occurred between students and faculty, students and administration, and faculty and administration.
6. However capable he was, he failed miserably in this case.
7. Oh, excuse me. I didn't hear you come in.
8. Nearby, an old oak lifted its gaunt limbs to the sky.
9. Mr. Smith, the head of the department, despite his vast knowledge of his subject, couldn't change a light bulb if his life depended on it.
10. I dressed, you will be amazed to learn, in two minutes flat and was out the door before his knock had stopped echoing.

9

1. After they had eaten, Big Tom pushed the cracked and dirty supper things to the back of the table and took the baby from its high chair carefully, so as not to spill the flotsam of bread crumbs and boiled potatoes from the chair to the floor.
2. He undressed the youngster, talking to it in the old dialect, trying to awaken its interest.
3. He stood for long minutes at the side of the bed, staring, trying to diagnose the child's restlessness into something other than what he feared.
4. For long minutes after the baby was asleep, he talked on, letting the victorious words fill the small cabin so that they shut out the sounds of the Northern Ontario night: the buzz of mosquitoes, the far-off bark of a dog, the noise of the cars and transport trucks passing on the gravelled road.
5. The trailer residents were not yet awake, so he sat down on the wooden walk leading to the shower room, his baskets resting on the ground in a half circle behind him.
6. This done, he stood and watched the headlights of the cars run along the trees bordering the road, like a small boy's stick along a picket fence.
7. Big Tom followed behind, all the anguish and frustration drained from him, so that there was nothing left to carry him into another day.
8. He was becoming worried about the baby, and her presence, while it might not make the baby well, would mean that there was someone else to share his fears.
9. The child was feverish, its breath noisy and fast.
10. One by one, as he waited, the lights went out, until only the sign lit up a small area at the gate.

10

1. Despite the negative feelings of some and the outright, often violent, hostility of others, the project will proceed on time.
2. Put the casserole in the oven at four o'clock, but make sure the roast is cooked before you do.
3. Josey, whom you know from last summer, has been asking for your address, but I thought I should ask your permission before I send it.

4. Prowling around the old cemetery, we came upon the grave of a young child who died during a flu epidemic.
5. Art is something I know little about except that oils, watercolours, and pastels require different skills and techniques.
6. Flattery, the old saying goes, will get you nowhere, but this has not been my experience.
7. Robert collects coins, listens to some types of music, and skis when he can, but otherwise devotes all of his time to his appearance.
8. Computers and robots are certain to be part of everyone's future unless there's a nuclear holocaust, in which case no one has a future.
9. Certain to feel better after a good meal, I left the party and went to a nearby steak house.
10. Before I left, however, I managed to offend the host, insult the hostess, and humiliate the guest of honour.

11

One of the teachers at our school, a mild-mannered man under most circumstances, burst into my office one day last spring, and he spent twenty minutes pouring out his frustration into my startled ears. Having spent several hours preparing for a class on stress management, he had been confronted by a student who asked if they were going to do anything important in class that day. Teachers are asked this question on a regular basis, and every time it happens, they wince. Most, however, are able to control themselves and make some sarcastic comment. This teacher had been asked once too often, I'm afraid. He ranted, raved, and roared despite my best efforts to calm him down, but gradually he ran out of steam and finally collapsed into a quivering blob. Seeing that he was now more or less under control, I told him that most teachers have developed defence mechanisms to counteract the trauma of being asked that question. My favourite response is to ask why today's class should be any different from all the other classes in the term; since we have done nothing of importance in any other class, it seems unlikely that we would be doing anything significant now. Some students take this as sarcasm, but others assume that I'm giving them permission to skip. The teacher found my reassurance helpful, I'm sure, because he smiled as he left my office, on his way to teach another class on how to handle stress.

12

The Canadian appetite for sports entertainment seems insatiable. In the past, three sports dominated the year for the sports fan, but now, thanks to specialty television, some very unusual and exotic competitions are finding fans in this country. Australian-rules football, a game that belies its name by seeming to have no rules, is gaining in popularity, though purely as a spectator sport. Triathlons, biathlons, marathons, mini-marathons, and a host of similar endurance events are now avidly watched by the armchair athlete and enthusiastically entered by the physically fit. Sumo wrestling, while not accessible to most of us as a participatory activity, seems to have a devoted following, and even darts and lawn bowling have their supporters. And then there is golf. To some, watching golf on television is as exciting as watching paint dry, but during inclement weather, when they can't be on the course themselves, golfers follow their heroes' every televised step and agonize with them over every shot for hours. The challenge for Canadian jocks of both sexes and all ages is to tear themselves away from these various spectator entertainments in order to play their favourite sports.

Chapter 19: The Semicolon

1

1. correct
2. incorrect
3. correct
7. incorrect
8. correct
4. incorrect
5. incorrect
6. incorrect
9. correct
10. correct

2

1. correct
2. incorrect
3. correct
4. correct
5. incorrect
6. correct
7. incorrect
8. correct
9. incorrect
10. incorrect

3

2. He sat down near a refreshing stream, for he was very tired.
4. It's a beautiful day, just right for a long walk.
5. Six of the Indian nations joined together in a loose union; they were called Iroquois.
6. The lawn, a little ragged, needs to be cut; the hedge, shrubs, and ivy need to be trimmed; the flowers need to be watered; and, not least of all, the gardener needs to be paid.
7. I'd like to help; however, I'm supposed to rest all day.

4

2. There are only a few who could catch him, and I'm sure she isn't one of them.
5. We'll have to go soon, for it's getting late.
7. If ever there were a time to act, it is now.
9. She disobeyed the rules, so she will have to be punished.
10. She is always late; however, she's worth waiting for.

5

1. There seems to be no end to the work that must be done; furthermore, there isn't enough time in which to do it.
2. There must be a way, or we're finished before we've begun.
3. I can't afford a Porsche; therefore, I drive a Volkswagen.
4. Shirley is one of my favourite people; she can always cheer me up.

5. There will be ample opportunity to finish your homework, but right now I need your help.
6. The flooring was all knotty pine, yellowed with age; the walls and furniture were of such design and colour as to blend with it.
7. Brock was killed early in the morning, but the Americans were driven from Queenston Heights by nightfall.
8. Canada's history is not a very violent one; however, there were several rebellions of note.
9. John has gone away to become a teacher; Martha now has twin baby girls; Kevin is unemployed; Julie is a lawyer or stockbroker (I forget which); and Paul is, as usual, drifting from job to job.
10. When the rain started, they were trapped in the open; nevertheless, they stayed where they were until it let up and then watched the game with enjoyment, despite being a little wet.

6

1. They are taken from twelve collections I have published during this period; except for retouching lightly two or three poems, I have left them stand as they were.
2. To these I have added the following poems: "The Warm Afterdark," which I wrote in 1957, and "Divinity."
3. My father was an ineffectual visionary; he saw God's footprint in a cloud and lived only for his books and meditations.
4. Luckily for us, she was not; she was tougher than nails, shrewd and indomitable.
5. At this point, Byron's contempt for the poet becomes understandable; my mother's commonsensical expletives begin ringing in my ears.
6. Not who is winning the Cold War is the big issue confronting mankind, but this: will the Poet, as a type, join the Priest, the Warrior, the Hero, and the Saint as melancholy museum pieces?
7. correct
8. correct
9. If he has the true vocation, he will take risks; for him there can be no "dogmatic slumbers."
10. correct

7

1. Computers are marvellous tools: fast, efficient, accurate, but dumb. They remind me of a secretary I used to know; she's now my boss.
2. To put the matter in perspective, I'd like you to ask yourselves a question: "What do I wish to accomplish?"
3. Taking a pad and pencil from the desk, he began to write; soon he was finished and showed us his creation: a limerick.
4. Push the concept of defeat from your mind; concentrate instead solely on victory.
5. If I could push defeat from my mind, there would be only a vast emptiness left; victory is impossible when you play on this team.
6. correct
7. If only jobs were as easy to get now as they were when our parents grad-

uated from school; then we'd get the same chance they had to prove what we can do.

8. Noreen wants to be helpful; it's just that she is so clumsy that one of two things always happens: either she breaks something or she hurts herself.
9. correct
10. Callous disregard for authority; an inability to apply patience to the solution of problems; and a fascination with the material, the trivial, and the impermanent: these are the legacies of the television age.

8

1. We're unhappy about our teacher's evaluation procedures, which are irrational, arbitrary, unfair, and often malicious.
2. Cornering at a dangerous speed, the police car swerved into the oncoming lane; luckily, no one was coming.
3. One of the products of the computer age is increased leisure, and this, in turn, has led to a vastly increased interest in one of the enthusiasms of this generation: physical fitness.
4. A glance at the calendar will reveal that there are only 212 shopping days left until my birthday; that's just enough time for you to find the present I deserve.
5. Put the coffee on the table and the sandwiches by the window; I'll eat when I've finished this exercise.
6. The Four Horsemen of the Apocalypse are Conquest, Slaughter, Famine, and Death.
7. They are another very good example of Biblical figures who have entered the language; others are Samson and Delilah, David and Goliath, and Solomon and Sheba.
8. After calling the meeting to order, the chairman voiced his chief concern: fund raising.
9. Public speaking has become one of my favourite activities; however, I'm still very shy when dealing with people individually.
10. The Canadian political scene has become much less interesting since the departure of Pierre Trudeau; whether you like him or not, he left his mark on a generation of Canadians who were influenced by the phenomenon of Trudeaumania.

9

1. One thing always returned to his mind when he thought of his tour of Europe: the delicious beer.
2. While France had excellent wine, the more northern countries were famous for their breweries, a fact he came to appreciate.
3. My diary tells me that on this date last year you gave me a dozen roses; I'm wondering if the romance is gone when I see that this year's gift is a potted geranium.
4. There's nothing wrong with potted geraniums; I know lots of elderly people who positively adore them. It just happens that I'm seventeen, that's all.
5. A fear of heights is consistent with your other phobias: fear of falling, fear of failure, and fear of flying.

6. correct
7. Sing another of the old songs for us; we enjoy reliving those years with you, even though we weren't born then.
8. The Math Department is offering a seminar for English teachers; I understand it deals with addition and subtraction.
9. Tax forms become my big concern every April; the deadline always finds me in the same state: terrified.
10. We have reached the end at last; now there is only one thing left to do: check our answers before continuing.

Chapter 20: Capital Letters and Punctuation Review

1

1. Henry Smith wants to be a prince when he grows up.
2. The Queen of England visited Ontario last winter.
3. Confident of victory, we marched on Paris, led by our heroic captain.
4. correct
5. Laurie tries hard, but she'll never be as good at typing as Frank.
6. *Silent Partner* was a Canadian-made film that featured international stars but also many young Canadian actors.
7. Do you think Fords are better than Chevs in the middle price range?
8. correct
9. High school is a time of growing and development for young people, a time for them to find a direction for the rest of their lives.
10. Office supplies are in great demand, so, if you need pens or paper, you'd better see Ms Carlo in Supplies right away.

2

1. Jamie Sue rode down Dufferin Street every day in the fall to look at the leaves.
2. I went with my English professor to the Calgary Stampede.
3. Alan goes to the city on weekends to see French films.
4. correct
5. I want to grow up to be a queen, or at least a company president.
6. Jane studied cooking, art history, and French in Europe last summer.
7. The committee we had elected deprived us of our human rights.
8. He considers himself liberal on matters such as the dress code.
9. Jim works for the phone company, which has an office on a street near his home.
10. correct

3

1. Following my failure in science and math, I renewed my interest in English and Spanish.
2. correct
3. On our trip to Alberta we were joined by Winnifred in Winnipeg, Reginald

in Regina, and Henry in Saskatoon; Henry really didn't fit in with our group very well.

4. While we think of ourselves as liberal-minded, we give our support to a political party that tends to attract the conservative element: Social Credit.
5. In Quebec, the premier is very influential not only in the policies of his province, but in the politics of the whole country.
6. All Canadians should learn French and English to retain the historic cultural uniqueness of their nation.
7. correct
8. Few teachers and even fewer students really have a firm grasp of the art of poetry, though many think they can write poems and judge the work of others.
9. Among Canada's great historic waterways, the St. Lawrence River, the Mackenzie River, the Fraser River, and the Red River are, to me, the most interesting because of the great historic figures who are associated with each.
10. Putting partisan politics aside, we decided to follow the advice of Governor General Ray Hnatyshyn and view the candidates with an open mind and vote for the best person, rather than for the party that promised the most.

Punctuation Review

I

1. "Enjoy the view," we called out as they left for the mountaintop; we had wisely decided to wait for them in a meadow halfway up.
2. To be a millionaire by the time you are thirty, you will have to take large risks, be lucky, and have creative ideas.
3. High school was, indeed, the best time of my life, because I met the friends there that I would continue to see for many years and I learned the principles that were to guide me through later, more difficult years.
4. The question of whether there is evolution doesn't worry most of the people in my class; they're more concerned about whether there's a dance on Friday.
5. "Why won't he listen?" Marsha whispered tearfully.
6. With the crowd chanting, "Out! Out!" the referee had a hard time justifying his decision: a ten minute misconduct.
7. Typing as though his life depended on the completion of the assignment, Ted managed to get through the first chapter before supper; this left him with Chapter Two, "The Next Day," to complete before bedtime.
8. The rain looked as though it would never let up, so Gary and the two girls packed up to go home, their vacation plans ruined.
9. "Don't go," Angela fell to her knees and begged her friend to stay. "Why must you leave now," she asked, "just when we're about to succeed?"
10. You'll find he has just one fault, my friend: he snores.

2

1. "Jump! It's the only way out!" she cried.
2. Since there is so much time left, why don't you go for a swim or have a sauna?
3. correct
4. Pushing past the horrified onlookers, the police officer entered the building within minutes of the blast and encountered chaos!
5. The Toronto Blue Jays, like the Montreal Expos before them, are winning friends among baseball fans in the United States.
6. "Don't go near the water," warned the twins' mother; however, they were far too busy playing with the alligators to hear her.
7. My computer is a big improvement on the old typewriter I used to use; it still makes the same number of spelling errors, though.
8. "You'll never make it, Stella! We've got the whole building surrounded," the detective yelled through his bullhorn. "You might as well come out with your hands up!"
9. Her lips curling into a sneer, she replied, "You'll have to come in and get me, copper!"
10. The director, his patience at an end, screamed, "Cut! That scene is too long, too boring, and too bad. We'll have to take it again."

3

For having saved the leprechaun's life, Douglas was granted three wishes. The first he squandered on a mere one hundred dollars, because he didn't believe the little man when he told Douglas that his wishes would come true. After more careful consideration, Douglas wished again.

"I want a bank account in a Swiss bank," he shouted, "and enough money so that I will never run out."

The leprechaun frowned and looked very disappointed in Douglas' wish, but he screwed up his face, went very red for a minute and then announced, "It's done," but under his breath he muttered, "Greedy young cub; he needs a lesson."

Douglas was all ready with his next wish; it was his greatest desire. He stared sternly at the leprechaun and in a loud voice said, "My last wish is the most important; I want to live for one thousand years."

The tiny old man grinned, then he screwed up his face and went very red for a minute. Finally he relaxed, sighed a deep satisfied sigh, and, very pleased with himself, walked twice around the young redwood tree that had just sprouted in front of him.

4

All too often, it seems that the Canadian national pastime is complaining about the weather. Our hot summers are criticized because they're too hot, while our springs are too wet, our autumns too cool, and our winters too long. If the climate is so bad here, why does anyone live north of the U.S. border? Perhaps the problem is not that Canadians don't like living in Canada, but rather that they love to complain.

The most popular sports teams in Canada were at one time those with the worst records: the Argonauts and the modern Maple Leafs. Could this popularity be due to the ample opportunity and scope they gave to their fans for complaint? Not only do we bemoan the losing record of such teams, but, when they do win, we dwell with glee on the possibilities of disaster for next year.

The same syndrome might be seen in our attitude towards our Canadian heroes. It has often been said that we are a nation without heroes, but I suspect that we have plenty of candidates; it's just that we enjoy complaining so much, we try to find fault wherever we can and love pointing out the clay feet of our great figures. One cannot help but wonder how Canadians fare in heaven, where everything is perfect. Surely we must be desperately unhappy in such circumstances.

Chapter 21: Finding Something to Write About

1

1. Not specific. It's too large a topic.
2. Not specific, nor is it supportable without a great deal of research.
3. Not significant. Every child knows what they are.
4. Not significant.
5. Not single. Choose one.
6. Not single or specific.
7. Not supportable. How can we know?
8. Not significant.
9. Not specific. Whole books have been written on this topic.
10. Not single.

2

1. Not significant. It's a commonplace fact.
2. Not specific or significant. Again, it's a simple fact.
3. Not single or specific.
4. Not specific. Nor is it supportable for most of us.
5. Not specific.
6. Not significant.
7. Not supportable.
8. Not specific.
9. Not significant. (Big deal!)
10. Not specific.

6

1. glue-sniffing (not a reason)
2. large bakeries; saving money (not part of the process)
3. improved looks (overlaps with "improved appearance"); improved social life (not directly related to S)
4. *General Hospital*; largely female audience (unrelated); quiz shows (overlaps with "game shows")
5. making travel plans (overlaps with "planning itinerary"); getting passport (client's responsibility)

6. may be dangerous; weight is often gained back (unrelated to S — not "diets")
7. white shark; hammerhead shark (species, not characteristics)
8. surge in birth of children from 1947–1965 (unrelated — it's a definition of "baby boom," not an effect)

7

1. they are fun to play; Lottario, Lotto 6/49 (unrelated)
2. practical training (offered in both); college students can smoke in the halls (not significant)
3. medical process by which person learns to control autonomic body processes; autonomic responses are involuntary, self-regulating processes (these are definitions, not benefits)
4. football requires helmets; football is more of a spectator sport (unrelated to S — these are contrasts, not comparisons)
5. intensely active; cannot concentrate for long (unrelated to S — characteristics, not treatments)
6. finding a job may take a while (unrelated to S — not part of the process); buy a suit (not significant)
7. in-laws; family breakdown (unrelated to S — not structures)
8. to ensure regular health checkups (overlaps with "to control spread of venereal disease"); to decriminalize prostitution (not related; it means exactly the same thing as S)

9

Topic	Order	Main Points
1. why pornography should be banned	chronological	__1__ it degrades the people involved in making it __3__ it brutalizes society as a whole __2__ it desensitizes the people who view it
2. differences between spoken and written language	climactic	__3__ speech is transitory; writing is permanent __2__ speech is direct and personal; writing isn't __1__ speech can't be revised; writing can
3. some causes of World War II	chronological	__2__ World Depression in early 1930s __3__ Hitler comes to power in 1933 __1__ heavy reparations demanded of Germany at end of World War I __4__ German aggression in Europe

4. effects of malnutrition	logical	__3__ malnutrition affects the productivity and prosperity of nations as a whole
		__1__ malnutrition impedes the mental and physical development of children
		__2__ undernourished children become sickly adults unable to participate fully in the economy of their society
5. how to start a gas lawnmower	chronological	__2__ make sure there is enough gas in tank
		__3__ turn switch to start
		__1__ put lawnmower on flat ground
		__5__ when running, adjust to proper speed
		__4__ pull cord
		__6__ mow!
6. how colleges benefit society	logical	__2__ they provide the individual with a higher level of general education
		__3__ society benefits from increased productivity and commitment of an educated populace
		__1__ they provide the individual with job skills

7. Decide on your own climactic pattern for this topic. Be sure you can defend your choice.

8. how to write a research paper	chronological	__3__ read and take notes on selected research sources
		__4__ write the paper
		__2__ compile a working bibliography of research sources
		__1__ narrow and define subject
		__7__ type and proofread paper
		__6__ prepare footnotes and bibliography
		__5__ revise the paper

Chapter 22: Writing the Thesis Statement

1

1. There are three kinds of students whom teachers find difficult to teach: whiners, snoozers, and disrupters.
2. The most prolific producers of unnecessary jargon are politicians, sports writers, advertising-copy writers, and educators.
3. Pay television has faced challenges in Canada because of the relatively small market, the high monthly cost, and the stiff network competition.
4. Political violence has become ingrained in the social fabric of many Latin American countries including Nicaragua, El Salvador, Chile, and Argentina.
5. Dining in the cafeteria should be avoided if possible, for the food is high in cost, low in nutrition, and unappetizing in taste.
6. The Canadian national character was shaped by early conflicts such as the battle for Quebec, the rebellions of 1837, and the Riel rebellion.
7. Canada is little more than an American satellite, for the United States influences our foreign policy, dominates our culture, and controls our economy.
8. Because they lack basic skills, study skills, or internal discipline, some students run the risk of failure in college.
9. The major improvements Western medical technology has made in impoverished parts of the world consist of widespread immunization, the availability of antibiotics, and improved sanitation.
10. Two cheers for democracy: one because it admits variety and two because it permits criticism. (E.M. Forster)

2

1. d. packed up and headed for Rome
2. a. strong
3. c. ugly
4. b. intelligently
5. b. by boat
6. d. trusted by the media
7. c. watching less television
8. a. increase appetite
9. d. unnumbered bank account in Switzerland
10. c. that fair-minded police are visible

3

1. not parallel
2. not parallel
3. parallel
4. not parallel
5. not parallel
6. parallel
7. parallel
8. not parallel
9. parallel
10. not parallel

4

1. His basement apartment was small, damp, cold, and dirty.
2. To be a good marriage counsellor, a person must have insight, patience, compassion, and experience.

3. correct
4. Too much coffee can give you nervous days, sleepless nights, and heart palpitations.
5. We require our employees to be honest, reliable, disciplined, and knowledgeable.
6. correct
7. correct
8. Inflation is down, interest rates are up, and unemployment is still high.
9. correct
10. Writing acceptable college-level prose involves applying the principles of organization, sentence structure, spelling, and punctuation.

5

1. Do you know the difference between polygamy, bigamy, and monogamy?
2. Mr. Bumble had given up not only on the Liberals but also on the Conservatives and on the New Democrats.
3. Elmo decided he'd rather be a plumber than a teacher.
4. A good coach must train, discipline, and motivate the team.
5. Two features of the semester system are flexibility and economy.
6. Going to college is good for broadening our social lives as well as for developing our career skills.
7. Compared to those of ten years ago, cars these days are smaller, more efficient, and more expensive.
8. We find it's more exciting to explore the tide pools at the seashore than to lie in the sun all day.
9. Children who are brought up in the city have a very different outlook on life from those who are brought up in the country.
10. Do the people of Canada want to be dominated by their neighbour to the south in economic, political, and cultural terms?

6

1. The four kinds of prose writing are narration, description, exposition, and persuasion.
2. College fraternities and sororities have become less popular in the past twenty years because they are expensive, they are time-consuming, and they discriminate against some students.
3. Freud's psychoanalytic theories, developed in the early years of this century, not only have affected the course of psychology but also have had profound implications for education, art, and literature.
4. The *Star Wars* trilogy consists of three George Lucas films: the first is *Star Wars*, the second is *The Empire Strikes Back*, and the third is *The Return of the Jedi*.
5. These movies have been enormously successful because of their action-filled plots, engaging characters, and superb special effects.
6. Intramural sports offer three important things to college students: a way to get involved in the school, an opportunity to meet friends, and a chance to stay fit.
7. Medical scientists have studied the link between weather and such diseases as colds, arthritis, and cancer.

8. Many English words have similar meanings, but they come from very different root languages: for example, *spectre* comes from the Latin *spectrum* (appearance); *phantom* comes from the Greek *phantasm* (image); and *ghost* comes from the Anglo-Saxon *gast* (spirit).
9. Geologists are exploring several phenomena that may lead to an early-warning system for earthquakes: the variation of electrical resistance of rocks under pressure, the release of gas trapped in the crystal lattice of a rock, and the appearance of eerie lights, or luminous flares, in the sky before a quake.
10. It was the best of times; it was the worst of times; it was the age of wisdom; it was the age of foolishness; it was the epoch of belief; it was the age of incredulity; it was the season of Light; it was the season of Darkness; it was the spring of hope; it was the winter of despair.

Chapter 23: Writing the Outline

I

I. Antagonize your teachers
   A. Aim an occasional snort or snicker in the teacher's direction
   B. Wear your Walkman to class and turn up the volume when the teacher speaks

II. Disdain your studies
   A. Don't buy the text for the course
   B. Never take notes in class
   C. Stop going to class

III. Cheat on your work
   A. Copy research assignments out of an appropriate library book
   B. Sit at the back during exams and try to read your classmate's paper
   C. Tattoo your answers on your forearms

3

"Flunking with Style"
Introduction
   Attention-getter: paragraph 1
   Thesis statement: To fail your year in the grand style, antagonize your teachers, disdain your studies, and cheat on your work.

I. Antagonizing your teachers
   A. Teachers like enthusiastic students
   B. Show you're bored
      1. slouch in the back
      2. wear your Walkman
      3. talk with classmates
      4. snicker at teacher
   C. Never answer questions in class

II. Disdaining your studies
  A. Buy your books late or not at all
  B. Never take notes
  C. Stop going to class

III. Cheating
  A. Copy out of a library book
  B. Adopt “appropriate” exam behaviour
    1. sit at back, read over classmate’s shoulder
    2. write answers on your forearms
    3. stash cheat sheets in washroom
    4. send in a substitute to take test

Summary and memorable statement: paragraph 5

Chapter 24: Writing the Paragraphs

I

Paragraph 2: *introduction of topic* *supporting sentences* *conclusion of topic*	I have sought love, first, because it brings ecstasy — ecstasy so great that I would often have sacrificed all the rest of life for a few hours of this joy. I have sought it, next, because it relieves loneliness — that terrible loneliness in which one shivering consciousness looks over the rim of the world into the cold unfathomable lifeless abyss. I have sought it, finally, because in the union of love I have seen, in a mystic miniature, the prefiguring vision of the heaven that saints and poets have imagined. This is what I sought, and though it might seem too good for human life, this is what — at last — I have found.
Paragraph 3: *introduction of topic* *supporting sentences* *conclusion of topic*	With equal passion I have sought knowledge. I have wished to understand the hearts of men. I have wished to know why the stars shine. And I have tried to apprehend the Pythagorean power by which number holds sway above the flux. A little of this, but not much, I have achieved.
Paragraph 4: *introduction of topic* *supporting sentences* *conclusion of topic*	Love and knowledge, so far as they were possible, led upward toward the heavens. But always pity brought me back to earth. Echoes of cries of pain reverberate in my heart. Children in famine, victims tortured by oppressors, helpless old people a hated burden to their sons, and the whole world of loneliness, poverty, and pain make a mockery of what human life should be. I long to alleviate the evil, but I cannot, and I too suffer.

7

1. definition
2. examples
3. specific details
4. examples
5. examples
6. process
7. descriptive detail

9

Though I'm new to college, I've discovered three ways of achieving the academic success that most of us desire. First, although going to class is not mandatory, regular attendance enables the student to master course content more readily. Second, the student must take personal responsibility for notes and assignments rather than relying on prodding by instructors. Third, the workload increases significantly by the middle of each term. Unless the student has made consistent efforts to stay on top of the material, he or she is in real danger of failing. Hence, the key to academic success is self-discipline and responsibility for one's studies as a college student.

Chapter 28: Wordiness

1

1. Basically, I prefer the genuine article to an imitation.
2. Although small and an ugly yellow, the car was, in fact, identical to his last one.
3. The conclusion wasn't known until he was free to announce himself elected.
4. I will repeat, for those who disappeared, that we are now free.
5. They circled behind the enemy and, at 04:00 on July 12, surrounded them and eliminated the threat of an invasion.
6. There was nothing they could do except repeat the facts.
7. In my opinion, this innovation won't see the light of day.
8. There comes a time of final reckoning, and you reach a conclusion.
9. Although his ideas seem unique, we must be positive that we don't repeat the mistake.
10. I think she is pretending to be sick so she won't have to go to work.

Chapter 29: Abusages

1

1. I could have done many things, but I chose to become rich and powerful very quickly.
2. Regardless of what you say, I think the media are generally reliable.
3. The reason Dennis came home was that he couldn't do anything more to help at the hospital.
4. They teach us many irrelevant things at this school.

5. correct
6. Mark was supposed to be in the race, but he fell off his bike during practice.
7. I should have stayed home, but I went anyway.
8. The reason you are failing is that you don't do any homework.
9. The police department was accused of prejudice against minority groups.
10. correct

2

1. correct
2. She and Craig tried to build the fire themselves.
3. "Those are they," we said when we found the canoes.
4. Everyone went swimming but her and me.
5. We and they heated beans on a Coleman stove.
6. She and I took a flashlight and went looking for bears.
7. I think she was more scared than I.
8. Back at camp, they waited; she was more worried than he.
9. Two porcupines chased her and me through the woods.
10. correct

Appendix C

List of Grammatical Terms

adjectives: words that modify (describe, restrict, relate to, make more precise) nouns and pronouns. They answer the questions *What kind? How many? Which?* — e.g., the *competent* student; *five* home runs; my *last* class.

adverbs: words that modify verbs, adjectives, and other adverbs. They answer the questions *When? How? Where? Why? How much?* — e.g., Elmo talks *fast* (*fast* modifies the verb *talks*); he is a *very* fast talker (*very* modifies the adjective *fast*); he talks *really* fast (*really* modifies the adverb *fast*). Adverbs often — but not always — end in *-ly*.

antecedent: the word that a pronoun refers to or stands for. Literally, it means "going before, preceding." The antecedent usually comes before the pronoun that refers to it. E.g., *Karen* believes *she* is possessed. (*Karen* is the antecedent to which the pronoun *she* refers.)

clause: a group of words that contains a subject and a verb. If the group of words can stand by itself and makes complete sense, it is called an **independent clause** (or **principal clause** or **main clause**). If the group of words does not make complete sense on its own but is linked to another clause (depends on it for its meaning), it is called a **dependent** or **subordinate clause**. E.g., *The porch collapsed*. This group of words can stand by itself, so it is called an independent clause.
But: *When Kalim removed the railing with his tractor*. This group of words has a subject, *Kalim*, and a verb, *removed*, but it does not make complete sense on its own. It depends for its meaning on *The porch collapsed*; therefore, it is a dependent clause.

colloquialism: word or group of words that we use in casual conversation or in informal writing. E.g.,

Steve *flunked* his accounting exam.
Did you *get* what the teacher said about job placement?
I can't believe that *guy* is serious about learning.

comma splice: the error that results when the writer joins two independent clauses with a comma. E.g., *The comma splice is an error, it is a kind of run-on sentence.* See chapter 6.

dependent clause cue: word or word phrase that introduces a dependent clause. E.g., *when*, *because*, *in order that*, *as soon as* See p. 55.

modifier: word or group of words that adds information about another word (or phrase or clause) in a sentence. See **adjective**, **adverb**, **dependent clause**, and chapter 7.

nouns: words that name persons, places, and things and have the grammatical capability of being possessive. There are **concrete** nouns that are **proper** (*Calgary*, *Beijing*, *Gaza*, *January*, *Sharon*); **common** (*woman*, *man*, *city*, *car*, *animal*); and **collective** (*group*, *audience*, *swarm*, *jury*, *committee*). There are also **abstract** nouns (*truth*, *softness*, *pride*, *confidence*). Unlike their concrete cousins, abstract nouns refer to concepts, ideas, characteristics — things we know or experience through our intellect rather than through our senses.

participle: form of a verb that can be used as an adjective (the *completed* work, the *weeping* willows) or part of a verb phrase (am *succeeding*, have *rented*).
The present participle of a verb ends in *-ing*.
The past participle of a regular verb ends in *-d* or *-ed*. For the irregular verbs, see pp. 39–40 and a dictionary.

person: a category of pronouns and nouns. **First person** refers to the person who is speaking (*I*, *we*). **Second person** refers to the person being spoken to (*you*). **Third person** is the person or thing being spoken about (*he*, *she*, *it*, *they*, and any noun or pronoun that may substitute for these).

phrase: a group of meaning-related words that acts as a noun, verb, adjective, or adverb within a sentence. Phrases do not make complete sense on their own because they do not contain both a subject and verb. E.g.,

Behind the garage is the best place. (phrase acting as noun)

I *must have been sleeping* when you called. (verb phrase)

Travelling in Spain, my friends saw some monuments *of the Spanish Civil War*. (phrases acting as adjectives)

In this weather, portaging is a chore. (phrase acting as adverb)

preposition: a word that connects a noun or pronoun or phrase to some other word(s) in a sentence. The noun or pronoun is the **object** of the preposition. (That is why the **subject** of a sentence is never found in a prepositional phrase.) E.g.,

I prepared the minutes *of the union meeting*. (*of* relates *meeting* to *minutes*)

One *of the parents* checks the children every half hour. (*of* relates parents to *One*)

prepositional phrase: a group of grammatically related words having the function of a noun, adjective or adverb and beginning with a preposition. See the list on p. 32.

pronouns: words that are noun-like. They usually substitute for nouns, but sometimes they substitute for other pronouns. E.g.,

He will market *anything that* brings in money.

Everyone must earn *her* badges.

There are several kinds of pronouns:

personal: I, we, you, he, she, it, they, me, us, him, her, his, hers

possessive: theirs, ours, my, mine, its, his, hers, your, yours

demonstrative: this, these, that, those

relative: who, which, that, whom, whose

interrogative: who? whose? whom? which? what?

indefinite: all "*-one*, *-thing*, *-body*" pronouns such as *everyone, something, anybody; each, neither, either, few, none, several.*

subject: In a sentence, the person, thing, or concept that the sentence is about — the topic of the sentence. See chapter 3.

In a paper, what the essay is about — the topic of the paper.

tenses: Verbs indicate past, present or future time. The different forms of the verb used to indicate time are called **tenses**. The verb ending (e.g., play*s*, play*ing*, play*ed*) and any helping verbs associated with the main verb (*will* play, *has* played, *had* played, *will have* played) show the tense of the verb.

There are simple tenses: **present**: ask asks
past: asked
future: will ask

and perfect tenses: **present**: have (has) asked
past: had asked
future: will (shall) have asked

The simple and perfect tenses can also be **progressive**: am asking, have been asking, etc.

transitions: words or phrases that help the reader follow the text smoothly from one paragraph to another, or from one sentence to the next. See pp. 174, 182, and 233–234.

verbs: words that say something about a person, place, or thing and whose form may be changed to indicate tense. They may make a statement, ask a question, or give commands. They may express action (physical or mental) occurrence, or condition (mode of being). E.g.,

George *hit* an inside curve for a home run. (physical action)

Laurence *believed* the Blue Jays would win. (mental action)

Father's Day *falls* on the first Sunday of June. (occurrence)

Helen eventually *became* interested in English. (condition)

For verb forms, turn to chapter 4, pp. 38–40.

Some verbs are called **linking verbs**: they help to make a statement by linking the subject to a word that describes or explains it. E.g.,

William Hubbard *was* Toronto's first Black mayor. (*was* links *William Hubbard* to *mayor*)

Mohammed *looks* tired. (*looks* links *Mohammed* and *tired*)

In addition to *am*, *is*, *are*, *was*, *were*, and *been*, some common linking verbs are *appear*, *become*, *feel*, *grow*, *look*, *taste*, *remain*, *seem*, *smell*, *sound*.

Another class of verbs is called **helping verbs**. They show the time of a verb as future or past (*will* go, *has* gone), or as a continuing action (*is* reading); and they show the passive voice (*was* completed).

voice: verbs may be **active** or **passive**, depending on whether the subject of the verb is **acting** (active voice) or **being acted upon** (passive voice). E.g., In 1988, *Brian Mulroney introduced* another set of tax reforms. (active)

Another **set** of tax reforms *was introduced* in 1988. (passive)